This is the love story of Yatindra and Sadhana – nearly 55 years of sharing cheers and tears, facing odds and overcoming them, together.

It's a story of reaching great heights in their fields – he in journalism and she in painting and sketching. He also wrote books and poetry. She couldn't lag behind – she too wrote articles and poems.

They did not stop there. He did thousands of radio and TV programs. She also was on radio for numerous programs.

He traveled extensively. She also did quite a bit. They were one of the most popular couples in India's capital city of New Delhi, and later in Indore, mingling with Presidents and Prime Ministers, top diplomats and business people. They were invited by various foreign governments to visit their countries.

Yatindra wrote books, Sadhana contributed for some. They collaborated in some more.

Sadhana raised their two lovely daughters, mainly by herself, as Yatindra got busy in reporting, writing books and traveling.

She also wrote poems about him, and he did the same about her and about others too.

They were always on the same page; were two bodies and one soul.

With all that, she was also an excellent cook, an expert in sewing, knitting, crochet work, embroidery, singing, hospitality, making life-long friends and helping others. Together they raised good children, brought good sons-in-law and spread love far and wide.

In return they got love from far and wide.

They both remained love-birds, till the last day for her. Those days, he would sit by her side, hold her hand, look into her eyes, and whispered sweet nothings in her ears.

This is their Fairytale Love Story. There is a vast treasury of historic events, and quite some biographical details like childhood and growing up, jobs in newspapers, marriage, sweet and sour memories, tough challenges and admirable achievements.

A
Fairytale Love Story

Sadhana Bhatnagar
Yatindra Bhatnagar

Volume 1 – India to USA
Yatindra Bhatnagar

Deepsadhana Publications
Los Angeles, California

Ashi (Sadhana),

Our Story, Dedicated to you
[Hamari kahani, tumhe hi samarpit]

Cover: painting: Sadhana Bhatnagar

First Edition: March 2018

@ Copyright 2017-2018: Yatindra Bhatnagar

Printed in the United States of America

Published by:

Deepsadhana Publications
P.O. Box 8011
La Crescenta, CA 91224
USA

Price: US $14.95

Grateful thanks

This is the Fairytale Love Story of Sadhana and I. Our children, their children and their children, the extended family and close friends are an essential part of our story.

They kept on asking me to do it, and do it soon.

I could not have been able to write this love story but for this loving family that would not accept No for an answer.

The persistent pressure came from granddaughter, Tamanna Roashan, and daughters, Sujata and Seema. Other dear ones were exerting indirect pressure and giving me ample time to complete the work.

My great granddaughter, Aliya's birth proved to be an added inspiration and encouragement to write the book.

Sujata, in particular, was a great help, as usual. She assisted me in various ways in compiling and completing this labor of love. She went through the entire manuscript carefully, proof-read, and also gave me valuable advice and suggestions. She played a significant role in formatting and producing the beautiful book.

Seema and Sujata both reminded me of some anecdotes I was forgetting. You know, age is fast catching up with me and I am fighting it.

I can't thank you all enough for your constant encouragement and great help. Your persistent pressure speeded the project.

Papa-Nana-Bade Nana (Great Grandfather)

Special thanks to Julie Ward (Sunland Printing) and Jenny Wannier, for doing a remarkable job in guiding us with the production of this very personal narrative.

Yatindra Bhatnagar

(Sadhana's birthday, October 14)

CONTENTS

1

My Word

Fifty-four years, seven months and one week. That's how long my marriage to my beautiful, talented wife, Sadhana (nee Ved), lasted. I knew her for a little over a year before our marriage. However, I only saw and met her a few times, all with her brother, Dr. Indrajit Kumar – and my friend of nearly four years.

I saw Ved for the first time, probably sometime in 1960. It was a chance meeting in a market in Karol Bagh, New Delhi. Indrajit introduced us. She was visiting him from Dehradun, where she lived with her mother, another brother and his family. Dehradun is a city in the foothills of the mighty Himalayas, nearly 150 miles from New Delhi, then with a little over 120,000 people. It's now the capital of Uttarakhand state with nearly 600,000 people.

[A year later we got married.]

The year 1961 was also memorable for another reason – Her Majesty Queen Elizabeth II was on her first visit to India, Ved (Sadhana) was among the million people that welcomed the Queen and her party, driven from Delhi Airport through the famous Connaught Place/Circus to *Rashtrapati Bhavan* (the Presidential Palace). Ved was at Connaught Place, saw the Queen, and waved.

The Queen was accompanied by the President, Dr. Rajendra Prasad on the 12-mile route, decorated with festoons, flowers and banners.

Little did Ved know at the time that her future husband – me – in the Press van with our newspaper's photographer, unintentionally, had, somehow become a part of the Queen's large motorcade. With dozens of vehicles carrying senior civil and security officials we went on merrily from the Airport to Rashtrapati Bhavan on the long drive. Our van was fifth or sixth in the motorcade and we had first-hand and close view of peoples' reception all along the way. [About that a little later.]

1

Six months before our marriage on October 8, 1961, I wrote to Ved and suggested a meeting (call it a 'date' if you will). She agreed and I went to Dehradun, met her at a beautiful natural picnic area – *Sahasradhara* (the thousand streams.) We didn't want a secluded place, a hotel or the like.

It was April 21, also the birthday of the Queen. It was a coincidence but these have occurred frequently in my life, our lives. Ved and I named the day as *Milan Divas* (The Day We Met).

Princess Elizabeth, the older daughter of King George VI, became Queen Elizabeth II, in 1952.

The year 1952 is also very special for me. It's because I had the honor and privilege to be interviewed for an editorial position by none other than Devdas Gandhi, the youngest son of Mahatma Gandhi, and a freedom fighter in his own right. He was happy with me and signed my appointment letter, himself.

[With Devdas *Ji* marrying Lakshmi, two great families of India forged a closer bond. Lakshmi was the daughter of C. Rajagopalachari, another top freedom fighter, and a close colleague of Mahatma Gandhi. He was also the first Indian Governor General of India after Independence, after India's last British Governor General, Lord Mountbatten left.]

I had the honor of meeting and interviewing CR, or Rajaji, as he was also widely known. I am also fortunate for having seen Mahatma Gandhi on a couple occasions, in both Delhi and Bombay, and out of respect, touching his feet.]

At Sahasradhara, dangling our feet in water, sitting on the ground, under a tree (though not like a Hindi movie scene of dancing, going around and singing), we talked about us, about families, we ate, exchanged views on a few other subjects. The talks, interestingly, included the Queen's visit earlier. She told me about her waving at the Queen, I told her my story.

I was reporting a part of the Queen's visit for my newspaper, *Hindustan*, and had attended Prime Minister Jawaharlal Nehru's press briefing about it. The briefing was arranged by Foreign Secretary R.K. Nehru. Also a couple days later, I was in Agra to report the Royal party's visit to the world famous Taj Mahal.

[It became a subject worth talking about with my would-be wife, especially the visit to Taj Mahal. No visitors, no lovers, would miss that for anything. We also made a visit, a few days after our marriage.]

Ved (I named her Sadhana – *the desired one*, with her consent, after marriage), was always a patient listener and was interested in my story; so was I, in her.

The remarks by Jawaharlal Nehru at the press briefing were memorable. Felix Naggar, the cigar-smoking ace French journalist and New Delhi Chief of his country's news agency, AFP, asked:

"Mr. Nehru, are you a Republican or a Monarchist?"

The question was weirdly provoking, but quite interesting, and Nehru was naturally taken aback – for a second only, then said:

"Why, I am a Republican."

Shot back Felix with another:

"Then why have you invited a Queen?"

We had a good laugh but we waited for an appropriate answer too. Replied Nehru:

"Three reasons: She is the Queen of England, a country we have had long relations with; she is the Head of the Commonwealth of Nations [a group of countries that were, before their independence, a part of the British Empire]; *and third, she is a pretty young lady."*

There was another round of laughter.

The rest of the information about the Queen's visit was given by career officials of the Ministry of External Affairs.

Ved and I had so much to talk about that memorable visit on our 'date.' How she wanted to see the Queen and how she, on her own, took a bus and rode for miles to reach the vantage point in Connaught Place. It later became a frequent and interesting topic of our conversation. I would tease her saying that you thought you were waving to the Queen, but it was also to me in that motorcade, and so on. And she would respond by remarking that you were more interested in the Queen than me.

In any case, we were not done with Her Majesty and things related to her.

In 1972 we went on a visit to Europe, including UK (London and countryside) and Sadhana made a sketch of Buckingham Palace to renew our interest in the Queen. Sadhana squatted on grass in front of the Palace and spent better part of two hours to draw a beautiful sketch (still a valuable possession with me). She also drew Big Ben and Parliament House, another beauty, another prized possession.

I met the Queen again, on her second visit in November, 1983, at a reception the British High Commissioner, Sir Robert Wade-Gery, arranged in New Delhi. I was the Chief Editor of *Dainik Bhaskar* (now the largest circulated daily newspaper in India.) I flew from Indore to New Delhi and had the honor to see-meet-shake hands and talk to the Queen, in small groups. A remark I made was: "The first time you visited India, I wasn't married; this second visit is when I have a wife and two grown daughters, one already married."

The Queen smiled and said: "I know, it has been a long time."

Another group of journalists and others was more informal. I mentioned that I am the founder-president of Two Daughters Club (never formally founded) and since the late King also had two daughters (*Elizabeth and Margaret*) he qualified to be a member. It was funny and the group enjoyed it.

Since then, I learnt that Presidents Richard Nixon, George W. Bush, Barack Obama and many other celebrities also have two girls.

I am in good company.

I digressed enough, thanks to Queen Elizabeth and Indo-British relations.

Back to my one and only 'Date.' The meeting at Sahasradhara was the start of our 'courtship' that lasted all those five decades plus of our wonderful marriage. Our friendship was great. Growing together was a delight. Sharing cheers and tears was a memorable experience. Encouraging each other in the pursuit of happiness and success was satisfying. Accepting challenges in various fields and reaching greater heights of accomplishment in our chosen fields were something to be proud of.

Of course, raising a loving and caring family was pure joy. And making a part of this big wide and diverse world OUR family was something not many have the opportunity to avail and honor to attain.

When I was in the US in 1965, I was interviewed by Fort Worth Star Telegram, a newspaper in Texas, and the reporter, Lynn Swann Davis, asked me how did I marry? My reply was simple, and very short: "I had a friend, he had a sister, and I married her." She persisted with, "you didn't have a period of courtship?" My answer was, "In India we marry first and then life is an eternal courtship." Her article had the headline: "In India they marry first."

Our courtship-marriage-love story lasted nearly 55 years. It is a long saga of love.

I would have loved to continue it as long as WE live but *someone* had different plans and I could do nothing about it. My love story remained incomplete, has not ended. I am still in love with Sadhana, and as I used to tell her (when she would frequently ask, why? how? still?) that I have fallen in love with you once again. I love you more than in early years of our marriage as now I have all the time in the world to love you, and see your inner beauty much more, and that you are mine.

Whenever I would tell her, "I love you," she would reply, "I love you two" and I would say, "I love you three." Pat would come her reply," I love you four," and this competition would continue till I would give up and accept that "You love me more." Yes, it was always like that and she would score over me. I do feel, with all my demands on her time, attention, care and posing challenges and creating problems and expecting her to face and solve all of them, take care of every adverse situation – often alone – and still loving me unconditionally, she had proven amply that she loved me more.

Nobody else could have done all that.

I can only compare her love to a combination of both Meerabai and Radha – two of India's own memorable historic characters in love with Lord Krishna. Radha, lived in the same village, and intensely loved Krishna. Thousands of years later, Meera lived far, yet loved him, worshipped him and craved for his glimpse, his presence before her. One was *prem diwani* (passionately in love), the other *daras diwani* (craving for a glimpse of God (in the form of her beloved Krishna).

[This relationship was repeated and depicted in a similar song in Hindi movie *'Ram Teri Ganga Maili'* (1985) by the top showman of Indian movie industry, Raj Kapoor. The nightingale of India, Lata Mangeshkar, sang it (written by Ravindra Jain who was also the music director of the movie.) These sentiments have been repeated by scores of other singers. Sadhana and I had the good fortune to hear Ravindra Jain at a private gathering in Vasant Vihar, New Delhi – home of one of our good Agrawal friends. He owned a transport business in New Delhi.]

Sadhana loved me totally and also intensely craved for my presence (I was frequently out on assignments far and wide, inspiring her to write love-poems.) Her love was unique, indeed a fine combination of both Radha and Meera.

We were totally in love with each other. If I was a song, Sadhana was the music. If I was a body, she was the soul. We were one, and we were in real love.

And now things are totally different, she is no longer with me, though I still love her, think about her, feel her presence and love all the time. That's why my love continues, OUR love story continues. Though it's incomplete (*hamari adhoori kahani*), it's not ended. It keeps on going from my side, is an unfinished, unending love story, and will ever remain embedded in my heart. It will always be on my mind, firmly planted in my memory, the fairytale love story people just imagine.

In our married life, Sadhana's support and inspiration, and her dedication and love enabled me to progress from a junior journalist to Chief Editor of a big daily newspaper in India, and of a couple of weakly newsmagazines in the United States. In the half century and more we were together, I wrote tens of thousands of news stories and interviews, feature articles and editorials.

In addition, I did thousands of radio and TV programs in India – some in America, Korea, England, Germany, and elsewhere. With all that, I also translated and compiled, co-authored and independently wrote 20 books on a wide variety of subjects including history, travel, biography, poetry and so on. My wife, my inspiration and my friend, was there all the way to help me go on with my career and accomplishments, and extensive travels. She would take care of me, our home, our kids and relatives, neighbors and friends – and also extend help to strangers in need. And they were in large numbers.

With all those things, Sadhana herself reached appreciable heights in several other fields. She flourished as an artist with her paintings and sketches, radio talk shows, hosted and organized events, and produced books and magazines. She wrote articles for various newspapers and magazines and also made her mark as a wonderfully sensitive poet, and a caring person for both humans and animals.

[We were able to compile a collection of her beautiful poems and show her an illustrated *sample copy* as she lay in bed in a California hospital, soon to depart in 2016.]

With all that talent she maintained her incredible skills in cooking, sewing, knitting, embroidery, crochet work, singing, gardening, swimming, and hospitality. She had actively participated in sports in her student years. She graduated from a college at 19 and had a post-graduate degree in teaching. Sadhana also taught classes in a high school for six months before we got married. She even improved the crop of guava fruit tree in our backyard with her own 'discovery' without spending anything.

In five decades of our marriage, she turned out to be an amazing woman. She proved to be a devoted and loving wife, a trusted companion and a faithful friend, an inspiration, a pillar of strength, a caring and loving mother, and an astute manager of family finances. I would give her everything I would earn, and she would manage things wisely, meet all our needs and even save for vacations and marriages of our daughters.

I couldn't have done that. My pre-marriage record speaks for itself.

In your life you often feel the absence of your mother, the way she took care of you, always thinking about you and forever keeping a 'hot-line' in her heart open for you. Sadhana was also like that, often playing the role of a mother to me, caring for me, thinking about me, feeding me and always asking me about my special preferences, and making those available to me. She knew my likes and dislikes, sensed my feelings, shared my problems and tried to come up with solutions. For us being married to one another did not only mean love in the physical sense. It was much more, much beyond everything.

Sadhana explained those feelings, and acknowledged my perception, in one of her beautiful poems. During the years she was sick and wheelchair-bound, I thought deeply about our relations and her qualities. Now that she is no more, I have more time and motivation to reflect, recall, re-evaluate, re-discover, re-assess, re-invent and re-live the magic of my wonderful wife, a remarkable woman. I can now realize and re-value my wife in a larger context and on a larger canvas of life.

She was perfection personified.

Things sometimes turn out and prove that life is not always fair. Often Sadhana would be the first to hear about deaths and other bad things happening in our family, with close friends, and in the neighborhood.

7

She was the first to bear the shock but the first one to show her inner strength and come out stronger to make it easy for others to face the situation. She was also my shield. She was strong. And she was considerate.

Of course we had our disagreements, we also argued and we also did 'battles.' But they were few and far between.

The 'ceasefire' was quick. Invariably with tears shared and sweet smiles exchanged happily.

The arguments did not last long.

The 'silent treatment' could not go beyond a couple hours.

I wouldn't have it any other way.

In early 1940s in India, I came across an ad for Brooke Bond Tea widely displayed everywhere. It said: "Two leaves and a bud, the standard plucking method of the high grade tea."

In our case, when we will patch up – and *I* loved that job happily – it was "two tight hugs and a kiss, the standard patch-up method of the highest grade of love."

The peace will be inevitably restored in no time to be followed by more tight hugs and more shower of kisses, enough to drown us in love and laughter for a long time.

Sadhana was an incredible human being.

We were indeed deeply in love with each other. Relatives, friends and neighbors cited our example and were all praise for us. They loved and respected us. They all, in turn, got ample love and support, care and affection from both of us. Still do.

Our daughters, Sujata and Seema and our first granddaughter, Tamanna Roashan, have been tenaciously and persistently prodding me to write about US, OUR love story and decades of OUR life of loving, sharing and caring.

How could I not do that after living with a most remarkable woman for so long? We all miss her, mourn the loss every day, every moment and wish she was still with me as my companion, my friend, my inspiration – as she had been all along.

OUR love story had to be written and shared.

Sadhana always wanted to go before me. One of Seema's friends, Sudhir Brahmbhatt, also interested in astrology, was visiting Seema-Randeep's home in Houston. We were also there and *that* was the only question Sadhana asked him. He examined her palm, did some more readings and made calculations and his reply was what Sadhana was anticipating, trying to confirm, and wishing for, all her life.

She did not have to tell me, I would have guessed. I knew that she loved me immensely and could never imagine a life without me.

I had wished both to *go together*.

Her wish reminded me of a touching quote attributed to Lori Voskuil-Dutter:

"I can't promise that I'll be here for the rest of *your* life, but I can promise that I'll love you for the rest of *mine*."

Sadhana loved as nobody could. She lived for me, and she left fulfilling her wish to go before me, many would not want that. Her love was unique, unconditional, unselfish, exceptional, and also unequaled. I could only try to match her love, and I always tried to do that. I tried to treat her as a queen, and she was a match. She also shared with me the good and bad days, cheers and tears, with a smile on her lips and courage in her heart, always.

[In 2012 she was in a Houston hospital after a major surgery and doctors advised a feeding tube for her. She was naturally, hesitating but after some cajoling, agreed.

The specialist doctor was excited and told Sadhana:

"You made the best decision in your life."

Without wasting a second, she pointed to me and said: "He is."]

Sadhana, the love of my life, left me, and all of us, on May 15, 2016 after a valiant fight against all kinds of ailments, infections, surgeries and procedures for five years. She had to gulp down tons of medicines and take hundreds of insulin shots too. She was in-and-out of hospitals dozens of times in Houston, in Northern California's San Leandro, and in

Los Angeles area in Southern California where we moved just four months before, on January 21, Mujtaba's birthday.

In 1986 we had moved to America from India and started our life together in the greater Los Angeles area with daughter Sujata and her husband, Mujtaba Roashan and their little daughter Tamanna. Younger daughter Seema was already here as Sujata brought her after her visit to India with Tamanna, in 1985.

Thirty years later we came back to Los Angeles to be near Tamanna. She had earlier moved here from Northern California. Tamanna loved her *Nani* (grandma) very much and had a 'deal' with her about promising a baby *if we all moved to LA*. As things started to fall in place, Sadhana's health deteriorated. Soon everything turned this loving reality into a painful event of a treasure lost, forever, irreplaceable, and leaving lasting memories.

As Jagjit Singh sang after his son's tragic death with the deepest feelings:

> *Chitthi na koi sandes,*
> *jaane vo kaun sa des,*
> *jahaan tum chale gaye.*

[No letter, no message, don't know the place, where you went away]

That's my feeling – our feeling – all the while – *jaane vo kaun sa des*....

Sadhana left us mourning this immense loss. Her life was a shining example of what love and togetherness mean. What's sharing and caring is all about. Why we celebrate a life. And why we can't erase memories from our mind and hearts.

With her leaving us, I felt I was old. While she was with us, I never thought I would ever grow old. Now I feel the 'juice' has disappeared from my body, that I do not have the strength that propelled me to happily push her wheelchair, bring it down the stairs (with help) most of the time, and that whenever needed, I was able to lift her from her bed onto the chair, and so on.

Her absence, I feel, has drained me a whole lot.

On the other hand, the inspiration that she was, the strength she gave me and the encouragement I always got from her, are the *most important* reasons, and the *main* motivation, to embark on this project and complete this big book – a tribute to my beloved wife.

Looking at her 41 photos adorning the walls and dressers of my room, and several in the rotating digital slide show gadget (more will certainly be added soon), I will not stop writing.

As I read somewhere: 'All it takes is one song to bring back a thousand memories.' And they are plenty, countless, never going to fade.

[Tamanna kept her promise to *Nani* – but it was a little late. Probably that was the planning of all the three – Tamanna, *Nani* and God. We got a cute little baby girl about nine months after Sadhana left us. That says it all. Tamanna desperately wanted *Nani* to come back.]

That's my life, our life, our joys, our challenges, our successes, and also my regrets. And that's what I share today with you all.

This is a long story, a fairytale love story. And yes, I can also say that *"teri meri, meri teri, prem kahani hai lumbi, kuchh pannon mein bayaan na ho paaye"* (ours is a long story, cannot be told in a few pages).

But I will try my best.

2

How the Whole Thing Started

Talking about pairs, arranged or love marriage, marrying in our own community (caste) and region, with similar customs and language and habits, family background – and of course comparing the horoscopes are common. None of these figured in our marriage at all. We did not try to find commonalities. We did not create, perceive, and try to find or force compatibility. Ours can neither be called an arranged marriage nor a love marriage – it could be described as a beautiful combination of both, and we loved it that way.

Of course we did have many things in common, like the love of Indian culture, pride about India's ancient glory and heritage, as well as Hindi, the national and widely followed language of India. Our families were followers of the reformist line of Hinduism, called Arya Samaj. This branch of Hinduism, in essence, adhered to the fundamentals of the religion as enunciated by the Vedas and other scriptures. It, however, did not strictly and blindly follow idol worship and rigid rituals but had the utmost respect for the great icons of Hindu heritage, history and culture in all their glory.

In any case, even these similarities did not play a dominant role in bringing our two families closer. I did not even bother to know the surname, or 'caste' of Sadhana's family. It was my friendship with Indrajit, the brother of Ved (Sadhana). We knew each other for at least four years before we sealed this sweet relation.

And Sadhana was one of a kind.

As we did not care about extraneous things we also didn't bother about family background. I knew very little about Ved's, and her family didn't care about mine. It was a little later that we became somewhat familiar with a lot of diversity but that didn't discourage us, on the contrary, was enough to take our relations further.

A little bit about how I came to know Indrajit.

His family was then living in Dehradun and Indrajit was a student of DAV College. Another young man, VK Sharma, was also there, though pursuing different subjects. Indrajit was a science student and VK had opted for arts (humanities) as his line. They were friends and keenly interested in students activities. VK had become a family friend and also knew Ved.

It so happened that after I moved from Bombay to Delhi and did my two-year college course (Intermediate, Board Examination), and as I was working full-time my further studies were interrupted. After a few years gap, I took up further studies, while working, and passed my BA examination. After that I joined the Journalism course (an evening college of Panjab University) for my post-graduate studies.

I met VK Sharma, also pursuing Journalism, at the same college.

VK contested and won the secretary's post at the students union, PUJA (Panjab University Journalists Association). The famous Punjab University at Lahore was uprooted after Partition of India in 1947 and had started its campus in New Delhi as Camp College to help working people to pursue their studies. As a 'refugee' it changed its name to Panjab U to distinguish itself from Punjab University, Lahore.

[From New Delhi this University shifted to Solan (Shimla Hills) and later to Chandigarh for a permanent campus.]

Some interesting things about the Journalism department: It was headed by Prof. PP Singh, the pioneer in teaching Journalism – he started the course in Punjab University, Lahore (now in Pakistan), in 1941, the first in India, and in South Asia.

Top members of the Faculty included Rana Jang Bahadur Singh, former Editor of reputed newspapers and Jamnadas Akhtar among others.

Prof PP Singh was a dynamic teacher and extremely knowledgeable about people, things, events and also had the impressively unique style of teaching.

I would only give two very interesting quotes from him:

1. Experts are not BORN, they are MADE. A child is born an idiot, he/she learns everything after birth.

2. The press release/news report/article should be the length of a woman's skirt – short enough to attract attention, but long enough to cover the subject.

I had fabulously good time at the school, though I was a 'nine-year veteran journalist' when I joined the post-graduate Journalism Department at this refugee Panjab University, in New Delhi.

I shared the stories of my time at the journalism school with Sadhana and she was amused. She also had the privilege of meeting with most of the faculty members and some of the alumni, including Sharda Puri, and of course VK Sharma.

Sharda, later married and settled in Germany. We came to know her parents also who lived in Pratap Bagh, the same colony where Sadhana also stayed with her brother Dr. Indrajit Kumar whenever she came to Delhi prior to our marriage.]

I became friends with VK, also because I came to know that he was the younger brother of DK Tyagi, (who preferred his family name and not Sharma.) Tyagi joined *Janasatta* newspaper in 1952 where I was a senior staffer. DK and I became good friends; VK was then in Dehradun. He came to New Delhi after completing his studies there and enrolled with Panjab U.

VK introduced me to Indrajit and soon the trio became very close. VK and I were closer as he was my classmate and lived nearer my house but the three would meet often. With VK, after we both graduated from the Journalism Department, and he got a job with the government of India, we could meet almost daily. Our 'joint' was Milk Bar, a nice restaurant close to my office, in Connaught Place, New Delhi.

Our friendship grew. Indrajit took me as a good friend – and may be the right person for his sister. However, the issue was extremely delicate: if NO from my side, the friendship would be lost, so he must have thought). So, the hint was given through VK and even then through Kanta bahanji, daughter of a refugee family that had kind of, 'adopted' me as a son. I lived with them for 10 years.

The rest is history, as they say.

A few facts:

Ved (Sadhana) was born in Nowshera (now in Pakistan) before her family moved to Abbottabad (also in Pakistan), now also known for sheltering terrorist leader Osama bin Laden and his killing by an American Navy Seal commando group, in a meticulously planned raid, in 2011.

I was born in Indore (India), over 800 miles from Ved's birthplace.

She moved to Abbottabad from her birthplace and I moved to New Delhi – the distance was cut by about 90 miles.

When we got married she was in Dehradun and I in New Delhi - the distance was only about 150 miles.

We were surely destined to move closer and closer till we became one.

I came to know that Ved's father (who had expired in 1954 when she was just 14) was a highly respected, successful and exceptionally generous man in Rawalpindi and later in Abbottabad. He was a prominent building contractor who owned big plots of land in old Rawalpindi (now the major part of Pakistan's capital Islamabad). He later built a huge home in the city of Abbottabad.

The Jaggi home (I came to know much later that Ved's family name was Jaggi) was big, real big, so big that in 1973 when I was in Islamabad on an assignment, a local newspaper reporter from the same city told me that it was now a big college.

[Indrajit never used 'Jaggi' with his name. He was Dr. I.J. Kumar. So I thought she was Ved *Kumar*, and addressed my first letter as such.]

But life doesn't always remain permanent, constant and unchanged. Jaggi family had to leave everything, home, business, property etc. and escape death during the Partition of India. They left what became Pakistan and managed to come to India; settling down in Dehradun that was, climate-wise, similar to Abbottabad.

Ved's father, Ishar Das *Ji*, found himself with problems and very little help. Ved, only 7, and three older brothers (the oldest just married a few months back) and her mother all had to cramp themselves in a small place. What a contrast and terrible change from the palatial home and rich status! But they never gave up and tried to make the best of a bad political bargain that religious fanatics brought about in dividing a country and uprooting millions, on both the sides.

An interesting, though unfortunate, trait in human nature, depicts an episode related to Ishar Das *Ji*. He had given a lot of money – some donations and some loans – to many people in Rawalpindi and Abbottabad. One of those debtors was also in Dehradun. Mr. Jaggi one day asked him to repay at least a part of the loan but was aghast at the reply. The debtor told him that he didn't have even a quarter (rupee) to buy poison for himself. Mr. Jaggi did not lose his cool, took out a quarter from his pocket and said, please take this quarter and do what you want.

The government and the people of India had opened their hearts for millions of Hindu refugees uprooted from their homes and helped them as much as possible. The government set up a separate federal Ministry in charge of a man who was himself a refugee – Mehr Chand Khanna. Mr. Khanna was a Minister in the North West Frontier Province (NWFP) that was given to Pakistan at the Partition.

[Interestingly, NWFP then was ruled by the Congress Party that was opposed to the Partition of the country. But ultimately the British decision was final and binding.]

Khanna was a prominent politician and India made use of his talent.

In a few years the Jaggis were allotted a big place (partly in lieu of what they had lost in Pakistan). The senior Jaggi expired leaving a big family behind; the mother, Kartar Devi, took charge and continued where her husband left.

The Jaggis wanted their star son, Indrajit, to continue, and excel in, his studies. Ved didn't get extra facilities for her but was keen to study and make a mark for herself. I am told that sometimes she had to study under a street lamp but never gave up and came on top.

[Indrajit was a brilliant student who went on to reach great heights in his field and retired as Director of Scientific Analysis Group (SAG) of Defence Research and Development Organization (DRDO) under the Ministry of Defence, Government of India. Even after he retired from the government job, he joined as Principal of Bharati Vidyapeeth's College of Engineering and worked there for a number of years.

Dr. Kumar wrote a masterly book on his pet subject – Cryptology – regarded as an extremely useful, educative and authoritative textbook on the subject.]

From our side, my great grandfather and grandfather were big *Zamindars* (landlords) in what is now Uttar Pradesh state in India. They had vast agricultural lands and orchards. My grandfather, Dr. Onkar Prasad never put the family name/ caste – Bhatnagar with his name, and so did my father. He was also a Veterinarian surgeon. My father, Dwarka Prasad *Ji*, was more into writing, publishing, political/social/cultural activism and literary pursuits; never interested in farming or lands.

I inherited the same traits.

My father got written and published some monumental and history-making books such as *Pravasi Bharatvasi* (Indentured labor – the book that helped abolish the "slavery"system), *Dakshin Africa ke Satyagrah ka Itihaas* (the history of Civil Disobedience movement in South Africa – the book that introduced Mahatma Gandhi and his early struggles in South Africa), *Fiji Mein Baaees Varsh* (22 years in Fiji), *Arya Samaj Kis Ore* (Whither Arya Samaj) and *Arya Samaj ke Satyagrah ka Itihaas* (the history of Arya Samaj Civil Disobedience movement – Hyderabad) among others.

It is said that one of the prominent leaders among pro-India Englishmen 'Deenbandhu' C.F. Andrews read from the book *Pravasi Bharatvasi* that brought tears in the eyes of the Viceroy's wife. She was shocked at the situation and had reportedly exclaimed: Is this the kind of brutal treatment faced by my subjects in the overseas colonies of Great Britain?

The impact of this book hastened the abolition of this type of slavery.

By the time I grew up and visited our lands for the first time, grandfather had passed away and father, uninterested in *Zamindari,* was living in Bombay (now Mumbai) some 800 miles away. He had not visited our ancestral lands for decades and that habit continued with me.

However, after my grandfather's death in Agra, I rushed from Delhi and met a gentleman, Rajgopal Bhatnagar (my father's age), who claimed to be my uncle. I had never seen him; there was none to either confirm or deny his claim. I accepted him on face value as he said his lands were very near ours.

He took me to see OUR lands and standing at a place spread his arms wide and said, all that is yours. I didn't know the size of our lands, what was grown and the income it generated. I was reluctant to visit often and that made him happy as he managed to get power of attorney from father. I learnt later that he grabbed a portion of our property for himself. The 'extra' part was taken over by the government under a just passed Zamindari Abolition Act to end what was termed as 'absentee landlord' practice.

All the documents were maintained in Urdu language and I did not have adequate knowledge or practice – or even time – to read everything. I was also unfamiliar with the area and people managing the property, though many of them who met me at our *zamindari*, showed all the traditional feudal loyalty and respect for me.

I couldn't care less. I was already a working journalist of standing in a reputed newspaper *Hindustan,* of the *Hindustan Times* group. Father was even otherwise uninterested.

[In Rajgopal, I 'found' an uncle, but there was yet another distant 'relative,' cousin brother (Surendra) who also appeared on the scene. Sometime before the death of my grandfather, he and his wife came to live with him in his fairly big house. My grandfather was quite old and lived alone – my grandma had died years back. I had visited my grandpa and had met this 'brother.'

Surendra *Bhaisahab* was a few years older to me and so I respected him.

My grandfather had his own room where he slept. Next to it, there was another room that we, kids, had not seen from inside; I just had a peek from outside, one time, and saw some suitcases stacked one over the other, and dressers. The things that attracted my attention most were two beautiful swords hanging on the wall. He was a big landlord and had those decorated swords with red velvet covered sheaths. They left me wondering – and a hidden desire to own them – if grandpa will agree. I never asked him. I did not know, nor care, what other things were stocked in that good-size room, most of the time locked.

And the same thing happened after grandfather died, and I did not visit Agra twice. Just visited one time and that was not the occasion to claim anything. Naturally, Surendra must have taken over everything, including those swords. I don't know what the suitcases and dressers had. He did not have the decency to let me know about grandpa's things or ask me to visit, and share, if I wanted to. He must have assumed that *he* had all the rights to 'inherit' whatever was there. It was just like finders-keepers.]

Like my father I never wanted to build or own home or invest in real estate. There was a time when I was offered land for building home in Delhi/New Delhi across the Yamuna River at a ridiculously low price of a quarter rupee per square yard – I could buy 400 square yards for Rs.100 (about 7 or 8 dollars at the then rate).

A friend had advised me to go for it as he had done. I refused point blank saying I don't want to throw my hundred rupees in the river. He came back to me three months later and said now the price is half a rupee per square yard, don't miss this last chance.

My reply was the same as the last.

Seriously, I did not regret my decision about land and home, property and estate. Yes, while in America also I had a chance and I, as usual, passed up. The price shot up six times in 12 years and I felt not buying a home then was a mistake. But then again I thought why to bog down in a thing like home, for whom, why, may be for the kids who might not even live in that home, in that city. So it's all right.

What did I bring, what will I take with me? One headache less for me, one problem less for my kids to discuss, agree or disagree, and finally reach a settlement I might not have approved. So why do all that? In any case, it's always the hindsight.

I found Sadhana also shared my views.

Going back to our roots, on my mother's side, my grandfather (*Nana Ji*), Ganga Sagar Sharma (a 'high caste' Bajpai or Vajpayee Brahmin) was the Head Train Examiner in Central India but had retired much before my kindergarten years. However, the respect and regard he had earned during his career was awesome. You could experience it on train rides in the region. Ticket checkers at several railway stations acknowledged my mother and us kids, and never bothered to check our tickets.

[He also, like my father, did not believe in a rigid caste system. And also he did not leave land, house or any other real estate – one less dispute for heirs to handle.]

I felt proud of him.

My maternal uncle (*Mama Ji*) was Yamuna Sagar Sharma. I was his favorite. There was no uncle on my father's side so this *Mama Ji* was closer to me, and all of us kids. I did not see my mother's sister (*Maasee Ji*) who was married years ago and lived some 750 miles away from Indore and died young.

[The 'Sagar' word in the names of my *Nana Ji* and *Mama Ji* means 'the ocean.' ['Prasad' in my father and grandfather's names means divine gift, a boon, basically a *small part of offerings to an idol left for the devotees.*]

Mother, whenever in a mood to tease me when I was a child, would say: Your father's side are all 'Prasad', our side all are 'Sagar.' I felt bad but had no answer to that, for a change.]

About 80 years back when I was 7 or 8, I first stayed with *Nana Ji* for a few days. What I still remember about him was his morning prayers, walks and the popular chants from the scriptures,*"jahaan sumati tahaan sampati nana, jahaan kumati tahaan bipad nidaana."* [prosperity prevails where wisdom is present; troubles where the opposite rules.]

My mother, Shashikala, was a senior nurse at the largest hospital in Central India run by Canadian missionaries. The United Church of Canada (UCC) Mission hospital's chief was Doctor Elizabeth McMaster who had, kind of, adopted my mother and took her under her wings. We, kids, never knew any maternal grandma other than Dr. McMaster – our *Nani Ji*. I did not see her after I was probably 11 but I have the memory of a soft, kind and loving face of my *Nani* with all-white hair, firmly implanted in my memory.

I was told that days after I was born (before we went home) she took me in a stroller and went around the sprawling complex of the hospital much to the delight of my family and the staff at the hospital.

I was a precious little boy after three older sisters, and rightly deserved love from all the near and dear people in our circle, that was announced by my Dadi (father's mother.)

My good fortune! And that continued forever.

[I was born in this same hospital as my two older sisters and a younger brother. My other older sister was born at home and the younger in Mussoorie where we moved after Indore when I was about five years. Now younger sister, Priyalata, and I are the only surviving siblings out of seven (one still-born).]

All that background information about our families was not 'investigated' nor needed for our marriage. They never asked me about my salary, benefits and prospects for the future. They didn't ask me even for my education though must have guessed that I was at least a college graduate being a member of a reputed newspaper staff.

Both the families were happy with what we had then, what we were then. All what was relevant was that the two sides were happy to come closer by marriage between two people who, somehow, felt they were made for each other and hoped for a loving future and a happy married life.

By God, they were right, absolutely right.

I was 11½ years older to Sadhana; she was 21 and I was 32½ when we married. I told her she was just a kid; she said she wanted a mature person, not a boy. I had 11 times more stories to tell her; she had 11 times more patience to listen to them. The deal was perfect, the compatibility unique and the determination solid.

The path to this marriage, the merger of these two loving hearts, was paved by God Himself.

That's why I still fight God for taking my life-partner away from me.

3

We Married on a 'Bad' Day, Made a Good Life

October 8, 1961! The day in a period when no marriages take place in orthodox Hindu families in India, and I believe elsewhere also. That day is part of the *Shraddh* ceremony when traditional, orthodox Hindus remember their dead, pay respects to their souls, feed the Brahmins, and the poor and pray for the eternal peace for the dead loved ones in the heavenly abode.

We have no quarrel with praying or feeding anyone and praying for eternal peace. However, we don't believe any of those days are 'inauspicious' for marriages and/or other religious festivities and will not bring peace, joy, contentment and loving relations.

For the wedding, I hired a bus and off we went to Dehradun where Sadhana grew up, had her education and made herself a loving and caring part of the family. She was an active and well-liked popular young lady.

Our marriage on a *Shraddh* day!

We had defied those beliefs, and by God, we belied those doubts. Everything went well on October 8, 1961, and thereafter for nearly 55 years. Virtually, the whole city came to witness this 'unique' marriage. We had no difficulty in getting the best hotel for our party that traveled 150 miles from Delhi. We had one of the best bands available for our *Baraat* and caterers were happy to get our order on the day they were supposed to be sitting idle and not making any money. Incidentally, the name of the hotel the marriage party stayed is – or at least was – The White House.

We never consulted astrologers for the 'auspicious' day for the wedding. For us all days were auspicious. We didn't feel the need of matching the two horoscopes. The only consideration was mutual convenience – I should get a convenient Delhi-Dehradun bus and the bride's people could make suitable arrangements in their city. Indrajit and I consulted 'Mr.

Calendar' of 1961 and decided on the convenient Sunday (October 8). Everything right happily fell into the right place.

For want of time and unlimited resources, we did not plan to have an elaborate week-long Big Fat Indian Wedding ceremony running into several days – *mehndi* (henna), *sangeet* (music) and so on. The only pre-marriage ceremony was going to be *Roka* (formal 'Yes' from both the sides), and sealing the deal with the future groom by the girl's side. Sadhana's mother and brother with a box full of sweets and a basket full of fruits and nuts visited us a few months back and we 'sealed the deal.' As is the custom, Sadhana was not present; she was in Dehradun. I had already met her on my 'date' April 21, *Milan Divas* – The Day We Met.

During this six-month of waiting, dozens of letters were exchanged. Phone facility was not easy; it was also expensive. So we had the mailmen on both the sides helping us. In this case 'the middlemen' were welcomed. Letters were a big consolation. We never let our daughters read those love-letters;   thought they might do so after we were gone, or when they grow up and become our friends.

[They are now more or less friends but the letters are buried in boxes of books and folders. For years they have remained un-opened as we moved from India to the United States, and several times within the country. And also, naturally, our two married daughters with their families – and Sujata becoming a grandma herself – there are many more demands on their time, and more pressing duties to perform.]

It was late afternoon when our marriage party reached Dehradun. A little before our arrival at Sadhana's home there was a light drizzle, supposed to be very auspicious. Soon after it stopped and the ceremony started.

The groom's (my) party that stayed at The White House had a very pleasant experience. Nobody had imagined that one day I would live in America, the country whose President lives in The White House, in Washington D.C., the capital city.

The *gharatis* (my in-laws and their friends) included *Mataji* (Sadhana's mother – Kartar Devi; all the three older brothers, Ram, Balbir and Indrajit – the first two with their wives and kids – and other relatives. Sadhana's maiden name was Ved, with her consent I changed it after our marriage. She loved it as the word means something more than 'the desired one,' something you are rewarded after devoted and persistent *tapasya* (hard work).

23

The groom's party included some of my friends and co-workers and some 'adopted-relatives' like Kamal Bhaisahab, a father-figure, and a part of his family, Kanta bahanji (who played the important role in arranging our marriage), Saroj and Rattan, close friends such as Virendra Prabhakar (also a photographer-colleague), and other friends like Air Force officer, Sq. Ldr. Shashi Bhushan Chhibber and Vinay Narula (who joined the Army following the Chinese attack on India's Northeast region in 1962.)

Some in my party were persuaded to join us at the last minute when the bus arrived at their homes, unannounced. They were loaded *as they were* at that time without 'proper marriage outfits.' That only showed my love for and closeness to them, and vice-versa. Nobody cared for what they wore; it was love, and the joy of being a part of the ceremony *for me* and them all around.

We were well received by the *Gharatis* and were accorded the traditional welcome. We had a flower-bedecked car and the special band. A huge crowd turned up to see this unique wedding arranged on a traditionally inauspicious (*Shraddh*) day.

Unmindful of all those out-of-date traditions, we had a gala time.

Mataji gave away the bride, a break from the orthodox tradition. We liked and respected it.

Everything went off normally, no hitch or dispute, no deals and no expectations. It was a different deal of getting the two families closer as one. We wanted everyone to recognize that a marriage is an arrangement for two families to come together and become just like one. It's not a relation just between a man and a woman, but it's a close bond between parents, brothers, sisters, uncles and aunties and so on.

The families coming together in good faith and cooperation becomes a big support system, an extended family group; new relations forged between two different sets of people. They may be from different backgrounds, regions, cultures – or even religions but love and understanding, accommodation, tolerance, cooperation, fellow-feeling, mutual compassion and kindness are the keys for healthy and happy relations among people, families and communities. You can extend this concept to the whole world.

Okay, enough of these sermons.

The ceremony was joyous, happy, memorable and lovingly completed. Sadhana and I were married with the Vedic ceremony and all the essential rituals conducted by a renowned priest before the sacred fire and with chanting of Vedic *mantras.*

Ved (Sadhana) had written a *Shiksha* (words of advice, usually from parents of the bride) and had set its tune herself. She could not, obviously, sing it so her older sister Satya *Ji,* did the honors. It's a beautiful song about the raising of the beloved daughter with all the love and care, and also how she is expected to conduct herself in her *Sasural* (in-laws place). In addition there are some words for the groom.

It's definitely one *Shiksha* every bride and groom should hear.

[No wonder, Sadhana rendered the same *Shiksha* for our daughter Sujata when she married Mujtaba in America, in 1982. (Of course she did better than her sister, who was crying more than singing. But that's okay. The words remain meaningful).]

It was a beautiful beginning of a most loving married life many envied and admired. On our part, we supported each other in everything that happened in our life; shared cheers as well as tears and raised a loving, caring family. We kept the family bonding, made and kept friends and lent our shoulders and hearts to those in need of support in any manner.

We were lovers and admirers of beauty in everything, in ourselves, in other people, in animals, in nature and also our environment. Sadhana's paintings and sketches, writings and personal conduct – supported by me and vice versa – speak volumes about what we thought, did, preached and practiced.

The day after the marriage ceremony, October 9, a part of the wedding party went sightseeing and the rest spent time in familiarizing with the hosts. After lunch we started back to Delhi with the usual *Vidai* ceremony that becomes sad with parting, and weeping.

We, the *Baratis* (groom's party) – were well-fed and the bus well-stocked by the *Gharatis* (the bride's side) for the long journey. We didn't have to stop to eat, though we did to stretch our legs and so on.

Once we were all in the bus and on our way the dreams of a new future overtook everything and almost a non-stop singing session started. Sadhana was persuaded and she obliged by singing what became one of our favorite songs:

Nayee manzil nayee rahein, naya hai meherbaan apna,
na jane ja ke theharega kahaan yeh karvaan apna.

(New destination and new path, new partner-friend, I don't know where this caravan will end up.)

How appropriate was her choice!

Many others also sang but I don't quite remember as I was sitting with my beautiful young bride and never left her side during the several hours-long drive to Delhi.

An incident worth mentioning happened on our way to Delhi. As our bus drove on and entered the city of Meerut it was stopped by a police team. We were told that because of a serious situation inside the city, it was under a strict Curfew Order from sunset to sunrise, or something like that, and no movement of people or vehicles was allowed. We were right there between those hours.

That was the first time I left Sadhana and came down, along with a couple other team-members to explain to the police that we are a marriage party returning to Delhi from Dehradun.

With that genuine explanation we became VIPs. Our bus was allowed to pass but with a police escort till the outer border of the city, safely. We waved thanks to the police and merrily drove on resuming our singing, and laughter.

So much for the 'inauspicious' *Shraddh*-day marriage – a police escort ensuring our safety!

After a long two-day bus drive, hectic marriage ceremonies and eating to our heart's content, we finally returned to Delhi. It was past midnight but each one was dropped off at their homes and lastly Sadhana and I, Saroj and *behenji*, at our temporary home in Ramesh Nagar. We got the bags down with many extras as a part of dowry-gifts.

A few words about dowry. I was against the dowry system that usually puts an additional burden on the bride's family. The tradition was born out of love and due share going to all the kids of the family. Just because in farming community, if a part of the land goes to the girl (actually the girl's husband and in-laws) it gets divided and the source of income for the sons or their families that are supposed to remain in a joint family system decreases.

To avoid such a situation the custom adopted was to give as much as possible to the girl when she gets married. In fact, throughout her married life, her parents or their successor sons, keep on giving to their daughter/sister on every conceivable occasion – her marriage, related rituals in her in-laws home, her kids' birth, their many rituals, their marriages and so on. That was the obligation, a duty and a tradition – all that instead of sharing the ancestral land or property.

In course of time it became a burden with forced dowry, expectations of the in-laws, even if it would crush the girl's parents/brothers. Many cases of torture of the daughters-in-law and constant friction between the two families, suicides by the girls before and/or after marriage, all because of dowry demands have marred the healthy and loving ties that should bind the two families.

In my case, I did not want anything suggesting a dowry obligation. I told my friend – and future brother-in-law - Indrajit that I do not want any dowry. My father also did not want, and did not receive 'dowry,' as such.

So we both agreed. But, there was a little but... Indrajit said that what his mother wants to give with love and blessings should not be regarded as dowry. I said okay, provided it was not substantial and for which you did not have to borrow, make special arrangements or make it a ritual to show off to the community and relatives.

That 'deal' was satisfactory. Sadhana brought with her what she needed to make a home and run it as she liked. She brought her new wardrobe, two suits and the wedding ring for me, her jewelry, and a sewing machine. I had bought some jewelry and sarees for her and two suits for me. Indrajit had insisted on a polyester shirt for me (that kind of expensive imported cloth had just become popular) and I wanted one for Indrajit too. They included some useful furniture too.

By the time we reached Ramesh Nagar, we were dead tired. We had no strength or wish to do anything but to sink in our bed.

That we did as soon as we could with a quick good night to everybody.

I had returned from Dehradun with my lovely talented wife, but not yet fully aware of what more talents she had, for me, for everyone to know. There was plenty of time for all that, starting from the next day when our two-roomed apartment/house was transformed into a beautiful *home*.

4

Making of a 'Home'

The next day I had to run some important errands that took a rather long time. In the last few days I had changed residence and in those days without the cell phones (they are called Mobile phones in India) we had only land lines and it was not easy or quick to get phone lines installed at the new home.

So, I was not in touch with Sadhana during the few hours I was out. It was late afternoon when I returned and was instantly stunned – my beautiful wife waiting for me in her elegantly chosen lovely dress (she wore only sarees for years), simple yet lovely jewelry and the apartment transformed into an amazingly arranged abode called "home.'

I was wonderstruck and could only say: "*Tumne to ise swarg bana diya* (you have turned this into a heaven.) She had a lovely smile on her face as she led me into the newly decorated and re-arranged home. We exchanged glances that said more than we expressed. Indeed that was the beginning of the exhibition of her talents that started unfolding as our marriage turned into months and years and more than half a century.

Sadhana did not pursue an interior decorator's course, as we know these days. But she had the sense of beauty and the aesthetic sense of a high order and she made full use of it. She was always a keen observer, and a quick learner; she arranged the furniture and other things to make the small rooms look larger, bare walls look beautiful with photos and paintings, and corners seem calling people to be noticed. The home looked elegant and inviting; it bore the stamp of a lady with good taste, creativity and vision. She did everything with love and care to make it her home, *our* home.

So much for the home, the rooms and the décor! Yet another stunning thing for me was the decorator herself. My newly-wed, in an elegantly selected outfit, with charming looks, the barest of minimum make-up, and a sweet smile extended a loving welcome to me. I was apologetic for being away for hours but she put me at ease with a *phir kya hua* (no problem, that's okay).

I was stunned and could only look at her full of admiration and joy.

I fell in love with Sadhana, again.

Something more was yet to come, another important discovery.

After I freshened up, Sadhana laid the food and there was a fabulous banquet – all the dishes cooked by her. Before our marriage, I had visited her when she was at her brother's home in Rana Pratap Bagh colony in West Delhi; this was before we had said a final 'Yes' to our new relations. She had treated us to several delicacies – some she cooked herself. But they would be mainly described as part of the High Tea – snack food. But the one she laid on the table the day after I brought her as my wife to our home was full dinner with a wide variety of dishes that showed her cooking skills, manifold.

And that was the beginning of the exhibition of her culinary expertise that sustained and delighted me, the kids, other relatives and a vast group of friends (both Indian and foreign) and even strangers who became friends and admirers for more than half a century she was with me. [It was passed on to our daughters in no small measure.]

[There was much to unfold in the days and weeks, months and years, and decades in India and in the United States, all parts of a fairytale marriage cut short after just 54 years, seven months and one week. Some say it was a long time, for me, not so.

One could say that we had a full life – nearly 55 years of married life should be regarded as 'full.' But for me, it wasn't full, it was cut short. I am sure Sadhana would also be feeling just that. She never wanted our life together to end; she always wanted us to be together till eternity. For her, eternity came in about 55 years and I am left alone, lonely in a crowd, holding sweet memories, clutching all the feelings of love close to my heart and wondering if...why...and complaining and fighting with the Super Parent, why... why?]

5

Our Honeymoon and More

We didn't have a honeymoon in the traditional sense of making elaborate plans to go to a far off place for days or weeks, someone gifting us the honeymoon package, and the couple spending the first few days together and to come back with sweet – or sour – memories of the trip. We had made no plans and our resources were limited. Therefore, we kept everything limited and simple.

For us it was the beginning to know each other closely and intimately. As the part of a beautiful ceremony we liked, just a couple days after our marriage, we were off to Dehradun again for *Phera* (return). It's rather customary for the bride to go to her parent's home for a short visit. Sometimes the bride's brother comes and takes his sister back for the *Phera*. Sometimes the couple goes by itself. We were no followers of any rigid ritual and went together.

In any case, the *Phera* tradition serves two purposes for the parents and their family: One, to know first-hand from the girl how was she welcomed at the groom's place (and how does she 'assess' the groom?)

Two: To know the son-in-law better without his entourage (*Baraat*).

Mataji had already met me in Delhi and liked what she saw and heard. The others also fell in love, *Bhabhis* and their kids included.

We made it Three-in-One: A much needed part of our honeymoon.

And so it was. After spending a couple days in Dehradun, meeting Sadhana's family and a host of her friends, we went to Mussoorie, ostensibly for a day of outing, to have the time exclusively for both of us – yet another part of our unplanned honeymoon.

Mussoorie is a small but picturesque hill-town, around 7500 feet high, a part of the mighty Himalayan range. Early October it's not that cold.

Our trip to Mussoorie was memorable. Though the distance between the two towns is just about 20 miles (and there have been improvements during the last 50 years) the winding hilly road trip by bus, with a few stops, takes more than two hours.

Those two hours were full of fun for both of us.

It started with getting seats separately. What a start, I whined. All the window seats were taken up as the route is picture-perfect with hills, valleys and beautiful flowers and streams. We both were a little unhappy but what could we do?

At the first stop, some passengers got down and I started chatting with one, Mr. Kakar, brother of RK Kakar, a prominent football (soccer) referee of Delhi whom I knew. I told him we just got married and wanted to spend some time together in Mussoorie. He was gracious enough to offer his window seat and for the rest of the journey Sadhana and I sat together oblivious of the others on the bus.

I don't know what the other passengers thought – entertained or annoyed – but we kept on singing and singing.

It was sheer delight.
It was pure enjoyment.
It was unmixed affection.
It was uninhibited entertainment for others.
It showed that we didn't care for anything else when together on our 'honeymoon.'

It proved that we two were immersed in our own heartfelt joy and were intoxicated with love and had the ability to feel closer to each other even in a crowd.

That is the ultimate union of two hearts and two minds to reach the divine state of one.

That was the relation between Sadhana and I, and that was *just the beginning.*

It was to demonstrate *Khullam Khulla Pyar Karenge Hum Dono* (we will openly show our love for each other) – only singing and sitting together a little closely.

[There was much to come in the coming decades, in India, in Europe and in the United States till she breathed her last, 54 years, seven months and one week later. As on that trip when we began our life together, we were madly in love with each other till the last.]

As we got down from the bus in Mussoorie, many passengers on our bus did give us smiles and wished all the best to us. They say, "All the World Loves a Lover." We saw that love, we experienced that mood, and we felt that emotion.

It was a memorable 20 mile-ride on a public bus.

It was enough for us to make our one-day trip to Mussoorie and make it two-day. We sent a telegram – no phone connection then – to Dehradun and off we went to a cute little Raunaq Hotel to just freshen up and then to sightseeing. The same evening we went to a memorable movie, *Hum Dono* (We Two), released earlier that year starring Dev Anand, Sadhana and Nanda, three of the top-ranking movie stars of our time. Dev had a double role as a military officer.

Hum Dono has a cult status with its story, acting and melodious songs - some of the most beautiful evergreen songs. They include *Abhi na jao chhod kar, ke dil abhi bhara naheen, Kabhi khud pe kabhi haalaat pe rona aayaa, jahaan mein aisa kaun hai ke jisko gham mila naheen, Mai zindagi ka saath nibhata chala gaya* and a couple of others. Sahir Ludhianavi penned all those lyrics, with Jaidev's music and Lata, Rafi and Asha singing them, it was magic. We, two newly-weds, could closely connect and appreciate with the story of a soldier and his dilemma on the screen. We were moved, but thoroughly enjoyed the movie.

It was a fun evening that lasted till 11 at night with the movie ending late.

We had forgotten all about food till we were out of the theater. The markets had closed by then. We had carried no eats with us. Finding nothing in the nearby bazaar we reached our hotel hungry and headed to our room readying to go without food on our first 'honeymoon' night.

However, someone had planned otherwise. In a couple minutes there was a knock at the door. A waiter with sleepy eyes but eagerness to serve asked us if we were ready for dinner.

What a pleasant development it was, one of the sweetest questions the like of which are always welcomed, especially on that memorable late evening. We had given up hope and were resigned to go to bed hungry. And then from nowhere this guy appeared on the scene as our savior.

The young man served warm food and we had our fill. He deserved, and rightly got, a generous tip.

We had rounded up a very pleasant and enjoyable night of fun – the first part of our unplanned honeymoon that had to continue for decades.

Next day we spent walking up and down and beyond to see some nice places, like Kempty Falls and Gun Hill, and even Lal Tibba. [A few years later the Municipality installed Telescope there to look at distant mountain peaks of Badrinath, Kedarnath and others.] The small town is very scenic and picturesque with Doon Valley visible from some points. It was the ideal place for us, and quite affordable too though it's called the "Queen of the Hills."

We returned to Dehradun happy and full of sweet memories. We could safely claim to have our 'honeymoon' after all, even if unplanned and quite short, but most pleasant and enjoyable.

At mother's home – 8 Old Survey Road, Dehradun – that became our family's summer resort for years when the kids were growing - people were curious to know all about our trip. Especially the two *Bhabhis* and some of Sadhana's friends were waiting for a full – and juicy – report of our days and nights after marriage. What happened in New Delhi, and before our arrival in Dehradun, and in Mussoorie and all the details were eagerly awaited and devoured with gusto.

Sadhana, a great story-teller in her own right and when the situation demanded, must have entertained the curious group of loving relatives and friends, including a close one, Swaran Pratap, with interesting tales, true or made-up didn't matter. We had fun for real.

Mataji, her mother, my mother-in-Law whom I always addressed as *Mataji* (Mother), was happy to see her daughter very happy and cheerful. Her love for me must have been doubled.

The day we had arrived in Dehradun from Delhi, *Mataji* saw a glow on Sadhana's face and must have understood how things were with her dear daughter – the youngest in the family.

An experienced woman and mother of five she could guess that her daughter was happy and was being treated nicely by her loving husband. *Bhabhis* had to directly ask pertinent questions, as I came to know later.

Mataji was a little disturbed at first when she saw Sadhana laughing loudly and chirping all around. Before marriage, like a good thoughtful mother, she had given a word of advice to her daughter to curb her habit of laughing, always chirping and being talkative at home. After we landed at her home in Dehradun she did not notice anything different. She must have thought that all her advice was in vain. On inquiry, Sadhana told her mother that in her new home people are excited, chirpy, especially her husband, very jovial, and himself laughs with abandon.

Mother felt a sigh of relief. Since then *Mataji* treated me as her loving son and developed deeper affection for me. She called me *Kaka* (Punjabi word for son).

Her Dehradun home was quite big (though not as big as the home in Abbottabad they had to leave behind) but quite spacious with several rooms and over 70 trees of the best *leechies* in Dehradun. In addition, they had a few mango trees and also the best quality jackfruit etc.

Mataji used to send a boxful of the choicest *leechies* to us in Delhi every summer. During the goods (cargo) train journey in hot weather half the box would be spoiled but *Mataji* insisted on sending regularly saying that at least half would be fine when they reach my *Kaka* (me) and Ved.

During winters, she would send us a boxful of *Pinnies* (sweets) the like of which I have not tasted ever. She would make them from scratch with month's preparation. Made of pure *desi ghee* (high quality clarified butter), rich and healthy, her *Pinnies* were out of this world. She would ensure they reach me safely.

Her love for me was special and she trusted me very much, so much so that she wanted me to help her make her will. She had three sons and two daughters, including Sadhana, and she wanted a fair share for everyone.

In a traditional Indian family, sons get more than daughters from their parent's property. Now legally the share is equal, though in practice often a preference for sons is always seen. In our case, I politely excused myself from helping *Mataji* write her will. I thought it might be – just might be – interpreted as my interest in influencing mother in distribution of her property.

I had no intention of even Sadhana sharing in the property (big house etc.) Sadhana also shared my view and wholeheartedly and willingly decided to forego her share and preferred it to go to the elder sister.

Whatever mother did, I don't know, did not try to find it, but know for sure that Sadhana and I did not want any share in the property. We had already got plenty from mother and brothers in the form of love, gifts at our marriage and from time to time on festivals and other occasions. We were happy with whatever we had and capable of earning more. Sadhana and I were, and have always been, on the same page in these matters, and practically all the other.

Sujata, Seema, Balbir bhaisahab's kids Anju, Ajay and Ranjana (Kaki) and Indrajit's daughter Rewa and son Vineet were the regulars on their summer breaks they spent at *Mataji*'s home. Sadhana and the 'resident *bhabhi*' Mohini (Balbir's wife) and Indrajit's wife Usha, were quite close and would join in the fun. I would also join them for a few days but let them enjoy most of the time without me. My work in Delhi was demanding and so was Indrajit's. Balbir *Ji* was the 'resident brother' and would rule over the household.

The kids have many sweet memories of *Nani*'s home and the time they used to spend – without much home work from the school.

Things were different those days, the kids were not so much burdened with homework and various projects. Life was more soothing, calming and enjoyable without any stress.

Sadhana, with her amiable nature and deep respect for elders soon won over my father, sisters and brother, my brothers-in-law who were not part of my marriage ceremonies. Many were living in Delhi, father and a sister-brother lived in Bombay (now Mumbai).

We invited and visited those in Delhi and they were impressed by Sadhana, her nature and her respectful demeanor. She quickly became a favorite of my older sister Prem's kids, and they were several. My two older sisters and their husbands had only praise for Sadhana as long as they lived. Their children had the same feelings and respect for Sadhana as long as she lived. She was there for everyone who needed her – and there were several occasions when that happened. Prem lost her eldest son, Pravin, in an accident and we rushed to their city 150 miles from us.

Her second son was Naveen (fondly called Chhota or Chhote *Bhaiya*) who was working in Delhi. The third son is Vipin Bhatnagar who worked in Bhutan for years and was also a great help to his father.

He later worked and settled in Dehradun with his wife Renu and his family. Their two daughters, Sapna and Swati, loving and caring, are happily married; they are close to Sujata and Seema.

Prem's daughters, Savita and Suneeta were married the same day at the same place, in New Delhi.

Sujata recalled with some amusement the day when, Sudhir, the would-be groom – later husband – came with his family to see Suneeta first time, as is the custom.

Suneeta was asked to sing. She chose this song:

Rehte they kabhi jin ke dil mein hum jaan se bhi pyaron ki tareh,
baithhey hain unhi ke kooche mein hum aaj gunahgaron ki tareh.

(Today I sit as a culprit in this gathering for the one who once loved me.)

The song was beautifully sung by Lata Mangeshkar in the movie *Mamta* (1966), picturized on Suchitra Sen; Majrooh Sultanpuri wrote the lyrics with music by Roshan.

An interesting choice of song at an occasion like this!

Sarita (Guchcha) and Anita (Annu) were the youngest of the siblings. Sujata and Seema fondly recall the *qawwalis* they had heard these young cousin sisters sing often. Among them was:

> *Kisko laaoon jawaabe sanam mein,*
> *koyi nazron mein janchta nahin hai,*
> *Chaand ke mukh pe dhabbey hain lekin,*
> *unke chehre pe dhabba nahin hai.*

(Who should I bring forward as a befitting response to my love as no one else I really like. Even the moon's face has spots on it, but there are none on the face of the one I love.)

All the kids were very close to each other. Often driving when we passed in front of Coca Cola factory near our house on Nazafgarh Road, Sujata and Seema would burst out singing, "Coca Cola factory Munnu *Bhaiya* ki, Chhote *Bhaiya* ki, Vipin *Bhaiya* ki, Coca Cola factory, Coca Cola factory" giving the ownership to their three cousin brothers.

Following the tragic death of Munnu (Pravin), whenever we passed the factory, they still repeated the lines *"Munnu Bhaiya ki"* but with a lower voice and tears in their eyes.

A few days after our marriage we were invited to our sister's place. As soon as our cab stopped, a teenager walked up and as we opened the door and Sadhana looked up, he greeted her with, *"Namaste, Dadi Ji"* (salutations grandma).

A shocked Sadhana looked at me as I introduced Papla (his nickname), son of my older brother-in-law's nephew – like his grandson. Therefore, he was my grandson also. We, Indians, have this interesting relationship and Sadhana knew the practice but this unexpected welcome by a 'grandson' for a just-married young woman was something shocking. We had a good laugh following this episode but Papla would always address her as *Dadi Ji.*

I was lucky to have Prem's husband, PRK Bhatnagar (*Jeejaji*) always there when I needed him. With me, he also risked his life when he accompanied me, on foot (as there was no vehicle movement on that road) to take a short cut when I was filling up a form for my Intermediate exam, in 1947. As we were walking, a nasty-looking sturdy man walked toward us. He did not give us a friendly look but just about four feet from us he suddenly, as if asked by a Higher being, turned left and went across the road.

As soon as we reached a 'safer' road, we were surrounded by a group of people who wondered why we took that particular road – they told us about a couple murders just a few hours back. *Jeejaji* looked at me and just smiled.

[Prem was my favorite sister though Sneh Lata (Bobo) was the oldest and the fairest of all. Bobo was somewhat feeble-minded, though never ever fell sick, to my knowledge. She was raised by my paternal grandparents *(Dada-Dadi)* in Agra from her early childhood. We would only see her when we visited them. She loved me from my childhood and whenever we met she would pretend to put a *tilak* or *teeka* (colored line) on my forehead and say: go, get married and bring her.

In my childhood I loved Prem the most. I remember when I was five or six, I used to say that I want to marry Prem. She also loved and cared for me but Preeti Lata, the third sister was more caring and protective. I have mentioned about her later. Both loved Sadhana very much.]

When I moved to New Delhi from Bombay, in 1947, I lived with Prem and *Jeejaji* when they were themselves living with *Jeejaji's* cousin sister, Leela, her husband RL Bhatnagar and pre-teen daughter Munan (Kanta). I was welcomed to that big extended family with open arms and hearts. The same treatment Sadhana got from that family, especially Leela *behenji* and was close to her till her passing away, many years later. Afterward, Sadhana and Munan became very close – and so were the two sets of children. It was a very loving relationship.

Sadhana had made her place in that family and also the extended family.

The first time ever we all heard my sister, Prem, sing for us was indeed memorable. It was a beautiful song with soulful lyrics, written by Shailendra and music composed by Shankar Jaikishan. Originally sung by none other than the nightingale herself, Lata Mangeshkar, for a legendary actress, Nargis, in the 1953 film – *Aah*, produced by Raj Kapoor who also played the male lead, debut direction by his own assistant director, Raja Nawathe, this song captured the utter despair and loneliness of a young girl as she longs to see the one she loves.

> *Yeh shaam ki tanhaaiyan, aise mein tera gham*
> *Patte kahin khadke hawa aayi to chaunke hum*

(In the loneliness of this evening, amidst those sad thoughts of you, the wind makes the leaves rustle and startles me.)

Prem sang it so well that soon this song became our favorite and one of the most requested numbers that she just had to sing each time we would get together.

Years later, even now when Sujata or Seema hum this lovely song, they fondly recall their *Amma Bua* (mumma-aunty) and cherish all the memories associated with her and this melodious number.

6

Our Active Life and the Big Circle

Back after the *Phera* I immersed in my job and more active life of a
journalist. In the decades that followed, Sadhana's varied talents
showed in ample measure. From cooking to sewing, knitting to
embroidery, crochet work to gardening, singing to sketching, writing
articles and poems to painting, and what have you. She would take
interest in whatever I was doing, keeping pace with me in outdoor
activities, meeting with friends, attending parties and inviting people –
both Indian and foreign to our home. All that made *us* one of the most
popular couples among the big group of national and international
journalists.

We also became one of the frequently invited couples for government
and non-government functions/parties and also for diplomatic receptions,
lunches, dinners and national day celebrations of numerous other
countries. In addition, Sadhana and I were often invited by the Prime
Ministers and Presidents of India on various occasions. There were
several state banquets for visiting Prime Ministers, Presidents and Kings
at Rashtrapati Bhavan (the President's House) to which we were
privileged and honored to be invited.

Among some of the other occasions we both had the privilege to attend
were Bharat Ratna Lata Mangeshkar singing *'Ae Mere Watan Ke Logon,
Zara Aankh Mein Bhar Lo Paani'* at the Red Fort in Delhi soon after the
Chinese attack on India's Northeastern borders in 1962. Prime Minister
Jawaharlal Nehru was there in the front row – we in the second – and saw
Nehru also wiping a tear as Lataji sang the moving composition by one of
the great song writers, Pradeep. He was also there in his long white kurta-
pajama he traditionally wore.

Sadhana would wholeheartedly share my views on politics, nationalism,
civic affairs, religion, culture, India's ancient history and heritage, and
personalities, both Indian and foreign. She would give her input, ask
pertinent questions and raise her doubts also. We would enjoy going to
art exhibitions, and literary functions, poetry recitals by eminent poets,
meetings addressed by leaders, and actively participate in various events.

It was a life full of activities, mingling with people from all walks of life in the capital city of India – and later the prominent centers of activities in Indore (where I had taken over as Chief Editor of *Dainik Bhaskar*, now the most widely circulated daily newspaper chain of the country, and the fourth largest in the world.) Sadhana, in her various activities at home raising two girls, and with the extended family and friends, always found time to be with me at state, national and international functions. She was truly my companion at every step, all the way.

Sadhana was a regular radio broadcaster and writer, in her own right, despite being a full-time wife and mother. She was frequently invited by All India Radio to give her talk, lead and participate in discussions. Her views were precise, her radio-personality was impressive, her diction easy and clear and her opinions convincing and elicited respect. She was frequently on the radio for women's programs and discussions for both domestic and international services for AIR.

While on a foreign visit with me she recited her poems at the Writers House in Cairo (Egypt), and on BBC London, among other places. While at BBC where I had gone to record a talk, Sadhana was just whisked away to another studio, without notice, where she gave a talk and recited her poems.

Sadhana used to write for reputed newspapers and magazines, including *Saptahik Hindustan*, a *Hindustan Times* publication of New Delhi and *Dharmayug*, a Times of India publication of Bombay (now Mumbai). She also participated in *Kavi Sammelans* (poets and writers gatherings) in New Delhi, Dehradun, Indore, Ujjain, Dewas, and some other towns in Central India. While in the United States, she also participated in literary programs in Los Angeles, San Francisco and Houston.

Sadhana was a devoted artist and produced scores of paintings and sketches in India and other countries we visited. Most of the sketches she finished on-the-spot, while some paintings were completed at home. She was creative, imaginative and also prolific despite her manifold duties as a wife, mother, relative, good neighbor and friend and writer-poet.

Sadhana's loving and caring nature got her many friends. Even the servants working at our homes were touched by her generous and caring personality. At a time when TV sets were few and the poorer families and kids could not even dream of having one, she used to invite the less privileged kids and families of the neighborhood to watch movies and other interesting programs at our home. In those early days movies were shown on TV only on Sunday evenings and our home was a mini theater for the neighborhood's less privileged.

In addition to the movies, Sadhana would serve tea and snacks to everyone in the audience. The smiles, joy and gratitude on their faces were priceless rewards for her, and all of us. No wonder our daughters Sujata and Seema got it from their mother – no one leaves their homes without having something. The gardeners, pool-men, cleaning ladies, handymen, mail-carriers and others are treated the same. The list goes on and on, because Sadhana and my parents, and their parents had shown the way of sharing and caring.

Sadhana's caring nature had no limits. She was widely known and admired. Suresh, the helper-girl for cleaning and doing odd jobs in our home in New Delhi's elite colony of Chanakyapuri, belonged to the so-called untouchable community. Sadhana not only was fine with her doing the jobs in our kitchen but also helped her in learning table manners, serving and keeping her own modest home tidy.

One day Suresh (normally a boy's name), rather hesitatingly, asked me and Sadhana if we would honor her and her family by visiting and having tea with them. Her joy knew no bounds when we happily accepted the invitation. Suresh had everything arranged nicely with plates and napkins neatly placed on the table. We had a good time at their home with tasty snacks and well organized household.

[Suresh was one of the main helpers in taking care of the gifts and other things at the pre-marriage reception for Sujata in New Delhi, prior to our departure for her wedding in Los Angeles.]

We also attended the wedding of Suresh in her not-so-classy colony but that did not deter Sadhana and me. That was not in our nature and upbringing. For us superiority complex never existed; arrogance about education, status and money were meaningless. We believed in humanity, humility and lived accordingly.

There was another servant-couple working for us. Radha was a kitchen-help, and occasional baby-sitter for our pre-teen daughters, Sujata and Seema. Her husband, Rati Ram, was our gardener. They were also given all the care and consideration by Sadhana, so much so that when Radha became pregnant, Sadhana would constantly advise, guide and care for her. We took Radha to the hospital in our car and also brought her and her baby boy back home. The look on her face and grateful joy were priceless for us. She and her husband would not stop singing our praises in the entire neighborhood and in their own circle of relatives and friends.

Yet another servant-couple, Pappa and husband Arumugam! The woman was also a kitchen- help, and frequently Aru too. The man was expert in making many kinds of *Mithai* (sweets). One was *Balushahi*. I never liked it before I tasted what Aru made. I have not had the kind of *Balushahi* 40 years before Arumugam made them, nor 40 years after.

He made *Dosas* and *Idlies* too and we used to have these delicious South Indian eats whenever we wanted. These are no longer 'South' Indians as they have become popular all over the world.

Our first exclusive servant was Umeed Singh, a young man from India's northern hilly region, whom I had hired way back in 1947-48. He was fiercely loyal to me and after a few years of working elsewhere, I re-discovered him and brought him back home that had become 'our' home by then. Umeed Singh always wondered how much *besan* (gram flour) we were using as every other day we would have *pakoras (fritters)* for tea and snacks. He worked for us in the same loving and caring environment though after some time we let him go to seek better job and life.

We did not hear from him, or saw him, after that but would think and talk about him often. That had been our nature, together. We were mostly on the same page.

We did not forget the same nature when we moved to Indore and I became the Chief Editor. We had the kitchen-help, cleaning crew and others. The young girl from the neighborhood 'cleaning crew' was also treated by Sadhana and our family with kindness, generosity and consideration. Often I would drop the helper, Vishnu, at her home after work. When that young girl's wedding was planned, and we were planning to leave Indore and India, we gifted her several dresses, bedsheets, comforters and other household things. Her mother thanked Sadhana profusely saying that the girl's entire 'Dowry' is complete.

7

My Irregular Hours, My Patient Wife

B efore I joined, *Hindustan*, the Hindi daily publication of the reputed newspaper organization, *The Hindustan Times* (owned by one of the top industrialists, Ghanshyam Das Birla), I had worked for three other papers: *Janasatta, Amar Bharat* and *Dainik Vishwamitra,* in Delhi-New Delhi. *Vishwamitra,* the Bombay edition, was one of the five editions, where I started my career as a journalist in 1947. Later I moved to New Delhi and joined the local edition of the same paper.

Rewind a bit:

Working for these papers was a different experience with no fixed working hours, no set yearly wage increase, no defined set vacation or sick time, and sometimes, no weekends. In some cases no regular pay-day, except in *Janasatta*. Sometimes we did not get the full salary on pay day, after working for the full previous month. There was no weekly or fortnightly pay-day in India. *Amar Bharat* was the worst; when I left it after three years, the paper still owed me three months' full salary, a part of which I received after many tries in the following months.

Janasatta, of the *Delhi Express* group of papers (later *Indian Express*), was managed much better. The Editor, Pundit Indra Vidyavachaspati, was one of the top men in the profession and a member of India's Parliament. The Managing Director of the *Delhi Express* group was Feroze Gandhi, husband of Indira Gandhi (daughter of Jawaharlal Nehru, the first Prime Minister of India). [Indira later herself became Prime Minister.] Feroze was then a Member of Parliament, in his own right. Indira lived with Nehru at the Prime Minister's official residence, Teen Murti House and Feroze lived separately in MP's quarters.

I worked for *Janasatta* only for three months and then joined *Hindustan*. The *Hindustan Times* newspaper group is one of the oldest in India, co-founded by Pundit Madan Mohan Malaviya, one of the stalwarts of the freedom movement in India, who later became the main spirit behind a reshaped paper that became the foremost nationalist newspaper in India. G.D. Birla was its big financier.

Mahatma Gandhi performed the opening ceremony of *The Hindustan Times* on September 26, 1924. One of the first editors was his youngest son, Devdas Gandhi.

I joined *Hindustan* in September, 1952 with a five-year standing in the profession. I stayed with the paper for over 30 years and rose from sub-editor/reporter to the post of Chief of News Bureau, second only to the editor. That period was very significant for me and my professional achievements, extensive travels, book writing, and frequent radio-TV programs. [Nine years later Sadhana came into my life and witnessed all that progress and also played a significant part in those accomplishments. I did the same to promote her interests and cheered her all the way for her writing, poetry, painting/sketching and radio programs.]

My joining *Hindustan* has one more memorable event – the beginning. I was interviewed by no less a person than Devdas Gandhi himself. He was the managing editor/director of the *Hindustan Times* group. A simple-looking but impressive personality, Devdas *Ji,* as he was commonly known and addressed, asked me several questions about my experience and possible contribution, if selected.

I must have impressed him as within minutes, I got the appointment letter with his own signature.

He, probably, was also impressed because of my answer to his last question: What salary do you expect, or you would like to leave that to me? I replied, without hesitation: I leave it to your judgment as I am confident of my ability to serve the paper well.

During my three decades plus with the organization, I became an invaluable asset to *Hindustan.* In addition, I frequently contributed to all the other publications of the group, *Hindustan Times, HT Evening News, Saptahik Hindustan, Kadambini, and Nandan* – a record no other staff member of the group can claim.

Of course I had my tiff with not only one of the editors of *Hindustan* but also with K.K. Birla, who got HT from his father, G.D. Birla. HT now has KK's married daughter, Shobhana Bhartia, as the chief executive. She was the first woman-chief of a big news group in India. She became the boss three years after I left: my tiff was with her father, because he had succumbed to political pressure and denied me the post of editor of *Hindustan* that I fully deserved on merit, and also seniority.

But that is a separate chapter in my life.

My work with the daily newspaper was unlike other 10 to 5 jobs. Yes, there were duty hours – 8 to 3, 11 to 6, 2 to 8 and 8 to 2 (the night shift). I worked sometimes doing 'overtime' on my own. I would accept shifts that others avoided. I would take on other assignments, in addition to my regular shift. I would write extra columns and articles, reports, etc. I had a motor cycle, later a scooter and so was quite mobile. I did not ask, nor got, additional allowances for this extra work.

It was labor of love.

In addition to my newspaper job, I had other interests also; I became involved in Chitra Kala Sangam, a cultural organization started by my good friend and colleague, Virendra Prabhakar. An artist himself with regular training from the ace artist Sudhir Khastgir, he was the staff photographer of our paper. I joined him and helped in organizing events and press publicity etc. for the organization.

Within a short period, Chitra Kala Sangam rose from Municipal Committee level to a bigger, national level organization with succeeding Vice Presidents and Presidents of India as Patrons and Chief Patrons.

We were the first to organize an International Cultural Evening of music and dance in New Delhi where diplomats from about 10 embassies, including the American, participated, sang and danced.

In just a couple years, we became the pioneer institution to organize International Cultural Evening for Children every year with Indian and foreign kids participating. Select children welcomed guests, managed the stage, conducted and made short speeches. Every performance had a full house, totally free of charge, only by invitation. Kids came, families came, neighbors came, others came and enjoyed the programs of music and dance where kids were the stars and blessed by VIPs.

Sujata, then only 5, was one of the child-organizers, and was honored, rewarded and blessed by the then Vice President of India, Dr. Zakir Husain (later the President.) These organizers were each given a bronze statue of Mahatma Gandhi, made by the eminent artist – Ram Sutar.

While accepting the award from the Vice President we saw him talking to Sujata and she responding shyly.

Later we asked her about the conversation that went like this:

VP: *aap hamare ghar aaiye kabhi* (come over to our house sometimes.)

Sujata: *pehle aap aaiye hamare ghar* (first you come to our house.)

We thought we were doing a good job of raising a polite and a well-mannered girl.

Sadhana was an enthusiastic helper and handled many duties, voluntarily. She couldn't be anywhere else.

One of the other important programs Chitra Kala Sangam organized earlier was memorable for me for two things: the significance of the program and conclusion of the celebration.

That was the amusing 'finale.'

Indrani Rahman was one of the most prominent Indian classical dancers. Once she was invited by the then Soviet Union for a dance tour of that country. As one of the organizers and the Press Secretary (it was a multi-purpose honorary post), I proposed that Chitra Kala Sangam invite and honor her as she prepares for her Russian trip. The entire group wholeheartedly welcomed it but, as it happens, the task to get her to our function fell on me.

[She was also chosen Miss India (even when married and mother of a child) and also participated in Miss Universe contest. She was the daughter of a Bajpai Brahmin and freedom fighter/journalist, Ramalal, who later became India's Consul General in New York. Her mother was an American woman (Esther Sherman) who became a Hindu and took the name Ragini Devi. Both mother-daughter were famous dancers and performed in many countries. They were exponents of Bharatanatyam, Kuchipudi, Odissi and Kathakali and popularized these classical Indian dance forms in the West.

Indrani also performed for President John F. Kennedy and Prime Minister Jawaharlal Nehru, during Nehru's official visit to Washington, D.C. In later years, she also performed for the visiting Emperor Haile Selassie, Queen Elizabeth II, Mao Zedong, Nikita Khrushchev, and Fidel Castro.]

I called Indrani and met her and her architect-husband Habib Rahman, and their son Ram at their home in Sujan Singh Park, New Delhi.

[Indrani at 15, still in school and underage according to the Indian laws, had eloped with Rahman who was 30 and married him in 1945. Indrani was very fair (after her American mother) while Rahman was dark complexioned.]

Their marriage lasted for five decades; they had a daughter also, named Sukanya.]

I was welcomed to their home in Sujan Singh Park, and Indrani graciously accepted our invitation to attend our function, held at one of the popular restaurants, Wengers, in Connaught Circus in New Delhi.

[We were also honoring the eminent writer, Yashpal Jain, at the same function.]

Beautiful Indrani Rahman, in a pink saree looked simply stunning.

As most of the members and many attendees at the function had not met Indrani, and she herself did not know many of the attendees, I introduced her, welcomed her and was frequently seen talking to her.

The function went very well and Indrani was seen off by me and a few other prominent members of Chitra Kala Sangam's core group.

Now the amusing episode.

After seeing off Indrani I returned to the main hall, settled the bills and generously tipped the waiters. Not satisfied with what I had paid them, a few came to me and said; *"sahib aaj to aapka khas din hai, kuchh aur mil jaaye,"* (Sir, today is a special day for you, let's have some more).

Instantly it dawned on me and my dear friend and Secretary of Chitra Kala Sangam, Virendra Prabhakar, and we exchanged meaningful smiles. The waiters had thought that it was my marriage reception and that Indrani was my bride as I was frequently going to her and talking.

This was our private talking point for quite some time.

I met Indrani Rahman several times at her shows and in parties and she was always gracious and charming. Of course, Indrani did not have any inkling about what the waiters thought about that memorable evening.

I wasn't married then and I shared this story with Sadhana later and she too enjoyed it. She also met Indrani a few times and saw her perform those exquisite dances, at New Delhi's famous Sapru House, and elsewhere. We were lucky to have met this dancing diva and seen her perform to full house many times.

[Indrani later moved to New York where she died in 1999 when she was just 69. Habib had expired in 1995. I never had a chance again to meet with Ram and Sukanya.]

This was my hectic life and work as an active journalist interested in many activities. I became used to this kind of regular/irregular/busy schedule and liked it, enjoyed it.

And then I got married.

And then nothing changed – more or less.

I had already 'warned' Sadhana that my evenings would be spent in office, reporting and writing/editing news stories, attending parties and functions, and might not be home till late, sometimes around midnight. The reply I got was, that's okay, I'll wait for you. And she did it regularly, lovingly, happily and without complaints.

No matter when I returned, after 9, around midnight, or later, Sadhana would not eat. She would be waiting for me elegantly dressed, having cooked a nice dinner and the table set. Her usual sweet smile would greet and welcome me at the door and make me feel comfortable. She never made me feel guilty of keeping her waiting, being so late, and that sort.

Her mere sight in a charming bridal mode would make my day – or evening. All the stress would vanish. That way she was also a very effective stress-reliever for me and everyone around. My very busy, tiring, stressful and varied duties at the office could not make me grumpy and hyper, mainly due to my wife. This has been Sadhana's nature ever since I married her – no reason to doubt she was like that even before for her entire family.

My duties at the office did vary but at one point I was given assignment to report the proceedings and activities at the Delhi Municipal Corporation. The Mayor then was Bawa Bachittar Singh, a businessman with a flourishing pottery industry. He was accessible and helpful and my counterpart in the English *Hindustan Times* was too eager to avail of the facility and would never let go of any opportunity.

It was a strange assignment for the man from Southern India who did not know Hindi or Urdu, the main languages of the Corporation. As a result he only recorded and reported the speeches of the Commissioner and the Mayor, as they were mostly in English. He would depend on me to give him a gist of what the others spoke – if at all he was interested.

At the end of the proceedings he would be right near Mayor Singh who would graciously ask him to hop in his car. Sometimes, only sometimes, I would also join him. The Mayor would get off at his office in Connaught Place in New Delhi and ask his driver to drop him – and me – to our office, which was not very far.

That aside, my duties at the Corporation gave me time to take a break of a couple hours as I had to write the story for the morning edition; my deadline was around 8 in the evening. And from 5:30 or 6 pm for a couple hours, it was my free time, *My Time*.

After our marriage we were living in Ramesh Nagar, in West Delhi. My office was around 10 miles from home but took nearly half hour to drive and about one hour by bus during busy hours.

Sadhana would dress decently and elegantly as she was still a newly-wed. She even otherwise, was neat and tidy, always, and was admired by the neighborhood – and more so the inquisitive neighborhood.

There is an interesting story about that.

I would be out on my Corporation assignment around 2 in the afternoon. A couple hours later, Sadhana would dress up extra elegantly – though she had barely any make-up – and would leave home around five. She would be back around 7-7:30, a couple hours before I would normally come during the Corporation assignment. This was her routine four or five days a week.

Inquisitive and curious, doubting and suspicious neighbors started a gossip. How's that a newly-married wife, in her finery, would leave home after her husband is gone, and would return before he comes back home? Was she having an affair?

Many in the neighborhood felt it their *sacred* duty to find out.

A man was deputed and started a Sherlock Holmes type investigation.

We did not have a car then and I would take the two-wheeler scooter to office. Sadhana would usually take the bus, or sometimes the three-wheeler *auto-rikshaw* to go. The 'designated detective' – not so-well-known to us – discreetly followed Sadhana one day on the same bus, to a spot around Connaught Place, New Delhi.

There he got the shock of his life.

As the bus halted at the Connaught Place stop and a smiling Sadhana got out followed discreetly by the 'detective,' I was waiting, and smilingly extended my hand to welcome my sweet wife.

We didn't care if the 'detective' collapsed on the spot.

The interesting story of Sadhana's 'suspected affair' was busted. The whole neighborhood must have heaved a sigh of relief – you know the neighbors may be inquisitive but they also are well-wishers and concerned about things that might go wrong.

Our neighbors were, otherwise, good and loving and caring and knew one another closely. They did not want anything bad to happen to us, the newly-weds and were happy that they deployed a 'detective' to re-assure themselves. They were so happy that in the next few days many of them told us how they were worried and how they were now relaxed and relieved.

That was the talk of the neighborhood for a long time. We enjoyed it.

That was my routine and that was *My Time* I would spend with Sadhana. We would spend a couple hours, go to a restaurant for snacks and tea, or take a walk talking sweet nothings and laughing.

Those were carefree days and also peaceful and safe. Sadhana, well-dressed as a newlywed in all her finery with absolutely minimum make-up (she did not need any) but quite a bit of elegant jewelry, would take a bus and meet me a dozen miles away and sometimes wait at a bus stop for me to join her.

Nobody tried to harass her, take liberties with her or tease her. There were no safety issues and whatever would come her way, my strong and courageous wife was amply capable of handling the situation. I never got worried about her as I knew she could take care of herself and even teach a lesson to others on how to react to an ugly situation.

Sadhana did have many occasions to travel alone, arriving at dead of night and tackling situations when the bus, train or flight were late and nobody to receive her at the destination. She never felt scared, never felt odd about the inconvenience she faced in not being picked up from and dropped at home, instead did all by herself.

She had ample faith in herself, a confidence that she can do anything.

[Once, a couple weeks before my birthday she asked me what I wanted as a birthday present. My reply: Your driver license. (We were in America then and she did not have an American driving license.) To my delight – it was no surprise as I knew my wife very well – there it was. She had taken a test and got the DMV license before my birthday. In India she was driving; would come with me to the airport when I was leaving and drive back herself. She would pick me up when I would land.]

Where could you get such a nice, loving, and self-confident companion?

She never complained about this almost daily exercise of leaving the chores, dressing up and taking a crowded bus, or the auto, and spending at least 90 minutes traveling time both ways. She enjoyed also making the entire neighborhood suspicious. We often talked and giggled about it. She could have rested at home or spent time reading, writing or painting. But no, she, and I, found it more fun and joy to make the separation short. What a pleasant break for the newly-weds!

After this regular rendezvous I would see Sadhana off at the bus stand and go back to the office to write my report.

Sadhana would reach home and prepare dinner. In a couple hours I would be home for hours of laughing, talking, eating, singing, reflecting, enjoying each other's company, in various ways, and dreaming for a lovelier future.

To go back about a year, when I saw Ved for the first time I was not in a mood to select a girl for marriage. However, her innocent face and graceful demeanor impacted me so much that I can now say without hesitation it was:

> *Ik nazar nay dekha, hum to bik gaye,*
> *Sauda vaheen hua, umra bhar ke liye.*

[At the first site, I was totally sold. A deal right there, to last a life-time.]

Soon I was elected General Secretary of Delhi Union of Journalists (DUJ). That meant I was the main man to run the organization, keep record of meetings, membership and subscription, plan more meetings, and take up cases of harassment and victimization at various offices of our members. Then there was lobbying to do for issues pertaining to members' rights and privileges.

The President of DUJ was C. Raghavan, from the Press Trust of India news agency. A senior journalist and knowledgeable about the problems, he had good contacts with government leaders. He appreciated my contribution and dedication and gave me full support to handle the affairs of the Union. The financial health of the Union was not good and I took it upon myself to correct it. The solution was to bring out a souvenir with advertisements and hold an annual conference to promote our cause and increase membership.

I did both. The souvenir had good articles and the advertisements wiped out our debt and also made a tidy surplus. The annual conference was also a big success. Home Minister (later the Prime Minister), Lal Bahadur Shastri and the Information and Broadcasting Minister B. Gopala Reddy came and addressed the gathering.

For Union work we had to meet leaders of government, Members of Parliament and the management of newspapers to discuss issues. There was a lot of work and the regular staff was minimum – only two, including me, and I was still a full-time member of the editorial staff at the newspaper. All Union work was voluntary, unpaid and in our own spare time.

That meant more time away from home and away from Sadhana, my bride of only a few months.

Sadhana would not settle for that.

She asked me if she could come to the Union office and help me. Who would refuse such an offer? That meant she was there for several more hours assisting me in record-keeping, and various other tasks while I was in the Union office, or even gone out for some assignment. She was there volunteering as an office assistant. That suited me, she never complained, and we enjoyed each other's company – sometimes just looking at each other and exchanging smiles.

Frequently on Union duties and mixing with my official duties, I would not have time or opportunity to take her to a restaurant or even see her off at the bus stop. She would not mind even that, never complained, and always managed to keep her 'job' and my routine fully manageable. Members who came to know about this arrangement wondered how a newly-wed couple could manage all that. But with Sadhana at my side and willing, everything was under control and still enjoyable for us.

No wonder, the Executive Committee of the Union passed a unanimous resolution at a meeting praising Sadhana's voluntary contribution and putting on record her selfless work.

She had certainly made a mark and become popular among the journalist fraternity too.

Sadhana was practically always with me in social, cultural, literary or patriotic functions I would go. She was as patriotic and nationalist as I was and that showed. She had inherited this from her father, who, while working as a building contractor for the then British government and others in undivided India's Northwest, was a nationalist, a social reformer and proud of India's Hindu culture and heritage.

In 1962, just a year after we got married the attack by the Chinese shattered Jawaharlal Nehru's utopian ideals and vision of a friendly neighbor. He had full faith in China's friendship and never heeded the warnings and advice from others such as Dr. Ram Manohar Lohia, who was for a number of years the outspoken and pragmatic leader and the Congress Party's foreign policy expert.

[More about Lohia *Ji*, a little later.]

The Chinese attack devastated Nehru and broke his heart as well as shocked the Indian people as the political atmosphere in India earlier was full of *Hindi-Chini Bhai Bhai* (Indians and Chinese are brothers) slogans and feelings.

The Chinese betrayal changed India and Indians. The nation was united as never before. Meetings, demonstrations and fund-raising for the Prime Minister's National Relief Fund etc. were regularly organized. Sadhana and I would rarely miss them.

One such event was *Veer Ras Kavi Sammelan* organized by some of my friends of a local branch of a prominent Hindi organization in Delhi. That was a poetic recital, open to general public, mainly devoted to patriotic and nationalist poems. Many prominent poets participated at the sprawling Ramlila grounds between Delhi-New Delhi.

In the wake of the surprise Chinese attack on India, Nehru made changes in his cabinet and replaced VK Krishna Menon, one of his closest men, and brought YB Chavan, Chief Minister of then Bombay state as Minister of Defense.

Our group was the first in New Delhi to invite Chavan for the poets' gathering. He was presented with a solid gold sword as our contribution to the National Fund.

Several stirring poems were recited and were applauded by the huge audience. After about three hours of entertaining/encouraging/inspiring poems it was decided to ask the audience to donate, whatever they have or want, to the Fund.

Many poets volunteered to go around among the audience and collect. They had cloth bags to collect donations. People gave money, jewelry and other things. Sadhana was also excited and as poet Bal Kavi Bairagi, one of the most prominent poets that evening, approached the audience, Sadhana without hesitation, took off her Rolled Gold expensive watch and put it in the bag.

I fully endorsed her action.

As the collection was rounding off the organizers started auctioning things that came in the bags. Sadhana's watch got them about 250 rupees, in 1962 quite a big amount. But there was a very simple, inexpensive thing that got most cheers when auctioned.

It was a pair of knitting needles.

Instead of mocking the donation, the innovative genius of the organizers put the pair of needles to auction. The starting bid was 10 woolen sweaters for soldiers. The bid went up quickly and soon a lady got them for the highest bid of 108 sweaters. The lady was, Kaushalya Narula, the founder-Principal of Nav Hind Girls High School, in Karol Bagh (now a senior secondary school for girls.)

It was a sight to see the Principal going up on the stage to receive the simple knitting needles and promising the sweaters as soon as possible.

Less than a week later there was a sizable delegation at Prime Minister Nehru's official residence where we witnessed Miss Narula and a few of her teachers and student representatives present the Prime Minister with 108 large size sweaters for Indian soldiers.

Nehru was full of praise and admiration for the contribution from school girls who themselves, or their mothers, knitted the sweaters, and that too so soon.

[Miss Narula worked with the institution for 35 years. After the memorable event, I also met her later at many functions of the school that I reported.. A refugee herself, she was passionate about girls' education. She was one of the pioneer women in post-independence India for educating girls.]

That was the spirit of nationalism, and public service that Sadhana saw, inspired, lived up to and enthusiastically shared with me.

Sadhana was also ready to help me in whatever task I had on my hand. A prominent publisher in Delhi, S. Chand and Company, asked me to translate an 850-page history of the Far East by Prof. Paul H. Clyde of Duke University in the USA. It was the third edition of the book, a Prentice-Hall publication, and was an authentic and detailed history of East Asia and the impact of the West on the region. It was a big task of translating into Hindi the Far Eastern history book by a prominent American professor for college students in India.

Sadhana, as usual, was ready to assist in any way I needed her. And I did need her.

Those days in 1962-63 nobody was typing a manuscript in Hindi and I did not have the typing skills or access to a Hindi typewriter. My handwriting wasn't good. It had gone from being okay to bad as a result of hurriedly preparing news material and writing my copy for the compositors in the press to typeset. They were still using the old method of picking each letter of the alphabet and joining them to make a line, and then a paragraph on a metal sheet.

[I started using a Hindi typewriter soon after, was one of the first, if not the first, to do so in a newspaper.]

After typesetting, the handwritten copies were thrown in the garbage. So the compositors advised me to not bother about good handwriting but hurry with the copy as they were capable of deciphering whatever we, writers, produced in long hand. The result: my handwriting went from okay to bad and unfit to prepare a big handwritten manuscript ready for printing a book, not a newspaper.

Sadhana herself suggested a better alternative and I happily accepted the offer, a big one. Her hand-writing was excellent, and she got the job, of course very exacting and totally without pay. But she was happy to get another opportunity to be with me for hours helping me.

Where can you find such a loving, caring and devoted wife, totally dedicated to her husband, his work, his duties and passionately sharing his responsibilities?

I did.

We agreed that I would dictate the translation from the original English and she would write everything down in her own hand to make the Hindi manuscript. And my God, she would sit with me every night after I returned from work and had our dinner – and keep on writing. Often I would be reclining on the sofa and dictating, Sadhana would be sitting tight on the floor, and writing. There were no complaints, no murmur, no hesitation. The work must go on, was her mission and her promise.

I love you Ashi for that also.

(I had given my wife several loving pet names; Ashi was one of them.)

The big book was taking time and in between – may be on a break – Sadhana became pregnant with our first child. Any wife would have put a stop to that task that, by any standard, was a kind of torture for Sadhana. A pregnant young woman, sitting mostly on the floor, writing pages after pages till past midnight every day! In any similar situation, anywhere, this would certainly be regarded as 'domestic abuse,' a torture, but Sadhana was made of a peculiarly sacrificing mold. She never said no, never asked for a long break, and of course, never asked me to find another writer.

Well, I couldn't afford to get one who would be with me, in my home, till late in the night, working and writing in beautiful hand.

The big book's translation was finally complete in a few months well after Sadhana was in her advanced stage of pregnancy. I owe everything to her for getting the job done without any breakdown, mishap or argument. Pity, I could not get her name on the book as co-translator, or writer/copy preparer or something. None outside our close family – the kids were not yet born – knew about Sadhana's major contribution in completion of the task.

I am in your debt my love!

However, that was the first in a series of other books that I compiled, translated, edited and wrote – and she continued to help in various ways. She herself collected, compiled, translated and produced a book of poems about the freedom struggle of Bangladesh, a decade later. But that's another story of her sincere help, dedication, and contribution to make my life meaningful, rewarding and also very successful.

One more thing about translating the Far East history book and its possible effect on our first child, Sujata: *Mahabharat's* legendary character Arjun was telling her pregnant wife, Subhadra about the strategy to penetrate the strategically intricate and complex *Chakravyooh* (placement of troops – a war-maze) and how his son, Abhimanyu, learnt the strategy while in his mother's womb. Similarly, I think my dictation to Sadhana about history must have influenced Sujata as she showed ample interest in that subject in her high school and college.

While Abhimanyu learnt only the half (to penetrate and break the Maze) as his mother fell asleep, Sadhana never dozed off. Sujata therefore, had fairly full grasp of ancient and modern history and even asked me to get her extra books on the subject. I happily got them for her.

Thanks Sadhana, you taught Sujata the subject in your own style.

As I mentioned earlier, Sadhana was quite a patient listener; she was also interested in my stories, experiences, my earlier jobs and so on. I had much to share with her – and we never got tired of doing our part – she listening and me talking.

In between, eating and enjoying other things, it became a routine and fun for us both.

One of my old stories was about my job with *Amar Bharat,* a Hindi daily newspaper in Delhi (1948-51). I was lucky to have some seniors who were not only experts in their jobs but always willing to share their knowledge with me. They encouraged me to become a better journalist, a better writer and a better future editor. There were many who were jovial, funny and inspiring.

One was Jai Nath Nalin, the magazine section in-charge, who also had met my father while in Bombay; the other, Vishnu Dutt Sharma 'Vikal.' They both used to address me as *Balak* (young man). I was only 19 then. Nalin *Ji* encouraged me to write articles whenever I wanted, and he would find a place for them in his section. He was himself a good writer and also wrote humor/satire and let me also write humorous articles and commentaries.

'Vikal' Ji was always funny and also said meaningful things. One of his sayings I often quoted for Sadhana when she was sick and not keen to go out and do things was: *"Keh gaye das Kabira ke vela hatth naheen yo auna"* (Kabir Das has said that past will never return – meaning, say or do things NOW.)

[The prominent Hindi mystic-saint- poet in 15th century medieval India, Kabir Das, did not write *that*; it was the 'creation' of my senior friend 'Vikal' *Ji*.]

That's what I tell my young listeners also, "don't miss the chance, you may never get the opportunity again."

One of my other senior colleagues was P. Somasundaram, a Tamil (South Indian), quite good at English and Hindi (though some thought a man from Tamil background could not be that efficient with Hindi.) He had earlier, during World War II, served in the Azad Hind Government of Netaji Bose in Southeast Asia. A few years later he went to Moscow and joined the Foreign Languages department. He was a hardworking, jovial and knowledgeable person, learnt Russian and married a Russian woman and had kids. Somasundaram had not forgotten me and on a visit to India, during the Janata Party rule (1977-79) met with me. We exchanged views and re-lived the years we worked together.

I wanted to visit Moscow and reconnect with him. Sadly, I could not make a trip – adding to my other regrets – and later learnt that my friend Som was no more.

There was another, Pundit Satyadev Vidyalankar (Bhai *Ji*), one time my Editor in another paper, *Dainik* (daily) *Vishwamitra,* in New Delhi, before he joined *Amar Bharat*. He was one of the top Hindi editors and writer/author. My father had published a couple of books written by him on religious and social subjects more than 10 years before I worked for him in 1947-48.

I remember, and personally respect him, especially for the following:

- Soon after he joined *Vishwamitra,* he got me and a couple of other colleagues, a substantial raise;

- He would complete his editorial around the time my shift was about to finish and ask me to read the proof. (The proof would sometimes come to me an hour or so late and I had to wait to do the proof-reading (and correct if the compositor had made a mistake or misread it.) That would take quite some time if there were any corrections to be made; they had to be carried out properly.

I was, at first, a little upset that the editor wanted me to do overtime (without any overtime pay) but soon realized that he wanted me to learn the style of editorial writing and also to be familiar with his editorials as they represented the policy of the paper. That was my training and I thank Satyadev *Ji* for giving me those precious tips, indirectly.

- At one point I joined another paper on a slightly higher salary. Bhai *Ji* casually tried to dissuade me but I did not heed his advice, but accepted his offer to continue for a few days working for both the papers till he got my replacement.

- The other paper, *Bharatvarsh*, had to be closed down by a government order as the publishers were part of a group that was charged, in some way, to be indirectly connected with Mahatma Gandhi's assassination. Just before the government order was announced, the publishers gave us workers, the option – either resign and leave or risk arrest, if the government insists on the charges. (Of course the charges were never made, or remotely proved, but the paper had closed down.)

- I was then 19 and opted to quit. I went to Bhai *Ji* and told him about the situation. He promptly took out my resignation letter from his drawer, tore it and said I knew something like that would happen. He had not accepted my resignation and did not even tell the publisher-owner about it.

- That was the kindness and also the farsightedness of my editor who liked me and my dedication to work.

- Working for two papers full time for a few weeks told upon my health and I was sick for about a week. Satyadev Ji treated this as 'paid sick leave' though in those days there was no provision of any kind of leave, sick or otherwise, in the paper.

That was the humane side of the editor – besides being a good teacher. I learnt a lot by working for him. He additionally made me familiar with foreign news as he would specifically give me a few foreign items to handle and translate from English to Hindi. (Most of the news would come to us in English on the news agency tele-printer.) That made me aware of, and interested in, world affairs too.

I was lucky to have worked with many people like him, who, kind of, became my mentors. I learnt things from them that I value and remember those who showed me the way. I always tried to pass on that knowledge to my younger colleagues.

This was in 1948. While leaving *Bharatvarsh* we were encouraged to take whatever extra stationery etc. was in the offices and I opted for just one thing – a foot long thin brass divider (used to separate metal type lines on a full newspaper page). In Hindi we just call it *Peetal* – brass and it's still with me and is constantly in use to cut a paper sheet. This *peetal* has been lost – and found – a dozen times in the stacks of papers and books I have. It's one of my treasured possessions, moved with me to a dozen places in India and America. It's also used as a threat to beat up errant kids – though never used for the purpose.

Talking about my treasures, there are several other things also – money-wise may not be so valuable, but they are memories. One is some two feet long, black solid wood round stick my father had been using since before my birth, for putting lines on un-ruled pages. This rolling stick is also used as hollow threat just like my *peetal,* but with a much older history and memory.

The third is a pair of tiger claws from my father's possessions I got - don't know how. These claws also must be my age – 88 plus, maybe older than that.

I also have a snake-skin, left on a branch of a *chameli* (Jasmine) fragrant flower-tree right at the entrance of the front yard of our Chanakyapuri home, around 1980.

Besides, out of a few thousand books still saved in unopened boxes in the storage, there are hundreds of rare books – one of them is the first edition of The Godfather. Rare Book company, a decade back, had offered this 1965 edition for $3,500. There are several, 50 to 100 year-olds with me.

There are hair locks: One of my first when I was 2½ years. Also, a collection of Sujata, Seema and Tamanna's first hair-cut. I don't know how long I can hold on to them. [Hope someone would keep them, as

Seema managed to get some from her mother's and shared a few strands with us all, beautifully encased.]

Sadhana would eagerly ask for and always appreciated stories of my early years in the profession as well as of my life. She would sometimes probe me, and quite frequently, had questions and comments also. I was too willing to share them with her. She would never get tired or bored listening to me. I had an unending treasure of stories related to my early life (as early as 4 years of age), work, travels, meeting with all kinds of people, see history being made and sometimes contributing to making of history. I had to go on assignments far and wide, meet with and interview/report major events and leaders.

One of my childhood memories concerned a big agitation, *Satyagraha* (the civil disobedience movement), protesting against the ruling authorities and courting arrests.) Mahatma Gandhi also resorted to this type of protests against the British, quite often.

This particular *Satyagraha* was against the Nizam (King) of Hyderabad, a big princely state in pre-independent India. The autocratic ruler was a Muslim but Hindus were in a big majority in the state. With the aggressive support of many hardline Islamic groups, the Nizam put severe restrictions on Hindus and their religious and cultural activities.

The Hyderabad Congress and Arya Samaj started a protest movement but, soon after, Congress withdrew. Arya Samaj, a Hindu religious and cultural organization established in 1875 by Maharshi Dayanand Saraswati, a renowned Vedic scholar and a social reformer, continued their *Satyagraha*. They sent thousands of volunteers to protest and court arrest in Hyderabad.

The then Indian state of Central Provinces and Berar (now Madhya Pradesh) had a congress government (because of the 1937 political reforms) and put severe restrictions on Arya Samaj's *Satyagraha.*

In my opinion, this was primarily done for two reasons: Mahatma Gandhi did not want any other organization or group to resort to *Satyagraha* – his own favorite 'weapon of protest.' Secondly, Hyderabad *Satyagraha* was by Hindus against a Muslim ruler supported by more Muslim groups, so it was seen by him as a 'Hindu Communal movement.' Gandhiji did not want to tarnish his image of being a perfect 'secular,' leader. Consequently pressure was put on Arya Samaj to end the agitation. It ended with mixed results.

Speaking on the role of Arya Samaj, world-famous Yogi Arvind (Aurobindo) Ghosh (1872-1950) of Pondicherry said, "Dayanand was the real harbinger of the Indian Renaissance which opened up new directions and fresh hopes for millions of people who were groaning under the worst kind of slavery resulting from social, religious, cultural and political decadence."

The *Satyagraha* gave an impetus to the political awakening and paved the way for political emancipation in Hyderabad and impacted the people in the whole country.

What I personally remember was the *jatthas* (volunteer groups) going to Hyderabad that passed through Delhi and meetings at Arya Samaj Dewan Hall, in the historic Chandni Chowk of the old city, to give them a rousing send-off. We lived in the flats (apartments) of the Samaj, upstairs, and father would always take us to attend those meetings and listen to the speeches and devotional and nationalistic songs.

I was then only nine years old.

One of the Sikh groups of volunteers was also at the meeting ready to go to Hyderabad. They sang, and I remember the few first lines of the inspiring song clearly. They enthusiastically sang in Punjabi:

> *"Hyderabad chalo, dharma bulaee jaanda.*
> *Sandhya na karan denda, havana na karan denda,*
> *Hakim Nizam sadda huqq dabaee jaanda."*

(On to Hyderabad, our religion is calling us. We are not allowed to pray or do havan – sacred fire – King Nizam is suppressing all our rights.)

[A couple of my senior colleagues on the staff of *Hindustan*, including Kshiteeshji, while students, had also participated in the *Satyagraha* and were jailed in Hyderabad.]

After 80 years these inspirational lines are fresh on my mind. Sadhana would marvel at my memory, and I at her curiosity and patience. I also told her that since she was preparing to come into my life, I had to keep my memory sharp. We always ended up our serious conversations with mutual understanding and loving smiles.

An absolutely compatible and understanding partner!

All that did make a bunch of interesting stories and Sadhana would probe and listen while she fed me, took care of my needs and share her own stories and experience while I was away.

If this nine year-old boy's memory of that inspirational song heard only one time didn't quite surprise Sadhana, here's one when I was only four years old that not only amazed her but went on to become the most fascinating story for our children and their children.

I clearly remember a cute little girl, Tappu. She was just about my age, maybe a few months younger, and could be regarded as my first 'girl-friend.' In those good-old days, GF and BF 'titles' were non-existent, we were just good friends and happy to play together *jab we met*.

Tappu was the daughter of a senior Judge of Indore High Court, Siremal Bapna (the full name I came to know later), a family-friend. Bapna *sahab* was particularly fond of me and would ask me riddles and tease me in various ways.

One day when the Bapnas were visiting us he asked me a riddle. (Mother frequently used to ask me riddles to sharpen my brain, and I liked it.)

The riddle he asked me was: '*bandar thha par dum naheen thhee, ulloo tha par per naheen thhay,*' (a monkey but no tail, an owl (dim-wit) but no wings), and I started seriously trying to figure it out what it could be. Then he added the punch line and the game was over. He said: '*aur ek ladki se zara bada thha,*' (and just a tiny bit older than a girl.)

I got it and, somewhat sheepishly, said: '*aaahh, aap to mujhe chhed rahe hain*' (you are just teasing me.) The families had a good laugh.

That was my last meeting with Tappu as we moved soon after to distant Mussoorie, some 750 miles away. I don't know if now she is also a great grandparent like me. Anyway, good luck my long-lost childhood friend from Indore.

I didn't know her real name then. I still don't.

Sadhana too had enjoyed that story and had a good laugh on how Judge Bapna caricatured her would-be-husband so long ago.

Talking about riddles and teasers started by my mother when I was not yet five – and used to share quality time with her - my all-time favorite is the following:

Kala thha par kaua na thha, bil khoday par chooha na thha,
patli kamar par cheeta na thha, Aur swarag chadhe par saamp na thha.

[It's black but not a crow, digs holes but not a mouse, has a thin waist but not a cheetah, climbs up but not a snake.]

I am proud to say that I had given the correct answer and got lots of kisses and applause from my mother.

The riddle had fascinated Sadhana also and our kids were asked the same when they were growing up though I doubt if they still remember the riddle fully and its answer.)

The answer is: Ant.

Around almost the same time, when I was not yet ready for Kindergarten, both my older sisters, Prem and Lata had discovered something to keep me entertained when they returned from school. Every day they spent time collecting something special and would hand over the box to me with clear instructions to open it very slowly and carefully. After the first day, I got a hang of it.

My sisters and my mother would watch my face light up as 4½ year-old, me, would open the box slowly and one by one, pick each colorful wonder of nature carefully and release it. It was an amazing sight to see a dozen or so butterflies fluttering away to freedom.

I was also curious about Ved's early life though she had not many memories of her childhood in either Nowshera, where she was born, or of Abbottabad, where she spent a few more years before the family fled to India, They had left Pakistan in a hurry, under grave threats to their lives and could not pack valuables while rushing to the railway station.

There were trains going to India but were extremely crowded with men, women and children, many already dead, many more severely injured and some even died on the way. The fanatics attacked, killed, maimed, harassed and looted fleeing Hindus. Something similar must have happened on the other side of the border also, but doubt, it could have reached that scale, ever.

[Pakistan was created on totally religious basis, brainwashed-notion – the extremely fanatic theory – and the 'burning desire' to have a separate Muslim country, for themselves. The result: more hatred, more conflict, more poverty, more terrorism and less development for Pakistan.

Meanwhile, even a divided India has prospered many-fold and is much more organized, educated, prosperous, democratic, strong and developed – and a lot more peaceful.]

Sadhana was little and the only thing she remembered about Nowshera was that their trusted Muslim employee would take her for a walk along the canal and on the way back, insist on buying her an apple himself.

About Abbottabad, she remembers a few things like the big, big home with scores of rooms and that her father would keep huge amount of money in cash, in big jute bags. He had to pay to his dozens of workers in cash and buy building material (as he was a big building contractor). In addition, he would give generously to the needy people he knew in and around their home or work place and would leave packets of cash at their homes – unasked for and un-noticed. That's why a lot of cash was always kept at home. And that was the man I got as my father-in-law, many years later, and whom I did not have the honor and good fortune to meet.

After fleeing to India, Ved's family got a small place where they lived for some time. What she remembers of that Cement Road home in Dehradun was that sometimes she had to study under a street lamp. But she never gave up and was always interested in studies, sports and helping her mother with the household chores.

Later when they got a huge home, she was happy but also sad at her father's demise when she was just 14. She told me that her father loved her the most and asked mother to love and care for her more than what she got from her earlier for various reasons. *Mataji* more than made up for whatever happened earlier.

[It was said that Ved's older sister suddenly died around the same time the youngest child of the family, Ved, was born. That so upset *Mataji* that consequently she became indifferent toward Ved.]

As for other members of my own family, my younger sister Priyalata and the youngest brother Virendra, both lived in Bombay, with our father. Both had done their Masters and also worked while they were studying. They also took care of father.

Priyalata came in contact with a bright young man Radhakrishna Prabhu and after some time both decided to marry. For some reason, my father was not in full agreement with this idea though all of them came to Delhi. Sadhana and I met them and tried to handle the matter smoothly. When the situation did not change, and Prabhu and Priyalata were keen to get married, we decided to go ahead with the marriage. Sadhana and I performed the traditional *kanyadaan* (giving away the bride) instead of our father.

This was just a couple months after we were married. This couple is in their 80s and still happily married. God bless them.

[Prabhu went up the ladder of success and held a very senior post at the Industrial Development Bank of India (IDBI). Later he was Managing Director of the Bank of Mauritius, spent 11 years in that country and contributed a lot to help its economic growth. Prabhu attended meetings at the World Bank on behalf of Mauritius. They now live in Mumbai though their two sons, Vivek Prabhu and Vinay Prabhu live in California with their families.]

Priyalata is the only sibling I have now.

We had been doing things like that whenever the situation demanded. *Kanyadaan* is regarded as a special sacred duty and an act of higher religious conduct to, kind of, act like parents and give away the bride. We felt fortunate to do this sacred duty. There were many more such occasions in our life.

The second was Sadhana's brother Indrajit's own wedding.

It came after vehement opposition from the girl's side despite their many years' friendship and even engagement that was arranged on a chance visit of Usha to Delhi. Indrajit and I visited Usha's ancestral home in Singhai State (where her maternal grandparents were king and queen.) Usha's mother was a scion of the princely family and so Usha herself was a princess. Our visit was futile and we returned empty-handed but we struck friendship with a neighboring prince who knew princess Usha and regarded her as his sister. Of course that also didn't help.

Indrajit and I returned very sad and disappointed, but safe and in one piece as anything could have happened in that state – though it was no longer a princely state with Rajas and Maharajas after India's independence and merger with other states. However, their influence and clout existed and we could have had trouble. Luckily we got away before any such thing could happen.

Back in Delhi, Indrajit immersed in higher studies and got his Masters and also Ph.D, and that opened doors for his further promotion. He had utilized those years of separation but ultimately got what he wanted and waited for. We encouraged and supported him wholeheartedly.

Finally, after a few years, Indrajit and Usha were married – without anyone from the bride's family present. Sadhana and I, by then, had become, kind of, experts in traditional rituals and happily did the *kanyadaan* for Usha. So she has dual relations with us – Sadhana's older brother's wife as *Bhabhi*; and because we gave her away, she is also like our daughter.

[We continued this sweet relation ever since. Both of them are very dear to us, have been solid supporters for us; our children and their children grew up together sharing time, interests and vacations.

However, life plays cruel games also and Indrajit-Usha lost their very bright and talented and very promising daughter, Rewa in an accident. She was only 28, and married just a year back. She was one of the brightest, newly appointed researchers in the Defense Research Department and was officially sponsored for higher studies at Roorkee University, one of the top Universities in India. Rewa was very close and dear to Sadhana, and all of us, and her sudden departure was too tragic for words.

She was deeply mourned by the family, her friends and colleagues. She is dearly missed.

In her short career she had developed circuits and other top scientific instruments, a part of which were used in India's prestigious space exploration projects.

Rewa was only 16 days older to our younger daughter, Seema, and shared a very special relationship with her. To this day Seema makes sure to send *Rakhi* to Vineet, every year, on behalf of Rewa. One of the reasons for this special bond is that Rewa's mother, Usha, also nursed Seema when Sadhana was badly burnt.]

Rewa's younger brother, Vineet is married and has a sweet wife (Sushma – Sweety) and a cute son, Archit. They still live in Delhi in the same home and with their parents, both retired. Usha *Bhabhi* retired as a senior school teacher.

8

Blessed with Two Daughters

In my profession and with my duties it was normal to get assignments out of the city, out of state and sometimes out of the country also. Sadhana had to be prepared for spending time alone. It would normally be uncomfortable or in many cases unacceptable as we were the only two and would be alone when I was on long distance assignments. For some time Saroj (my 'adopted' *Maasee*'s 'adopted' daughter) was with us to give Sadhana company. They got along very well.

Our first new year together was 1962. We got a New Year card printed and mailed to some of our friends – colleagues and seniors.

One card was sent to Dr. Harivansh Rai Bachchan, one of our very respected and beloved poet/writer. Both Sadhana and I had read many of his books, and heard his poetry at poets meetings which he frequently participated – and dominated with his famous poems. We also knew his wife, Teji *Ji*.

We were pleasantly surprised to receive Dr. Bachchan's reply to our card and his good wishes in the form of two lines of poetry – sheer beauty. It said:

> *Naya varsh le naya harsh ghar aaye,*
> *Jeevan ke path mein kaliyaan phool bichhaye.*

[May the New Year bring new joy to your home,
And may your life's path be strewn with buds and flowers.]

We were delighted to get such beautiful and meaningful good wishes from the eminent poet/writer who later became my mentor, inspiring me to write books.

This message was special for the beginning of our journey as a married couple. We had many occasions to meet and hear Dr. Bachchan and enjoy and enrich our life by his inspiring writings.

[Dr. Bachchan's son is the legendary Indian movie star, the icon, Amitabh Bachchan, and his wife is also a famous star, Jaya. Their son Abhishek and daughter-in-law, Aishwarya are also famous actors making this the First Family of Stars still active in the industry.]

A little after the first year of our marriage, I had the opportunity to go to another state, a thousand miles from New Delhi, on an assignment. I was a little concerned to leave Sadhana alone but the event was also special for me. Sadhana, as usual, did not question, and persuaded me to accept it willingly and cheerfully as the trip was important for me.

The conference I was to report in Hyderabad was organized by one of my heroes, the prominent freedom fighter, Dr. Ram Manohar Lohia. [I had followed his solid contribution to the freedom struggle, and also active public life after India's independence.]

There was another connection with Dr. Lohia. He and I graduated from the same high school – Marwari Vidyalaya High School, in Bombay. Of course, he was much too senior to me having graduated in 1927; he stood first. I did my high school in 1946. Our close bond was forged later in the fifties and sixties when I was an active newspaper reporter in Delhi and he was a prominent politician and a member of India's Parliament.

[Marwari Vidyalaya had many kids from millionaire Rajasthani (Marwari) families as in those days Hindi was hardly taught in any other school in a Marathi-Gujarati-dominated region. The other predominant group was from Uttar Pradesh – both were basically, Hindi areas. We had English as a subject in our school from the early stages; it was the medium of education for higher classes till the final High School Exam (Matriculation.).

It was all boys' school on Sandhurst Road, Central Bombay.

Among my classmates (Class of 1946) were sons of Daga, Somani, Rungta, Seksaria, Ruia, Gupta, Vaidya, and many other families of big industrialists and businessmen. They owned huge mills and factories. Some lived in extra affluent areas like Napean Sea Road, Pali Hills, Malabar Hills and Marine Drive. We selected Luxmi Narayan Rungta as Captain of our Cricket team; he was not *the* best but quite a good batsman and would treat all of us for lunch on the day of the match.

Mahatma Gandhi, while in Bombay, stayed at the Birla House but held his evening prayer meetings at the Rungta's, the neighbors, as their lawn was larger.

However, we were very friendly, nobody threw his weight around. I would be invited to play table tennis at Vinay Ruia's home – he had a table. I would sometimes meet the Somanis – Venkatesh and Vijay, and Dagas – Madho and Udho, Padam Chand Jain for extra study, at their homes that proved to be very helpful for me.

Most of these Rajasthani classmates were very good with Arithmetic, Geometry and Algebra – all Math subjects – and scored 100% marks.

Suresh Gupta, though not a Marwari, was later made our Cricket Captain. Ramgopal Vaidya, was 'custodian' of our private Cricket kit to bring it when we played matches at the Oval grounds or at Cross Maidan (grounds) near Dhobi Talao area where he lived. Prem Kishor Begraj Gupta – later became a doctor and lived in England – was a cute little boy when he came to our school and class for the last two years and the teacher asked me to share my seat (always a two-seater) with him in the front row.

The playground was rented for a day-long game from the Municipal Corporation for just two rupees.

We, cricketers, were 'highly paid.' For an 'official' game (between school-teams) each player was paid one rupee (16 *annas* made a rupee.) I would spend two *annas* from and to my home by tram-car,12 *annas* for lunch, one *anna* for tip and one *anna* for either a *'paan'* or as my saving.

Wow! What an era!

Yes, for *Kabaddi* matches the team was given just two pounds of lemons to suck. Cricket is still the richest among all the sports in India.

Rupee was then in 1946 probably at par with the dollar. (Even in 1965 one dollar was 4.75 rupees.) Now the rate is nearly 66 rupees for one dollar. Sadhana had a good laugh when I told her the story of our 'big' payment and expense.

It was great fun. There was friendship all around, never any fights or animosity. The teachers – Mulye, Thampi, Bhende, Ramchandra Shastri, and Principal Jakhie, and many others were great.

Sadhana met a couple of my classmates in Delhi and enjoyed dozens of our interesting stories from the past. (She had some of her own.) Udho Daga had moved from Bombay and settled down in Delhi; Vaidya visited often from Lucknow that he had made his residence and business.]

Lohia *Ji* had substantial differences with Nehru on many domestic and international issues. In his writings and speeches he had warned about the Chinese designs on India's northeast but Nehru totally ignored his views. The 1962 Chinese attack vindicated Lohia *Ji* but it was then too late.

Lohia *Ji* died in 1967 at the age of 57 and his followers raised suspicion about his treatment and death but nothing came out of it as the Congress Party government was not interested in the matter. India had lost a passionate patriot, an excellent orator and an ardent advocate for social and political reform.

I lost an inspiring senior nationalist leader I could relate to. I would faithfully cover his meetings and other functions in Delhi as a reporter. He always had a soft corner and affection for me and would call me if he was making an important speech or organizing an event.

I felt honored.

It was in 1962 when Lohia *Ji* organized the conference in Hyderabad. The city also was important for me as uncle, Capt. Surya Pratap (my father's sister's husband) and his parents had settled there for a long time. Uncle served as a very senior official in pre-independence government of Hyderabad's Nizam (King) under its Prime Minister Sir Akbar Hydari.

I met my extended family after about 15 years.

After the conference I returned to New Delhi and the re-union with my wife of one year was something for the stars. We laid the foundation for the start of our family. This was also the start of a more active and successful career.

It was also the 'book project' that I got and completed with Sadhana's invaluable assistance.

Sujata was born on July 11, 1963, about nine months after my return from Hyderabad. Sadhana was absolutely sure that she embarked on a new, happy journey on October 20, 1962, the day I returned. She had told me the very next day, and I believed her instincts, as I did about so many other things and instances in our long and happy married life.

She was remarkable.

[That was also the day China attacked India and shattered Nehru's dreams. The whole passionate and close friendship with China ended and

Nehru could not recover from the shock. He was totally disillusioned, lost and heart-broken.]

Sujata was born at Victoria Zanana (women's) Hospital, exclusively for women, situated in a thickly-populated area of old Delhi. It was mostly a maternity hospital. It was quite 'ancient,' named after Queen Victoria, one of the longest serving monarchs of England during the British rule over India. She was also proclaimed the Empress of India, so it was only appropriate that a hospital be named after her.

[The present Queen of England, Elizabeth II, is a great-great granddaughter of Queen Victoria, now the longest serving monarch in the world. She became the Queen on Feb 6, 1952 and completed 65 years on the throne. She is 91.]

However, little did Queen Victoria know that during the reign of her great-great granddaughter India will no longer be a part of the British Empire and even the hospital named after her would discard her name. Now it's Kasturba Gandhi hospital, named after the wife of Mahatma Gandhi. It's reported to be one of the largest maternity hospitals in Asia with 450 beds. It's one of the busiest in the world with a reported birthrate of 12,000 per year. The 112-year-old single story structure has been expanded into a sprawling nine story complex of several buildings.

Our younger daughter, Seema, was also born at the same hospital. One of the reasons was that my older sister, Preeti Lata, was a doctor at the hospital and so was one of her classmates, Daya Bailey. With these two 'doctor-sisters' we were, kind of, royal guests and enjoyed a private ward for a number of days.

I converted the ward into our 'home' with at least three suitcases, radio (there was no TV then) and some other household things. I would go to work from the hospital ward and return after office to spend more time, and even the night there.

I did not have a car then, only a two-wheeler scooter. One of my good friends, senior journalist S.R. Bahl, working for the French News Agency (AFP) insisted on giving all of us a ride home in his Ambassador car that could also carry our luggage, radio and other items in the big trunk.

It was Sujata's first car-ride, repeated after 15 months for Seema. For both the girls Bahl uncle and Bahl aunty – and their young children (son and daughter) – were nice and close family friends.

We were overjoyed when we brought Sujata to our modest home. What we lacked in space we made up with immense love and care. The main task of caring and raising, naturally, fell on Sadhana who showed that she was an expert in that field also. She was youngest of her siblings but her brother's kids, especially the older daughter, Anju, had always been her favorite and close to Sadhana since her birth. She had been, kind of, her mentor and guardian.

I was, as usual, busy in my work and would not give as much time to home as is normally expected. But Sadhana, made of some peculiar material, never expected me to share either baby-care or household chores. She knew my schedule and kind of work, and so handled everything, herself. She even made cotton-cloth diapers herself, soft, milk-white, washed by hand and extra-cleaned with the whitening powder Tinopal, and were always neatly ironed. The neighboring mothers marveled at Sadhana's skills, concern, love and care in raising her children.

Sujata, being our first child, had her share of rewards like a good birthday celebration and more than six months of breast-feeding. Sadhana used to say that a healthy 'mother- cow' gives the best nutrition to her babies. Sujata had a grand first birthday party in the famous Constitution Club in New Delhi where relatives, fellow journalists, several senior officials, and politicians were among the 300 or so guests present.

The kid was smart and exhibited her love for gifts right at the ripe old age of one year. She reserved her big smiles for guests carrying gifts, and sometimes looked the other way, as if totally disinterested, when she found some arriving empty-handed.

It was a hilarious scenario, though a little awkward.

Seema, on the other hand, had a subdued birthday celebration: no big first birthday party and not even mother's milk beyond 16 days.

More about that a little later.

Some of our close relatives were anxiously waiting to welcome a boy but somewhat disappointed that it was a girl. We were not. We were happy to have our first child. Sadhana and I joyfully welcomed our second girl-child without any reservations.

[My parents had three girls before I was born. They were fine though my grandmother (father's side) was reportedly a little disappointed. This was the old custom, especially in the farming community. We were big landowners with extensive farms and many orchards. But there was no widespread or big disappointment, as such. My grandparents even took my oldest sister with them and raised her with love and care.]

To come to Seema's birth and celebrating her first birthday: At that time our finances, and/or my work did not permit a second big birthday bash. (We compensated with several big parties and celebrations for Seema later on in life.)

Seema not getting mother's milk for a longer period was more disturbing. A little over two weeks after Seema was born, Sadhana, working in the kitchen with a kerosene oil stove caught fire and was burned quite badly – waist down. Sujata, not even 16 month-old, was also in the kitchen and, in her own way, tried to warn her mom that her saree had caught fire. She also tried to put out the fire with her tiny hands. I was in the other room, heard a scream, ran to the kitchen, doused the fire and rushed Sadhana to the hospital leaving the kids with neighbors.

My dear wife has always been a fighter. She had changed into a fresh saree and her face did not betray any discomfort. When the doctor came to the waiting room and asked 'where is the patient?' I pointed to Sadhana. She couldn't believe, and thought if she was the patient her injuries must be minor.

On full examination, the doctor saw the extent of burn injuries on her body and was almost speechless. Sadhana had big blisters on the lower parts of her body and the skin was peeling off. The doctors at the hospital were very good, took care of her, treated the injuries very carefully, gave her antibiotics, and specifically told her to discontinue breast-feeding Seema for fear of infection.

Poor baby! She still complains.

The doctors discharged Sadhana a day later satisfied with their treatment and her response. They gave her a very effective cream to apply on the burn injuries that became our 'miracle treatment' since then.

Cetavlex cream really worked like a miracle cure. That white cream in a toothpaste-like tube helped quick-healing. In a week's time the body healed well, helped, in no less measure, because of Sadhana's own will-power. She had to care for two toddlers and also look after her husband. In less than three weeks she was fine without any burn mark on her body, thanks to Cetavlex medicated cream.

[We still depend on Cetavlex for burn injuries and related problems. The cream is hard to get now even in India; the last time we got it was from England; it's worth the trouble and cost.]

So, Seema did not have her adequate quota of mother's milk but the lack of it did not show. Seema has been good at studies, also sports – some continue even now. She has a Black Belt in Taekwondo, and has done half Marathon while raising her kids. She now plays tennis. In addition, her nine-year old twin girls keep her running from one errand to another, from one project to another. With all that she is maintaining a big house and its inmates cool. In addition, she has more than her share of parties and big celebrations in her life with a very successful cardiologist-husband, Dr. Randeep Suneja.]

Sujata has consistently been very good at studies and, like a big sister, always tried to guide Seema in her studies. Sujata, habitually, would ask Seema after every exam how she fared. She would ask for the question-paper and check Seema's answers much to her fright and total reluctance to do so.

But that's what big sisters are for.

Sujata scored very high marks in her studies at school and college. However, she got married early and moved to America in 1982 and Seema moved with us to Indore in 1983 to continue her studies.

[Sujata had to raise, and care for, the family, 10 years later also to look after her very sick husband, and a decade and a half later, a very sick mother. She and her husband, Mujtaba, are now caring for an 88 year-old man (me). Sujata kept her full-time Kaiser Permanente (hospital) job till the last year.

God bless the two kids, and their kids, and now Sujata's grandkid, Aliya, the latest addition that has brought sunshine to our extended family, less than nine months after Sadhana passed away.]

Rewind to when the girls were born. I want to clear a couple of rumors and misconceptions, doubts etc. about both the girls. Seema, especially, has the complaint that Sujata was very much wanted, but she, somehow, was 'unwanted.'

The first part is true, the second very much untrue. Both the girls were very much wanted. The only difference – if it could be termed as a 'difference' - was that in case of Sujata the initiative and urgency were from Sadhana; for Seema, mine.

I was 35 years and six months, and wanted to have kids no later than that. I had figured that I could retire at 55 or so (in our office the retirement age was 58 and then raised to 60.) For Sadhana and I, boy or girl didn't matter. To us girls are embodiment of *Lakshmi* (the goddess of wealth and prosperity) and *Saraswati* (the goddess of learning and fine arts). That's the belief according to Hindu heritage, culture and scriptures. We both had decided to have only two kids and we had them, both very much wanted. According to Hindu scriptures the symbol of valor is also a woman, *Durga*. So, girls were always welcome in our home, our life.

Now dear Seema, once for all, don't ever think that you were in any way 'unwanted.' You were very much 'wanted' then, same as your older sister, and more 'wanted' now, both you and Sujata.

Both the girls have proved their worth in ample measure and continue to do so. They have blasted the traditional thinking about having a son – the traditional yearning, wish, and expectations. We did not share the old thinking. We have always maintained that good girls will bring good sons to us in the form of good husbands. We are right. We are blessed with good sons – sons-in-law, Mujtaba Roashan and Randeep Suneja.

I am not in any way suggesting that there are no good sons and that good sons do not bring good wives who could be like good daughters for the in-laws. Examples for both the situations are in plenty, some good and some not- so- good. In case of Sadhana's nephew Vineet, who grew up with Sujata and Seema, his wife is more than a daughter to Indrajit and Usha *Bhabhi*. Sushma (Sweety) treats and cares for her in-laws like her own parents. Of course it's mutual, though I would give more credit to the girl who comes from 'outside' and makes the husband's home and family 'her own.'

Coming back to our daily life early in our marriage, we were still in Ramesh Nagar. For some time it was not that hectic. My job as a reporter was to cover the City and its administration, the Municipal Corporation and local functions. Though all that kept me quite busy, there was ample time for the family and friends.

One of our neighbors was O.P. Bhagat, a colleague working for the English *Hindustan Times,* a sister publication. They had three apartment units – one for him and his small family, the other for his big brother and his family, the third for his parents. All of them were very close to us.

All the Bhagats became a family for us. Sadhana had endeared herself quickly to them, especially to the Bhagat-grandparents. Both of them loved us, had the utmost affection for us, both. I can't forget how the senior Bhagat would hug me tight, give me his loving blessings and say in Punjabi, *Thand Pai Gayee* (this is so soothing).

Real grandfatherly blessings for us we both cherished.

This was something out of this world, so much love for an unrelated neighbor, in ample measure! The Bhagat-grandma would similarly give a loving hug to Sadhana that echoed the same sentiments for us both.

The senior Bhagats had grandkids also. One of them Neelu (Neel Kamal) and as life moved on, his wife Santosh and their son Sonu (Nilesh) and his wife, Aparna, and their daughter, Rewa are very dear to us. Neelu's parents, and his older brother Raj and his wife, were also close to us.

[Ours is a 56-year-old relation and we treat each other as family. This extended family has lost some members but those that remain are still close. The Bhagats live in New Delhi, India, and so we now only have long-distance relations, but still quite close.]

We spent eight years (1961-69) in Ramesh Nagar, West Delhi, in between in Jore Bagh, South Delhi, but then were back in Ramesh Nagar. (Earlier also I lived in Jore Bagh for over six years. In 1969 we moved to nearby Rajori Garden where we had a bigger house and lived there for five years till 1974 to move to Chanakyapuri (Diplomatic Enclave) in a prestigious area.

While in Ramesh Nagar we used to have parties -- birthdays, Lohri, Holi, Diwali and other festivals and special occasions. The Bhagats, and many other neighbors, and our family had a lot of fun. Singing, reciting poems, a little dancing and lots of eats were the highlights.

Among the two top singers were Sadhana and OP Bhagat's wife, Premi. Among others was a young man, Rajpal Sharma, who had the routine of singing his favorite song *(Vrindavan ka Krishan kanhaiyya sabki aankhon ka tara, man hi man kyon jale Radhika, Mohan to hai sabka pyara)* on his daily morning walk. His singing was melodious and soothing; there was never any complaint from any neighbor about waking up by his singing.

One of Sadhana's favorite songs was *Mil gaye ho madadgar humumra tum* (I have found a companion/helper of my age.) The core lines of that song are: *swarthy vishwa mein hai kise kya pata, pyaar kitna mila hai tumhara mujhe* (the selfish world doesn't know how much love I have got from you.)

The other was, and continues to be our favorite, *tumhi mere mandir, tumhi meri pooja* (you are my temple, you are my worship).

[This is one of my all-time favorite songs from the movie *Khandan* (1965) sung by Lata Mangeshkar. Incidentally, *Khandan* is probably the only movie with all the three Mangeshkar sisters (Lata, Asha and Usha) singing. It had Sunil Dutt and Nutan, as the leading stars.

I would ask Sadhana to sing this song for me frequently and she obliged till about a year before she passed away – she had stopped singing, hardly speaking.]

This has been the intensity of our love.

Among the other Sadhana-favorites were a few Punjabi songs such as *Kala Doria* and *Meiyo tere naal vasiyan te hore koi vase vee na* (I am the one who lives with you, none else will do that) which sent the listeners laughing and enjoying endlessly.

Premi often sang, *Gaata rahe mera dil, toohi meri manzil* (my heart keeps singing, only you are my goal – destination.) This was a favorite of all of us, from the very popular Hindi movie, *Guide,* starring top actors – Dev Anand and Waheeda Rahman.

Indrajit particularly had his own – and ours too – favorites such as *Aataa hai jab bahaar mein mausam shabab ka* (when it's the season of love blossoming) and *bhala kisee ki muhabbat mein kya liya maine, jo doston ko bhi dushman bana liya maine* (what did I get falling in love, my friends have become my enemies.)

OP Bhagat would tell stories and I would recite my poems, some humorous, some romantic. It was fun all around. We used to have great time in our small, intimate neighborhood. The loving and caring, sharing and helpful neighborhood communities are the backbone of any community – the missing link here.

[Sadly both OP Bhagat and Premi *Bhabhi* are also no more.]

Things were very different then; we were young and full of life. But in Sadhana, I got not only a loving and caring companion but also someone who would share my life's experiences with total interest and attention, a rare trait.

Apart from poll-campaigns I also kept myself busy in work on the desk, for reporting as and when asked to go. I would often, on my own initiative, go the extra mile to write and report. I became well known in my journalistic fraternity, in the community, government offices, embassies and also public/private sector businesses and industries, arts and sports organizations and so on. There was no field of activity where I was not present to observe either as a hobby, or to report as a journalist. That made me popular – and was frequently invited to functions and meetings. It also got me rewards in various ways.

The first was right in my office. I was selected to work as a full-time reporter, my desk duties as a sub-editor ended. From basically in-office, I became one to crisscross the city and beyond, for writing, interviewing and reporting. I made full use of the new responsibilities and also make headway for myself. I got a larger field to work.

All that was possible as Sadhana took all the responsibilities of running the home, caring for everyone, working with the girls with their studies and other projects and pursuing her own hobbies of painting, sketching and entertaining, and so on.

One of my interesting assignments was a week-long first Inter-University Youth Festival, in the early 60s, at Talkatora Garden, a sprawling area in New Delhi. Over two dozen Universities from all over India sent their youth contingents. There were talented young men and women – the college students, artists, performers, actors and debaters. There were many youth activities, including plays presented almost daily on the stage at the Garden and we saw the young talent from all over the country.

Sadhana saw only a few events but, as a reporter, I was covering the Festival every day. Sometimes JK Jain would also be with me. Bombay University was one of the most prominent with some young men and women that shone on the cinema-screen soon after.

There was a handsome young man in his early 20s and a young woman about 18, who later became acclaimed actors in Bollywood. The young man who stole the show with his good looks and acting talent was none other than Amjad Khan, the latter-day villain par excellence who became an iconic actor with his memorable role in Sholay as dacoit Gabbar Singh. Amjad acted in scores of movies in his 30-year career and was acclaimed for his mannerism and dialogue-delivery.

He was, probably, the only villain who became the face of Brittannia Biscuits with the slogan: *Gabbar ki asli pasand* (Gabbar's real choice.)

The other was very charming Kumud Chhugani, a brilliant Kathak dancer even while in College. At 18, she was picked up by the ace Director Kishore Sahu and got her first role in Poonam Ki Raat opposite Manoj Kumar. Initially, she was reluctant to leave her studies but it was a good break for her.

Though Kumud was talented, somehow her histrionic skills could not be adequately exploited and though she did over a dozen films, she could not rise to stardom. Among some of her much talked-about movies were Laadla, Mujrim, Shart, Resham ki Dori, Bandhe Hath, and Hum Shakal. She acted along with Amitabh Bachchan, Balraj Sahni, Dharmendra and some others prominent actors of her time – some still active.

I had many occasions to see these talented young people and interact with them, little realizing that at least one of them – Amjad Khan – would rise to iconic heights and become the undisputed king of villainy, displacing the very talented and likable, Ajit, from the role. It's a pity that he passed away at a young age of 51 in 1992 – many other superstars are still appearing as heroes in 2017 at this age.

Apart from reporting on politics and other subjects I covered the cultural events, films, plays, and Indian and International Film Festivals. I have met a host of celebrities including Amitabh Bachchan, Shashi Kapoor, Jeetendra, Hema Malini, Zeenat Aman, the top European actress Gina Lollobrigida, and Waheeda Rahman with Dev Anand, the latter duo just a day before their top movie, Guide, was released.

It was an intimate group with only two journalists – Raghuvir Sahay and I. We had exclusive chat for over 90 minutes; 45 minutes Waheeda took to join us as Dev Anand smilingly remarked, must be getting ready, it's her big day.

Sadhana saw some of the International movies shown at the Festivals, usually at the famous Vigyan Bhavan, New Delhi.

She was with me when we met Dilip Kumar and Saira Bano when they came to attend a well-acclaimed documentary on the famous river Ganga and its nearly 1600 miles-long journey from the far Northern source Gangotri to where it meets the Bay of Bengal in far Eastern India. Dilip and Saira had an age-difference of 22 years but that evening it did not show. Both looked charmingly young and friendly.

There were numerous celebrities and dignitaries from every walk of life I met, many times whenever possible, with Sadhana. I wanted her company at these events. She enjoyed both – my company and the opportunity to meet with stars.

[As we were revising this book for a final look before it went for printing, the sad news of one of India's finest movie stars, Shashi Kapoor's passing away made us very sad. Memories came back to me, especially of my meeting with Shashi on a flight from Delhi to Bombay in 1978 when he boarded from Bhopal and by chance, had a seat next to me.

We talked just like a fan and a star for almost the entire duration of the flight, nearly an hour. He told me about his trip to Bhopal for getting entertainment exemption for his new film *Junoon* (Obsession) pertaining to the period of 1857 when Indians fought against the British for their freedom. He told me the story (I had not seen the film.)

Junoon was produced by Shashi; his whole family (wife Jennifer, and their three children, Sanjana, Kunal and Karan) was featured in the movie. Naseeruddin Shah and Shabana Azmi were the other main actors. It was directed by Shyam Benegal, one of the best directors in India.

The film received several awards though was not a money-making blockbuster. But Shashi never cared for money.

As our plane started descent for landing, I thanked Shashi for the pleasant time and talks and said: *hamara aur aapka bahut nikat ka sambandh hai* (we have very close relations.)

I thought he got that 'relation' as between an actor and his fan and said, yes, yes. I added: *Mai Sewakji ka putra hoon* (I am son of Sewakji – as my father was widely known.)

Hearing that Shashi gave me a sweet smile and a tight hand-shake, and said: *Voh to phir ghar ki baat hai* (oh, then it's like a family.)

My father was a friend of the Kapoor patriarch, Prithvi Raj Kapoor, and was helping him with Hindi-Urdu language for his Prithvi Theatre plays.

81

Shashi and Jennifer took keen interest in Prithvi Theatre, much more than his two older brothers, Raj and Shammi. They had revived it.

Sadhana was thrilled with my meeting with Shashi, was happy for me; and also once again, was all admiration for my father who had close connections with the First Family of Hindi movie industry.

Among Shashi's notable movies are Dharmaputra, Kabhi Kabhie, Namak Halal, Deewar, Jab Jab Phool Khile, Kala Patthar, Sharmeeli. He had 61 solo leads in movies, the most among the Kapoor clan, out of nearly 148 films, 12 with Amitabh Bachchan.]

We were still in Ramesh Nagar when a bigger chance came my way and made a big change in my – our – life and opened a vast field for me, nationally and internationally.

It was 1965, when Seema was just about a year-old and Sujata 26 months, I was invited by the US government for an extended study-work-observation tour. That Multi-National Foreign Journalists Project was handled by Indiana University (Bloomington, IN). With an ever dependable and capable Sadhana by my side, I accepted the invitation. My father, in his seventies, came from Bombay to stay and give moral support to the family in my absence.

That also meant one more person to be cared for and looked after but Sadhana rose to the occasion. She never complained, never protested, never whined and never had any gripe. On the contrary, she proved herself to be an ideal daughter-in-law willingly and respectfully caring for my father and keeping him comfortable.

All this was done despite the fact that father was not, in any way, a part of my marriage plans and the actual ceremony. He did not even know that I was going to marry – he and some other members of my immediate family had, kind of, given up on me and lost hopes that I will finally marry. So this topic lost its importance in our dealings, meetings and conversations though we still were meeting and carrying on normal relations; there was no such thing as being 'estranged.'

Sadhana, soon after our marriage, started 'rebuilding' and strengthening our relations. She gave all the required, or expected, respect and regard to all those family-members who were deprived of the chance to be a part of my marriage plan and attend the ceremony. She created such a good impression on father that he must have totally forgotten any gripe – if he had any – about not being made an important part of my big day, as the father of the groom.

All that happened because my wife was exceptional. She was made of a different material, in a different mold, with special qualities of love and care. God Himself created her.

[That's why I still quarrel with God for taking her away from me.]

Sadhana had endeared herself to all the other blood relations – none of whom were a part of my marriage. My father, my sisters and my brother all fell in love with Sadhana the moment they met her and never had any cause for complaint for the rest of her, and their life.

Sadhana's humane side: This is a story of Sadhana's humane side and her compassion for animals also. I came to hear about this from some of our neighbors on my return from office and later confirmed by her also. OP Bhagat wrote an article for *The Hindustan Times* about the episode.

As is common everywhere in India, there were a couple stray dogs in our neighborhood sustained by food from homes. One day the neighborhood kids – with excellent communication skills – spread the news that one of the females, had given birth to six puppies. This was big news almost like the birth in the family.

The dog – kids had named her Veena – had dug a pit in one corner of the big vacant space in front of our homes, a playground for the kids. The pups were comfortable in their 'maternity ward' till the fateful day when it rained very heavily.

The kids and their families were comfortably confined to their homes. Sadhana was nursing Seema – just a few days old – upstairs in our home. Suddenly she heard some puppies crying, louder when rainwaters entered their pit. Veena had wandered elsewhere, may be for food. Sadhana peeped from upstairs and didn't see anyone. Instinctively she came down and was shocked to find the pups inside the pit that was quickly flooding. She knocked at a couple doors but none wanted to come out in the heavy rain. Sadhana didn't worry about anything – a nursing mother out in the heavy rain unmindful of her own health!

Without wasting another minute, Sadhana brought a straw stool, turned it upside down, put her hand inside the pit fast filling up with water and began taking out the pups, one by one. She had put five inside the stool but suddenly recalled that kids had mentioned six pups. She put her arm and her shoulder deep inside the flooded pit and finally, felt the sixth, caught it and filled her upturned stool.

Right at that moment Veena arrived huffing and puffing in search of her pups and saw what Sadhana was doing. The animal instinct, she realized and out of gratitude started licking the feet of the savior.

Sadhana brought the pups upstairs, Veena dutifully followed. First things first; Sadhana cleaned the pups with warm water, then dried Veena. Next she gave some warm milk to her and laid down all her pups beside their mother to have a hearty lunch away from the pouring rains in a warm compassionate home.

That act of kindness was a part of Sadhana's nature. In that process she had won over Veena like anything. Since that day, Veena had become a sincere and dedicated bodyguard for our family, especially for Sujata, our first born.

Years rolled by. Sadhana cared for the two girls very much and was there for them every step of the way.

One late evening, little Seema, just about 4 years, excitedly told her mother that tomorrow they have the sports day at school and that she needed white shirt, white skirt, white socks and white shoes.

Sadhana, naturally, was a little concerned – just a few hours and so many requirements?

Next day Seema had everything that she wanted, participated in the beads race and surprised us all. Half way down, we saw that she was well behind the pack and we didn't have a good feeling. But in an instant, we found Seema putting the beads quickly on the string one after the other, finishing the job and sprinting toward victory.

We, parents, and Sujata were ecstatic. Seema had made us all proud.

Little did people know that Sadhana worked almost the whole night to personally stitch her dress, iron it, found a white pair of socks and polished her shoes to beautifully dress up her little girl ready to compete.

The prize Seema won was a real reward for Sadhana's hard work.

[Like Sujata, her sister too was very much attached to Sadhana, so much so that she *had* to see her mom's face every morning when she woke up.

One day, while in Indore, Sadhana was talking to our neighbor, Narindar, in the yard when Seema woke up in her room. She didn't see her mom and was quite upset. She went outside and seeing Sadhana, told her in no uncertain terms what she needed every morning – to see her mom's face.

Seema was then about 20 years old.]

There's an interesting story in contrast to Sadhana's rescue act for the pups. I used to have regular 'encounters' with a thief who had cultivated the habit of helping himself to the inviting vegetable garden in our front yard. He had mastered the skill of opening the latch of the iron-gate by using his God-given tool – his horns. He was a full-grown bull.

Many times we had seen the vegetables that Sadhana had planted simply disappear. And then we discovered the thief. Our helper, Vishnu would try chasing him away by swinging a stick only to find him more defiant and reluctant to leave.

It may sound strange that an editor found a way to tackle the beast and drive him away whenever he witnessed the attempted robbery. As soon as I would hear the opening of the latch, I knew the culprit had arrived. I would appear on the steps of our home, and in a stern voice order the bull to go away. And lo and behold, he would stop, look up, obediently follow my order, retreat and turn away only to come back another day.

Unfortunately, he would not wait for the second part of my order – put the latch back on as you leave.

And this one is not a 'bull' story. We did have several pets ranging from pups, dogs, kittens and yes, a whole bunch of rabbits.

Many of the pups became our house-guests, one at a time, courtesy Seema, most of the time. She would bring a puppy from here, another from there, some from somewhere, of course with a high pedigree of some stray dog.

But they were all gifted, novelty, record-holders, sort of.

This one dog in Rajori Garden had the gift of recognizing the sound of the horn – only of our car. Jackie will not bark at any other horn – in India blowing of car horn is a common thing. He will only extend a friendly barking welcome whenever *I* would approach home and sound the horn.

In Chanakyapuri we had Moti. This one was extremely fond of balloons. He would immediately get up as the balloon-seller approached our home and started his *peepari* (crude flute of vendors.) He would act like a child anxious to get one. We would buy a couple and he would play with one till it popped. He will then give it a satisfied look and go away.

The rabbits were fun. They would multiply quickly in our big backyard and we will give them away.

The birth of baby-rabbits is a fascinatingly touching example of motherly love. Weeks before the delivery mother-rabbit would pull out her fur (rabbit-furs are the softest) and make the softest bed in the world. She would look ugly without her beautiful fur and with blood spots clearly visible. After a few weeks of 'post-partum' love and care of the babies, she would eventually get her full coat of fur back.

What a sacrifice! Paradise regained!

Lastly, who could forget our tiny kitty cat that was abandoned at – or around – birth and Sadhana became her 'foster mother.' She would feed the kitten with a small one-and-a-half inch bottle and nipple till its tiny tummy would be full and show. It was so little that it would climb on to my shirt pocket and sit there. Sadhana had made a small 'bedroom' for her in a little basket and every morning as it would hear her 'mother's' voice it would come rushing to be picked by Sadhana.

The curious thing about this kitty was it did not grow much and remained a very small cat even after about four months – a rare dwarf specie weighing not more than ¾ of a pound. At four months the cat is more than half-way to adulthood. This one 'refused' to grow – as many grown-ups would wish recalling their happy childhood.

Before we could seriously think of taking it to a vet to find out more about any dwarf cat, it was brutally killed by, probably, its father who sneaked into our house through an open window near father's bed. It's said that the male cat is jealous of the offspring and often kills them for depriving him of the time, love and attention from the mother-cat.

We all were very sad but Sujata, Seema, and their cousin Rewa (who was spending a few days with us), were mad. They had a 'mother of all battles' with their grandfather whom they blamed for keeping the window open and getting *their* cute kitty killed.

RIP Kitty!

9

My Memorable Visit to America

The year 1965 brought a sea-change in my life – our lives. The invitation for the visit to the United States came through a letter from Ambassador Chester Bowles who was one of the finest and friendliest American ambassadors to India. His wife, Dorothy, was equally respected for her dedication and love for India; so was their daughter Cynthia (who later wrote a book *At Home in India*).

Mrs. Bowles used to wear a saree when out in public – social functions organized by Indian groups.

Ambassador Bowles had good personal relations with the first Indian Prime Minister, Jawaharlal Nehru, and strongly believed that the United States and India shared fundamental democratic values. This view is shared by other American Presidents including Kennedy, Clinton, Bush, Obama, and now Donald Trump.

This may be one of the reasons the program under which I visited America had been given added importance as that year we were three Indian journalists out of 13 in a group from eight other countries. Korea (South) had a special place those days for American planners and had four Koreans in our group.

Something about how I was selected.

I did not seek the invitation. (I heard that some of the very top journalists had virtually begged for invitations for visits to other countries.) I was chosen, probably, because I was among the bunch of newsmen who were active in the field, fair in their reporting/commenting and had created a good impression on those who mattered.

One day a couple of American officials from the United States Information Service (USIS), now US Information Agency, visited my Editor Ratan Lal Joshi with the proposal. They seemed to have already made up their mind about me and it looked like they just wanted to *inform* the Editor. Actually they did not give Mr. Joshi any option to nominate somebody else; he just might have done that given a choice, though it was doubtful whether that name would have been okayed.

However, the visit from US officials did not leave any room for Mr. Joshi and he had to welcome the idea. That job done, I had the invitation letter from the Ambassador on behalf of the US government in my hand and the following couple of weeks I was on my way to America, my first travel overseas.

Sadhana was ecstatic on hearing the news. Instead of making me worry about her and two small kids left alone for four plus months, Sadhana confidently said she will handle everything and encouraged me to go without any hesitation. She was very happy for me and took it as my well-deserved reward for hard work in my profession and immense love for her and our family.

My visit coincided with India's 17-day war with Pakistan (August-September in 1965) when Lal Bahadur Shastri was the Prime Minister of India. I asked my Editor if he needed me in India to report on the conflict and to decline the invitation from the US. He said no, you should go and utilize the opportunity to explain the Indian point of view to Americans.

That sounded fair and I did not have to think otherwise.

Everything went on well and I was on my official American visit as a staff-member of the newspaper *Hindustan*, but was not considered 'on-duty.' I was left to utilize the vacation I had earned. I had about 2 ½ months earned vacation and the rest was without pay. But it was okay for me. I knew Sadhana will manage, and she did, with added responsibility of my father who had come to stay with my family while I was away.

In my absence, Sadhana handled and cared for two small kids and my father. She also arranged a trip to her mother's home in Dehradun, a city with which my father was also very familiar in the 30s. We had relocated from Indore to Mussoorie in the Himalayan foothills sometime in 1934. The snowy winters did not suit mother so she would move to less cold Dehradun valley. We – mother, two older sisters and I – spent years in that city mainly during the extreme winters. As children we had fun-time in both the places, more so in Dehradun.

A thoughtful Sadhana was able to get in touch in the mid-sixties with one of our neighbors of the thirties. While visiting her mother in Dehradun, she took father, Sujata and Seema with her. It was a very nice and nostalgic meeting with our neighbor, Miss Edwards (who had continued to live in the same house). She loved us, children, and was pleasantly surprised and very happy to meet with the wife and two daughters of that naughty boy (me). My mother was her favorite neighbor and I her favorite child in the entire neighborhood.

I still remember what she gave me on Christmas – a box-full of marbles. My older sister Lata, then 7 ½, (very helpful to my mother) got a kitchen set; my other older sister Prem, 9, got a doll – she was not into much for household work.

[Unfortunately, I could not meet Miss Edwards after my return from the US as I got a promotion in my office and plunged head-on in my new and more exciting assignments on national and international levels. I started reporting the federal government, Parliament of India and major government departments such as defense and foreign affairs.]

Sadhana's support and willingness to manage our family and home during my long absence was in play, always. Her management skills were also amply proved with the fact that half of my 'vacation-visit' was without pay. The management of my newspaper, *Hindustan* and the venerable editor, Ratan Lal Joshi, did not agree to utilize my stay and travel in the US for the benefit of the paper. I had suggested to him that I would keep sending dispatches from America for publication (which would have benefitted the paper) but he sidelined it by saying "no, no you go and enjoy the trip."

Other journalists in my group sent news/views roundup to their papers which proudly printed them announcing that their reporters are touring the United States and sending special dispatches.

So much for the strange leadership at *Hindustan* I had to encounter and work with.

As I got selected and invited for the US visit almost all of my colleagues expressed happiness and congratulated me. Just two staffers had different reaction, something that happens – a little heart-burn, a little jealousy etc. One sulked (probably he knew he was never going to get selected), while the other, though congratulating me, could not hide his own feelings and said, "I will also go some day."

I did not mind that at all and hoped and wished him well. I said I will be very happy whenever you get a chance. He was then one of the junior members of the editorial staff.

[A few years later he did get a chance, though it was a very short visit but I was very happy for him and said so. He, otherwise, had much respect for me as he was one of the reporters in my section and worked under my directions. He was junior to me in years and in position in the office but both Sadhana and I, cared for him and his family. He was also impressed by Sadhana and respected her and would often convey her messages (when I was out of office) in poetic expressions.]

Sadhana would always reach out to my colleagues and their families. We were like family. We treated this particular staffer, Brahmarshi Kumar Pande, with extra care and concern when he got very, very, sick and passed away quite young. Both of us often visited him and Sadhana cared for him as her own little brother or brother-in-law (husband's brother.) We were also there for his wife and three children.

Sadhana, with her loving and caring nature continued to play a significant part in the life of this family after Pande's demise. A few years later, she helped the family by finding a good match and arranging the marriage of their older daughter. This young man was a brother of Sadhana's good friend, Saraswati (Saru) Sharma. This was something extra-ordinary but that was my Sadhana, always helpful, always caring.]

Before I left for the US, the Press Officer at the American Embassy, Kent D. Obee visited our home with his lovely wife. Sadhana, as usual, had some tasty Indian dishes ready for the American couple who enjoyed them and also wished me a very fruitful visit to their country.

The Obees also visited the famous Hindu place of worship in New Delhi, Birla Mandir (temple) and our photographer Virendra Prabhakar took their photos. [It's a sad story again, for me to not been able to contact the Obees while in the US. The story is being repeated, unfortunately.]

Sadhana was always curious to know how I was doing so far away from her and the kids, if I was taking care of my health and what were the highlights of my trip. I kept her posted and she would take delight, felicitate me and spread the word to other relatives and friends. She never complained about my not being with her and the kids and that she was left to manage everything by herself.

I am sure not many other wives in similar situation would be able to conduct themselves as my dear wife did. I felt lucky then, and blessed later too. Sadhana has left many valuable memories behind.

Coming back to my American visit, it was absolutely life-changing. It was educative and informative, definitely enjoyable and challenging, cherished and rewarding, in many ways.

The Multi-National Foreign Journalists Project was sponsored by the State Department and managed by the Journalism Department of Indiana University, Bloomington (IN) with Professor Floyd Arpan as the Director. There were other talented and helpful professors attached to the project like Associate Director Jim Callaway, Prof. Richard Yoakum, Prof. Ralph Holsinger and others. The Chair of Department of Journalism was Prof. John Stempel, a distinguished academician and an inspiration.

'Papa Floyd,' as he was fondly and respectfully addressed by most of the visiting journalists, was an experienced journalist-administrator-professor. His office was highly efficient in handling the project, dealing with multi-ethnic journalists from various countries bringing their expectations and hopes and peculiarities. The Faculty-members were knowledgeable, friendly and ever eager to share their skills and expertise. It was a learning- meeting- traveling-writing and working experience. We were exposed to events, their coverage and meetings with eminent media persons and civic leaders.

Mrs. Arpan – 'Mom Holly,' as some of us addressed her often, was an accomplished educator herself. She played host to all of us frequently, took us out for meetings etc. and also drove me to the airport for my journey back to India.

The project included two 'three-week stints' with two newspapers for each of us. We were expected to accompany the reporters on assignment and observe the working of the newspapers, radio and TV in the US and also write. In addition, we were frequently meeting with civic and other leaders, and traveling – also quite a bit of sightseeing as tourists. We were taken to Niagara Falls and saw the Wonder from both the American and Canadian sides. As a citizen of a member- Commonwealth Country – India – we three Indians did not need a Canadian Visa (those days were different), others had to get, though the Project took care of that business.

While in Los Angeles I had the opportunity to visit Disneyland and San Diego amusement park, Sea World and so on.

We also met with NBC and *The New York Times* editors, and had interesting talks with them. They admitted that American newspapers, by and large, are 'opinionated' and many of the stories they print are analytical, not straight news. They also said, American media was itself a big business free from big biz pressure. [Since then, things have changed a lot – the big biz controls most of the big papers and TV and the media is more opinionated and biased, and partisan.]

That was an experience for me; big Indian newspapers, in some cases, were owned by big businesses, also influenced through advertisements and many were also patronized by politicians. But, by and large, they did report straight news – only comments and editorials would express opinion. It was a clear demarcation.

One of the valuable experiences for me – and I am sure for others – was to meet with normal, regular people interested in international affairs and people from different countries who invited us for lunches, dinners and also to stay with them – individually. The program was chalked out in such a way that it was not a burden on us, financially.

Each one was paid $18 per day – regular periodical checks were given. This money was for our stay at a hotel, breakfast-lunch-dinner, and moving around. Now one would say: What! Only $18 a day for all those expenses! Right? Wrong!

For us it was $8 a night for stay in best of hotels, including Hiltons, and even Waldorf Astoria, in New York [now charges from $319 to $1800 a night.] And it was $6 if we shared the room with one of our own group-members. Breakfast-lunch-dinner for a preferred vegetarian did not cost more than another six dollars. Papa Floyd had told us at the start that, 'if you don't drink too much, not smoke too much and not indulge in too many other things, $12-18 would be enough.' Yes, that was correct.

Papa Floyd also advised us, and got our unanimous consent, for his office to withhold $6 from our daily allowance as long as we were in Bloomington, IN; that was for a little over a month. The University's 'guest house', Indiana Memorial Union, was a multi-story building and we shared rooms at subsidized rates. Eating at the University cafeteria was also inexpensive and so $12 per-diem was okay.

About 32 days later when we were going separately, without Papa Floyd with us, on our out-of-state travel and work, we had an extra (from our savings) $192 each. We were delighted and thanked Papa Floyd for the great idea.

Besides that, we had more savings as we were frequently invited for lunches and dinners by the Faculty members, some social organizations, newspapers, and a few prominent community figures. That meant more savings. For me that also meant I was able to send $200 to Sadhana during my four months plus stay out of India. [Sadhana returned the 'favor' by twice air-mailing big packets of India-made silk ties and scarves as gifts for my American hosts and other friends.]

Can you beat that! Such a thoughtful and caring companion of mine!

In those days you could get more for a dollar. My breakfast, normally, was one dollar plus, lunch-dinner not more than 2-3 dollars. Most of our transportation was either provided by the Project or community members who invited us for lunch-dinner or sight-seeing. We were picked up from the airports/railway stations by the hosts or volunteers.

That was the beauty of the project – if you were prudent you did not have to spend a single penny of the money you brought with you – 18 dollars a day were good enough for you.

This 'volunteer system' was interesting and useful. All over the country, in several cities, there were 'hospitality committees' manned by only a couple of staffers paid by the government or various organizations. They were mostly run by volunteers who gave their time and transport as good citizens. These men and women were willing and able, eager and happy to help foreigners. They also wanted to know more about others, and show them around, invite them to their homes and conduct themselves as messengers of peace, love, solidarity, and friendship all the time.

Not many countries have a system such as here in America. We loved it.

For me there was another 'achievement.' After a month's stay, and planned travels out of Indiana with Papa Floyd, we had to travel to some other cities as a group with another leader. With Papa Floyd's suggestion, and the unanimous opinion of my group-members, I was selected as the leader to officiate for Papa Floyd. That was an honor and a recognition that I was shaping up as someone popular and capable of handling responsibility in a diverse group. I was one of the most lively members of the group and friendly with all the others.

Generally, we were encouraged to share rooms with another member for two reasons – one to know each other better, and two, to save money. Papa Floyd had paired us fairly and I thought the arrangement was fine.

However, there was a serious complaint on the very second day of our 'independent' travel: one Korean member told me that he could not sleep as his roommate was loudly snoring all night. He desperately wanted a change in the rooming arrangement.

This was a challenge, and I had to do something about it to avert a crisis. The guy was adamant for a change and it was not proper for me to dump the 'offensive' roommate on somebody else. I decided to make him *my* roommate to solve the problem. I could handle his snoring - had no other choice. Well, I had to explain to Papa Floyd – who kept a track of everything that went on with us. He had a weekly newsletter (*The Little UN Gazette*) circulated to all of us wherever we were traveling. In addition, he would visit every one of us when we were working with the newspapers.

I made that complaining Korean a good friend.

Generally all the Koreans – and others too – were good friends. When we were on a bus from Bloomington to Chicago (about 230 miles, a 4-hour drive) I sang a couple of Hindi songs, and the Koreans sang Arirang, one of their very famous folk songs that I also learned to sing, of course partly, and in my Hindi-English-Korean pronunciation.

Arirang is also considered the unofficial National Anthem of Korea. The pleasant fact is both North and South Korea have given Arirang national and UN status by getting it included in UNESCO's Intangible Cultural Heritage list.

In essence, the song is about lovers, the girl is in love and the boy not-so. The young man goes away and the girl says that you will not be able to go far as you will hurt your legs. This simple story is woven into beautiful lyrics and set to melodious music.

Korean version (that the Korean group sang, and I learnt):
Arirang, Arirang, Arariyo...
Arirang gogaero neomeoganda.
Nareul beorigo gashineun nimeun
Shimrido motgaseo balbyeongnanda.

The English translation:
Arirang, Arirang, Arariyo...
Crossing over Arirang Pass.
Dear who abandoned me [here]
Shall not walk even ten steps
before his feet hurt.

Additionally:

> Just as there are many stars in the clear sky,
> There are also many dreams in our heart.
> There, over there that mountain is Baekdu Mountain,
> Where, even in the middle of winter days, flowers bloom.

[Arirang has somewhat changed in its 600 year-life.

The fascinating story about Arirang is that until 2013, the lyrics had not been translated into other languages, forcing singers to sing Romanized Korean lyrics. In late 2013, a group of professional translators and skilled interpreters from the famous Graduate School of Translation and Interpretation at the Hankuk University of Foreign Studies produced 'singable' lyrics of "Arirang" in nine languages other than Korean. On December 3, 2013, Professor Jongsup Jun directed a concert under the title of "Let the World Sing Arirang in Their Tongues," in which a student choir sang the famous Kyunggi "Arirang" in English, Chinese, Japanese, French, Italian, Spanish, German, Russian, Arabic and Korean. – *Wikipedia.*]

What an unbelievably enchanting show that must have been!

The impact of the song and its importance is that it's very much associated with the United States and its military also, that took part in the Korean War (1950-53) and still guarantees South Korea's security.

The South Korean government designated "Arirang" as the official march of the U.S. Army's 7th Infantry Division since 26 May 1956, after its service in Korea during the Korean War. The official Division song was the "New Arirang March," an American-style arrangement of "Arirang".

On February 26, 2008, the New York Philharmonic performed "Arirang" for an encore during its unprecedented trip to North Korea.

It's sheer beauty, and I have often pleasantly surprised Koreans since then whenever I happen to meet them, anywhere.

I traveled coast-to-coast in America – from New York and Washington DC to Los Angeles and San Francisco, from Niagara Falls in the East to Disneyland in the West, from Alaska to Texas, and in between.

I worked with two prominent newspapers also, *Philadelphia Inquirer* in Philadelphia, and *Fort Worth Star Telegram* in Texas, each for three weeks. Going out with reporters, meeting the local leaders and others and writing articles/reports for the papers was very useful.

In Philadelphia and Fort Worth, I attended court proceedings and was even invited by the judges to their chambers and discuss issues and cases they were hearing. It was gracious of them to ask for *my* opinion on the issues. What an experience!

While I was in Fort Worth, in Tarrant County, one day a staffer took me to the Sheriff's office. I couldn't figure out why, but soon the scene unfolded and I had become an Honorary Deputy Sheriff of Tarrant County. Sheriff Lon Evans gave me a certificate and a badge and said jokingly: "Now you can go out and arrest anyone you don't like."

It was an honor and I cherish the memory since that day in 1965.

[Sheriff Evans is no more. There is another distinguished officer, Sheriff Bill E. Waybourn in charge. After 51 years I wanted to visit Fort Worth and the Sheriff's office but could not. And that's another story.]

There were several other instances when I felt privileged to be invited to this country. Judge Byron Matthews asked me to join him in his court to celebrate Christmas *three days before* the actual festival as he came to know that I won't be around on The Day.

His court was decorated and there were lots of eats. As I entered two women staffers came rushing and kissed me – I was under the mistletoe. *[Mistletoe is a plant/flower and relevant to several cultures. It is associated with* Christmas *as a decoration, under which lovers are expected to kiss.]*

I was treated as a special person worthy of love. What a unique honor!

That was the kind of reception and hospitality I saw and received wherever I went. I saw greatness, respect, understanding and love for people from different countries. I don't know if all the other members of my journalist group had such a beautiful experience. I had, and I am both grateful and honored to have been given a chance that brought me closer to this country.

[Little did I dream that one day Sujata would be married in America and we all would live in United States leaving the country of our birth behind.

I also didn't know that Sadhana would breathe her last in this country she made her home for 30 plus years.]

Among the many memorable events in the US was the one at Albuquerque (New Mexico State) where I was staying with a nice little family of husband-wife and a baby. Dorothy Morse, the lady of the house and the home maker, was my main host as her husband was working.

One day Dorothy took me to the local radio station for an interview. We had the baby also with us as Dorothy could not leave her home.

That interview became memorable for a few reasons.

The radio station had just started an open-line program where listeners sitting in their homes or offices could dial the studio's number and ask questions. This was of course, in addition to the interviewer's questions.

The interviewer was a little perplexed when she saw a baby also with Dorothy and me who were ushered in the studio. However, without any delay, she made up her mind and said, it's okay. This was probably one of the rare occasions when a toddler was inside the studio for a live interview and questions-answers from the audience at homes or offices.

She started the program by introducing Dorothy and I, then added: In case the proceedings are interrupted or we go off air you should know that there is a baby in the studio who might have fiddled with switches and mikes.

It was very thoughtful and creative and we both were very much impressed by the interviewer's presence of mind.

[The baby did not take part in any conversation, did not interrupt, did not fiddle with anything throughout, as if she knew how to behave in a studio. I don't know if, as a grown-up she became a celebrity radio personality.]

After the initial introduction and a wide variety of questions about India, Indo-US relations and my impressions of the visit so far, it was the turn of listeners. One of the listeners happened to be a student from India who wanted to meet me afterwards and take me to dinner.

A young girl asked me how did I get married? I gave my pet short answer: "There was a young man who was my friend; he had a sister, and I got married to her."

That elicited much applause and response.

We could hear listeners enjoying and laughing at the crisp answer.

She persisted: "But how can *I* get married, *I* don't have a brother."

More laughter followed as I replied: "Don't worry, *I* can be your brother and find you a good match."

I didn't know if that sort of informal and amusing interviews were done in India those days. Things have changed immensely in the five decades since then.

With my hectic schedule on the US tour a few developments took place – both in India. One was that we added a new member to our family, a *Rakhi* brother of Sadhana. The second was – the details I came to know much later – that she had been writing poems in my absence; the hobby she continued later also and got ample encouragement from me.

More about the two developments:

'Rakhi' brother Brij Mohan Chhibber. He was the neighborhood chemist, a certified one, often addressed as Doctor as he knew enough to take care of normal and everyday ailments in the neighborhood. He had a chemist shop nearby.

One day the kids got very, very sick and Sadhana was concerned. She didn't have much money and desperately needed medicines and help. She went to Brij and said, brother, I need help. Brij not only gave her medicines and valuable advice but also visited our home to see the patients. He simply refused to charge anything either for the visit or the medicines saying you addressed me as 'brother' and how can a brother charge his sister for his (*newfound*) nieces?

Since that day in 1965, Brij has been Sadhana's brother, had *Rakhi* tied to his wrist for more than half a century till Sadhana was alive. Even now my daughters, Sujata and Seema, have continued the tradition; they sent *Rakhi* to Brij in India last year after Sadhana passed away. They sent *Rakhi* again this year as they couldn't see their two *Mamas* (Indrajit and Brij) without *Rakhis* from their sister.

Brij has been a brother for Sadhana and *Mama* (maternal uncle) for Sujata-Seema ever since. In a few years after this development he married and his wife, Hem, has also treated us as close relatives. Not only that, his two daughters, Madhu and Ritu – are like my daughters – they were named by Sadhana. Besides that, Sadhana also made the final choice of names for Madhu's two daughters, Medha and Aadya.

[Sadly, Brij passed away Aug. 27, 2017, deeply mourned by us all. This is a very close and deeply loving relation with his family that, I hope, will continue for generations. Madhu, for all practical purposes a single mother, took care of her mother – who had a stroke last year - and her father who was unwell for a long time. She is caring for her pre-teen daughters also. Ritu, married and working in London, keeps helping in other ways.]

Sadhana's older blood-brother, Dr. Indrajit Kumar also lives in New Delhi and had been a source of strength, support and help for us. He has always been like a father-figure for Sadhana and played the leading role in arranging our marriage. He lived quite far and on that day Sadhana could not inform him and get him to help. Later we had moved to another area – Chanakyapuri (Diplomatic Enclave) that was further away.

However, we used to meet quite often and his two kids, Rewa and Vineet, and Sujata-Seema grew up together. Sadhana knew his wife, Usha, years before they got married and who is also well liked by us all. Vineet got married in 1999 for which Sadhana and Sujata's husband, our older son-in-law Mujtaba, and Seema with little Arjun visited India and attended the marriage. Vineet-Sweety have a 9 year-old very sweet son, Archit, whom Sujata and I saw for the first time in 2016.

The other significant development was Sadhana's writings. I knew that she occasionally wrote poems before marriage. My absence gave her an incentive to write more, more so when she didn't get my letters from America for a couple of weeks. Phone calls were not that easy or cheap, and air-mail was the more convenient communicator. She wrote most of her poems in Hindi, her choice, my Mother Tongue and India's National Language. She had a unique grasp of the finer points of the language, her emotions, and the word-pictures she painted have been out of this world.

I used to write to her quite often but there was a big gap, thanks to a confusion between air-mail and surface (sea) mail. When she wrote to me about it I vowed to write to her every day. After finishing my day's programs and activities I would write a letter every night and post it, without fail, the very next day.

Later I came to know that all the neighborhood kids knew about my letters and as the mailman came he would be followed by kids announcing "Aunty *Ji* you have many letters from Uncle." It was fun for them but excellent news for Sadhana, eagerly waiting for my letters. Sometimes they were delivered in a bunch. She would regularly write to me and would often advise me about my food. She was concerned about me as this was the longest time I was spending far away from her and her cooking which she knew I relished.

My letters were rays of sunshine for my dear Sadhana. The time she waited for my letters gave birth to some of the finest poems in Hindi language I have come across. One is *Jo mil pati teri paati* (only if I got your letter) and then she went on weaving a fine web of beautiful similes and painting exquisite word-pictures.

These poems are so very touching and out-of-this-world.

[We got a sample copy of the collection, *Samarpan* (Dedication) and showed it to her as she lay on her hospital bed, in May, last year.]

My US trip made me a little wiser, a little braver in facing the audience with more confidence. It also made me more curious to explore things and develop a 'larger nose for news,' as we say, and that makes a big difference about how we chase and discover news/articles ideas. I applied these with enthusiasm and good results in my later life as a reporter, writer and editor.

Another idea Papa Floyd 'implanted' in me is, just ask, if you don't get it it's fine, but if you got it that's your reward and success.

This needs a little explanation.

As we wound down our visit, we were back in Bloomington, IN and were invited for a farewell dinner by the local Kiwanis Club. All members of our group, Project Director and his associates, prominent members of the Club and other community leaders were present. Papa Floyd selected me and Brian Cuthbertson, a tall, young Australian, and fellow journalist-member of the group, to answer questions from the audience.

[Brian was a staffer of *South China Morning Post,* a newspaper from Hong Kong, later its Editor.]

It was again an honor for me.

The after-dinner speeches and Q&A session were interesting. Both Brian and I praised our hosts – the Project and the friendly, cute little city of Bloomington, the US government and the American people, in general. We expressed our gratitude for the opportunities we got, the hospitality and the unique privilege of working with American newspapers and traveling coast to coast in America, we enjoyed.

The Q&A session was mostly handled by me. There were questions about our impressions, about the American political scene and our reaction and so on. I tried to answer them as best as I could and was able to create a good impression.

In my closing remarks I said that after my stay and travel and getting so much love, consideration and encouragement from the Project staff, and the officials in general, I feel very close to this country and its people. With such a good relation, I said, I would like to share some of my concerns also.

I then commented on the crime rate (it was nothing as compared to what it's now), and an unchecked proliferation of weapons. Of course, I was reminded of the Second Amendment of the American Constitution that guaranteed 'the right to bear arms.' A couple questioners then wondered how the government could curtail people's right and put restrictions on them.

To those questions my answer was simple: "if the government can put restrictions on your driving a car (with red lights, and double yellow lines, etc.) and riding a bus (with a yellow line near the entrance proclaiming, don't cross the line, it's the law) why can't there be reasonable restrictions on people having arms?"

One of the reasons I thought the crime rate was going up was unrestricted sale and purchase and owning of guns of all types by anyone, anywhere, any time. I had in mind the situation in India where there were very severe restrictions on buying and owning guns; even getting a license was not easy. That was probably, the legacy of the British government that didn't want more Indians to own guns and it was difficult – if not impossible – to make a weapon on your own.

America, its history and its Constitution are entirely different.

That was a ticklish matter and, there could be no consensus on that.

The matter had to be left there. Though my remarks seemed a little 'undiplomatic,' Brian and many in the audience, agreed with me. I asked Papa Floyd whether I had crossed the line and he said it was okay.

[I know there is a strong debate – and differences - on this issue despite the ever-increasing violence and use of arms. But some restrictions are definitely needed.]

Project Director Prof. Floyd Arpan had a final private meeting with the group and all of his associates and asked for our comments, suggestions, and any wishes that remained unfulfilled.

Some suggested a much longer project, six months instead of four, many more opportunities to work in other newspapers, etc.

[Prof. Arpan headed the Project for 29 years. He retired in 1981 as Professor Emeritus and died in 1990. The project was started just after World War II with training German journalists. After the war, Germany's work places did not have enough able bodied people to work. Millions had been killed or maimed and there was a severe shortage of workers everywhere.

The United States had taken up the gigantic task of re-building war-torn Germany, and the other countries liberated by the Allies. The journalist project was one of them. After initially, all-Germans, with Korean War ending it was mostly all-Koreans. Later it was extended to other nations also becoming truly multi-national project].

At that farewell meeting and stock-taking I mentioned about my wish. I thought of an interview with the late President Kennedy's wife, Jackie, but was hesitating the request might be turned down.

Papa Floyd's comments still resonate in my mind: You should have told me, what if she had agreed to it? I would have at least tried and even if she had declined, it was okay. At least we could say we tried. You should always try, howsoever impossible or difficult the idea or your wish-list seem out-of-reach.

That's a lesson I always try to follow and tell others to do just that – try. I often hear people saying, oh it's difficult, it's not going to happen, and you shouldn't hope to get it. I say: why don't we just try, if we don't succeed, no big deal, but why not give it a try, who knows, we just might.

Sadhana will always give it a try, and she did get what she aimed for.

[Just an example: a few years later, in 1972, I was stranded in Egypt when a part of our European trip went bad. Sadhana had a round ticket to India, I didn't. The option was she returns and sends me a ticket. Those days it was difficult to travel without express permission and a P form from the Reserve Bank of India (like the Federal Reserve in the US.)

The task, on the face of it, looked extremely difficult, if not impossible. Sadhana, determined to try, went to the RBI office, sought the senior officer and despite his reluctance and making excuses, finding fault with our tour planning etc., persisted. She told him point blank, and forcefully: an Indian citizen is stranded in a foreign country, is it not your duty to facilitate his return to his own country? I am not asking for money. I am paying for the ticket, you just have to give me permission on a piece of paper. She argued with him and succeeded in getting it.

Needless to say I was able to return with Sadhana's persistent effort. She never thought of the difficult task. She never gave up. She tried and got results. If you don't try, you won't get it. If you try, chances are you will be successful. She was.

Years later, in America, I got positive results after trying. I got a refund from US Customs in San Francisco for the import- duty we paid at the airport on our return from India in 1998. Later I discovered that we were not required to pay as we had not crossed the limit of spending in India. I took up the issue with the Customs. They put hurdles and wanted proofs/receipts of our spending. Meeting all their requirements – and the receipts I usually keep – I succeeded in getting the refund. Everybody had their doubts but I tried and I got results.]

Thanks Papa Floyd. I had learnt a valuable lesson and have tried to put it to work since then at every possible opportunity with good results. In case it did not succeed, I always have the satisfaction that at least I tried. I have tried to impress upon others also that trying is always better than not trying and regretting later.

A "big thank you" for the unique opportunity to scale greater heights and return to India well prepared for more opportunities and responsibilities that waited for me and successes were assured along the way.

While in Bloomington, IN, the major local daily paper, *Bloomington-Herald Telephone* printed several articles written by our group-members. I also contributed a couple and got a lot of good reviews.

The India-Pakistan war had ended and Prime Minister Kosygin of the (then) Soviet Union had played a major role in ending the hostilities. He also persuaded both Prime Minister Lal Bahadur Shastri of India and Army Chief-turned President Ayub Khan of Pakistan to visit Tashkent (now in Uzbekistan) for important talks.

After the talks (4-10 January 1966) a ceasefire agreement was signed and the very same night, Prime Minister Lal Bahadur Shastri died under mysterious circumstances.

[Surprisingly, no in-depth investigation was done in India or the Soviet Union. That, legitimately, gave rise to a conspiracy theory that has not died even 51 years after his death. It has become more suspicious as Shastri's personal physician, Dr. Chugh and his family also died in a road accident in India in 1977.]

Shastri was the Prime Minister after the death of Jawaharlal Nehru from June 9, 1964 to January 11, 1966. A very simple, but dedicated politician and an astute statesman, he had, in this very short period become very popular with his pragmatic leadership and peoples' causes he took up sincerely. His *Jai Jawan, Jai Kisan* (hail the soldier, hail the farmer) still resonates in India and emphasizes the importance of both.]

In Bloomington in our three-member Indian group the news came as a shock. I was interviewed on the local radio and paid tributes to the man who in a very short period put a stamp of his leadership on India. Not much had come till then and so, not much was said about the circumstances of his sudden death.

[I had the honor and privilege to meet Shastri *Ji* and also attend his several press briefings, a few under a big tree at his official residence. His achievements in a very short tenure were admirable. India then depended on American wheat under PL-480 but when Washington threatened to suspend supply, Shastri stood tall. He declared he would observe fast on Mondays to save food (just a symbolic gesture) and the whole country fell in line. Restaurants voluntarily closed Monday evenings all over India and people observed fast to join Shastri *Ji* in giving a fitting reply to American arm-twisting.

It was Shastri who brought about closer integration of Jammu & Kashmir during his term by changing the titles of *Vazir-e-Azam* to Chief Minister and *Sadr-e-Riyasat* to Governor in line with other Indian states. He also got extended several other federal laws to that state – an action long overdue. The state remained peaceful, no anti-India slogans were raised and no Pakistani flags were hoisted. He faithfully tried to implement the laws on orderly integration of Jammu & Kashmir state with the rest of India as envisaged under the agreement and the Indian Constitution. He was effective and he went about his business in his quiet way.

Before the 1965 war, Pakistani President Ayub Khan, had boasted that he would have breakfast in Lahore (a Pakistani city) and lunch in Delhi (Indian capital). To which Shastri *Ji* had replied: *Hum bhi tehelte tehelte Lahore pahunch jaayenge* (we can also leisurely walk and reach Lahore.]

This was Lal Bahadur Shastri whom India lost on that fateful 11th January, 1966. That was a tremendous loss for the country that ended up with decades of Nehru-dynasty rule with political complications, corruption, autocratic policies and more subversive acts in and around the country, especially in Jammu & Kashmir state.]

[In my stay and travel in the US I made several friends and continued my connections with many. Among them were Ben Dolin and his family in Los Angeles, John Maxson of Philadelphia, and Colorado Senator John Bermingham, who also visited India and stayed with us for a couple days. I lost contact with many and while in America for 31 years now, have been able to re-connect with only a few. The re-connection also could not last long. Some attempts failed badly.

I tried in a few cases and was able to connect with Papa Floyd's daughter Cheryl, and his son Professor Jeffrey and spoke to them on phone a couple times. I learnt only some time back that Jeff is no more. He was a distinguished professor and an expert on International business.]

While in Indiana our group had attended Cheryl's beautiful wedding – a very enjoyable and lovely function.

Prof. Callaway recorded a popular song for me on my recently-purchased tape recorder (the old type with spools). The song is:

> *Show me the way to go home.*
> *I'm tired and I want to go to bed.*
> *I had a little drink about an hour ago*
> *And that has gone to my head.*
>
> *Wherever I may roam,*
> *On land or sea or foam,*

You can always hear me sing this song
Show me the way to go home.

[Since then I have sung this beautiful song at several parties and groups of friends and got applause. I always remember Prof Callaway, who also is no more.]

While recalling this for the book, I wanted to look for the song's history, and, as usual, Wikipedia helped me.

It said:

"Show Me the Way to Go Home" is a popular song written in 1925 by the pseudonymous "Irving King" (the English songwriting team James Campbell and Reginald Connelly). The song is said to have been written on a train journey from London by Campbell and Connelly. They were tired from traveling and had a few alcoholic drinks during their long journey. The song is in common use in England, Ireland, Scotland, Wales and North America.

Thanks a lot Wikipedia, I enjoy the song, always, and your great help too.

10

Homebound

The other beauty of the US Project was additional allowance of $100 to each of us to buy books of our choice at the huge book-store of Indiana University. It was a good amount to buy dozens of books. I spent some of 'my' money and bought more books without thinking about the extra weight while flying back. I carried much below the limit when I flew from India. But spending about $200 and collecting scores of books in the US, I was a little worried about excess baggage.

However, my hosts knew these things happen, and so had a provision to help us. Papa Floyd told us to leave *all* our books at his office and the Project would pay for shipping and delivery at our homes in our countries. Wow!

Everyone was happy with this additional windfall.

For my return trip I had planned to break journey in London and Cairo. The friends in both embassies were anxious for me to visit their countries. However plans were changed as I was offered a choice to visit Vietnam where the war was on. I chose Vietnam. Wrote to British and Egyptian Embassies in Washington D.C. and India, expressed my appreciation for their offers but let them know of my changed plans.

I was anxious to visit the war-front though it was quite dangerous. That decision meant that the Project had to re-route my return journey to India. I made it a little more elaborate for them but I must express my gratitude to the Project and the US government for accommodating everything. Normally, it is supposed to be direct, and the shortest route, from America to India (with just one or two stops for things like change of planes). But our hosts were extra generous and arranged for any route I wanted, with as many stops as I preferred to have. It was 1966.

This was January-winter in America, and also colder regions of Indiana and the East or North for the return journey. The Project had learnt a valuable lesson and this year was not taking any chance of missed flights, stranded passengers etc. because of severe weather, storms, snowfall etc. So, instead of all of us departing together, our return was staggered and we were put on different flights on different routes, even different people taking us to different airports, wherever possible.

My final plans were like this: Bloomington (IN) to Chicago (stop for several hours because of the connecting flight, I opted for a little longer stop at Alaska as we all had visited Chicago earlier). It was cold and snowing and so I did not go out of Anchorage airport, but that was okay, at least I could boast of a visit to the largest American state, also called The Last Frontier. The interesting fact about Alaska state is that it was purchased [then less than a hundred years back, in 1867], from the Russian empire for a mere 7.2 million dollars – just two cents per acre.

[This is the story of unbelievably foolish Russian sellers, and incredibly smart American government led by President Andrew Johnson and the Secretary of State Seward (who negotiated the sale) and who bought the huge landmass!

The area is 663268 sq. miles. The state is so very rich in resources and what the US paid for Alaska it earned 100 times more in just 50 years.]

After a few hours at Anchorage my travel plan was Tokyo, Seoul, Hong Kong, Vietnam, Singapore and back to New Delhi. All the flights on various airlines were paid for by the American government's Journalist Project I was honored to be a member for four plus months. The other stopovers and stays were my responsibility; only stay and travel within Vietnam was all paid for by the US government.

Something more about the journey back home with so many stops.

As I mentioned above, when our visit to the US was winding down we were asked by Papa Floyd if any one of us would be interested in visiting Vietnam, then engaged in a war between the two divided countries – Communist North Vietnam supported by China, USSR (Russia) and other Communist countries, and South Vietnam, supported by the American military and some other countries such as Australia and others. [The 'Indo-China War,' was fought in both Vietnams, Cambodia and Laos. The 20-year war ended in 1975 with the fall of Saigon, over- run and later annexed and unified by North Vietnam into one Vietnam – Socialist Republic of Vietnam, now more friendly toward the US than aggressive China.]

Out of 13 journalists only I agreed to go. One Indian said it's too risky. The third Indian said he didn't have time but may stay for a day or two. I found out later that he went from the airport straight to Indian envoy's home, stayed there for less than 24 hours and next day took a flight back home. That was his choice, none should question. He may have his reasons and I don't wish to dwell on that more. But that was his 'Visit to Vietnam.' I am sure he must have written about 'The Visit' and got it prominently displayed in his paper. That's okay, he 'observed.'

[For me, I preferred a longer stay. It lasted about 10 days. I also wanted to go out of Saigon and to the actual war areas. I ended up visiting areas south and north of Saigon, right up to Da Nang and 17th parallel, the dividing line between the two states, and also saw a part of the action, firing etc. I was told that the Press center area I stayed in Da Nang was shelled the previous night by North Vietnamese (Viet Cong) military.]

I had written to Sadhana about my trip to Vietnam. Naturally she was also concerned, more so because I could not write and post letters for a few days while traveling back home. She was naturally worried, especially because of my Vietnam trip. She was not in a position to give her opinion or reaction but knowing me – and I knowing her – she stood by me and my decision to visit the war zone.

The only thing she could do was to remain strong and pray. She did both. And I shared her strength and her faith and benefitted from both.

Rewind to the journey back home from America.

My first stop after Alaska was Tokyo. I had, and still have, very high admiration for Japan, despite the fact that Japan was on the 'other side' in World War II. For Indian freedom fighters (I include myself for being a tiny part) Japan had given support in various ways since the early years of the 20th century, if not earlier.

Netaji Subhas Chandra Bose was one of the top freedom fighters, who had challenged even Mahatma Gandhi disagreeing with his methods and won the election for President of the Congress Party defeating Gandhi's candidate. Later, because of vehement opposition and non-cooperation by Gandhi he resigned from Congress.

When the British cracked down on freedom fighters, Subhas was one of the leaders arrested and then, because of ill-health was put under house arrest with tight security in his own home, in Calcutta (now Kolkata). He fooled the British and escaped, traveled a thousand miles in disguise and reached Kabul (Afghanistan.) From there it was European countries where he spent some time. In Germany, he met Hitler and asked for his help in freeing India. Bose was not toeing the Nazi line, he was interested

109

in India's freedom. He would accept support from the Devil if he could get India's freedom; that was his way of thinking.

However, Subhas Bose did not get a satisfactory response from Hitler but was provided with a German sub-marine to take him to Japan. Subhas, dodging the British and allied ships managed to reach Tokyo, and sought and received help from the Japanese government.

In the next few months he was able to mobilize Indians settled in Asia and set up Azad Hind Government (Free India Government) and formed the Indian National Army (Azad Hind Fauj) to fight the British Army on Indian soil and free India.

His slogan '*Jai Hind*' (Victory to India or Hail India) has become a popular greeting, even today, in the armed forces. Another of his stirring slogan was "*Chalo Dilli*" (March to Delhi) to encourage the INA volunteers preparing to march to the Indian capital and free the country from the British.

There was yet another clarion call: "*Tum mujhe khoon do, mei tumhe aazaadi doonga*" (Give me blood, I will get you freedom).

What a man! What a rousing message! They worked and the British were badly shaken.

While getting Japanese support he had made a clear stipulation that no Japanese troops would set their foot on Indian soil, only the INA would do that. He kept his word and his soldiers fought the British Indian Army on the soil of India and did capture a few posts in Eastern India.

Subhas Bose has always been my Hero. Sadhana shared my admiration for Netaji (as he was popularly addressed when he formed the Free India government and the Army). Sadhana and I have been on the same page, sharing the same or similar views on a variety of topics. In case of Subhas Bose I had the "upper hand" as a nine-year-old *I* had seen Bose (at Delhi railway station, and that image is firmly planted in my memory); Sadhana was yet to be born.

We shared the same admiration for other freedom fighters who gave their lives for the country. Also we both, and Sujata and Seema, have great respect for members of the armed forces and the Police. Both the daughters, when quite young, would always salute the men and women in uniform, especially of the armed forces. That they regard as a part of patriotism. Sadhana and I have set an example for them and have always been appreciative of the fact.

[Now 'Politically Correct" leaders and a big chunk of people have no such feelings for the uniformed forces or the National Flag, or the National Anthem. Shockingly, the US Supreme Court in 1989 had ruled that insulting the National Flag, in any way, is Free Speech. That was an absolutely shameful ruling and, hopefully, someday soon it would be changed to the delight of patriotic people.]

Back to my visit to Japan: Even at the age of six or seven I came to know about Japan, the Japanese language and its hardworking people. It so happened that my father had sponsored a young friend of his to visit Japan and learn to make good, yet inexpensive, toys. Japan was famous for that industry, among other things.

That friend, Ishwar Chand, sent a parcel of toys *addressed in my name.* What a thrilling, happy occasion for me – a parcel of toys from a foreign country in *my own name!* Wow!

That 'Wow moment' was recreated when he returned to India, visited us and also stayed for quite some time with us. He gave us – me and my two older sisters – a few lessons in Japanese language. We had learned counting up to 10 and about a dozen words in Japanese. That impression lasted and I was thrilled when I got a chance to visit Japan even if it was some 30 years late.

I spent three days in Tokyo, stayed first at Imperial Hotel, a regular Western style hotel and later at a Japanese style *Atami /Ryokan* – a new experience. I also dipped my naked body in the community bath (you couldn't join with shorts, a loin-cloth or a lungi.). Fortunately there was only one person – a male – in the bath that morning who exhorted me to drop my shorts and jump into the bath. I am not used to it but accepted it as yet another experience you have visiting places.

I spent a whole day sightseeing (Imperial Palace etc.) and left without visiting some more places I always wanted to go. I thought there will be a next time – I am still waiting for that 'next time.'

On that trip, the next was South Korea (Seoul).

My Korean visit has some real background.

It started with my meeting with one of the top businessmen, Sull Wonshik and his pretty artist wife Hisook (Limb Hisook), a well-known couple of South Korea, in New Delhi earlier in February, 1965. They were members of the South Korean delegation to the 20th Congress of the International Chamber of Commerce in India that I was reporting.

Practically all the top industrialists/businessmen and women of the world attended that big conference.

After a reception for delegates at New Delhi's famous Imperial Hotel, as guests were leaving, I saw Hisook and Sull waiting anxiously for their car. I went to them and was told that they have their embassy car. As they waited we talked and became friends.

We met again at some other event and renewed our acquaintance.

A week after the conference ended and guests were gone, I got a picture post card from Hisook on a visit to the world famous Taj Mahal, in Agra, India. I wrote back at their Korean address I had, and that cemented our friendship.

In the United States our group had four journalists from Korea. That made me more interested in Korea, its history and culture. From America also I kept in touch with Hisook and I had written to her about my return trip to India and the possibility of my stopping over in Korea's capital city. [The Vietnam trip was being finalized and I had to travel that route.]

My good friend Hisook lost no time in responding and enthusiastically welcomed the plan. Little did I know that she had made her own plans to extend a welcoming mat and offer me hospitality for my stay.

Hisook was at the Seoul airport to receive me. She apologized for not taking me to her home as their big mansion with tall columns was being renovated. Instead, she took me to Bando Hotel, a nice big hotel and told me that I was their guest. I did feel a little guilty, kind of, imposing myself on them but Hisook with her charming and friendly smile disarmed and silenced me. She also said her husband, Sull, would be delighted to meet me at the earliest opportunity.

Sull Wonshik was a prominent businessman. I knew as he was one of the delegates to ICC Congress in New Delhi where we had met. When I had mentioned this to my Korean journalist friends on the American trip they were impressed. They told me about Wonshik being a very successful businessman, and that I am lucky to know him and his wife.

I felt honored, respected and loved. Indeed they were nice and caring couple, so down-to-earth, and extended all hospitality to me throughout my stay.

As a matter of fact when I first wrote to Hisook from America I had asked my friend Hong Yong Ki about the correct form of addressing a lady, in Korean language. He wrote it down and I copied it on my letter. Hisook's reply came in no time and she, kind of, complained saying that the address was too formal, I should instead just address her as friends do. Since then I always addressed my letters to Dear Hisook. I was Dear Yatindra for her.

While in Korea, Hisook was my guide. She with a chauffeur-driven car would take me sight-seeing, to a radio/TV interview and to a meeting with the editor-publisher of the English language daily, *The Korea Herald*. Next day I saw my interview printed in the paper. The editor gifted me a beautiful black tray with Korean engraving and the name of the paper.

Two days later, Hisook came to the hotel and told me that in the evening her husband, Sull Wonshik, would take me some place as she would be busy. It was okay with me and I thought Hisook needed some time off. Sull took me to an exclusive club with a couple of his friends. We had a Korean style, sit-down dinner and watched beautiful young Korean women dancing. It was a fun-meeting for which Hisook had given me a friendly alert: this will be a men-only place.

It was, except that the hosts, the dancers and entertainers were mostly women. We were the only three or four men. But it was fun and a new experience for me.

After the memorable days of my first visit to Korea (I had one later as the guest of the Korean Government), my good friend Hisook came to my hotel with several beautiful Korean and other gifts before taking me to the airport. Some gifts were especially for Sadhana. Hisook's other gifts included beautiful Korean style tray with shell-inlaid work, a golden Parker pen and pencil set, a cute little powerful transistor and a dozen 9-volt batteries – in case they were not available in India.

I was overwhelmed with this Korean hospitality and love. My admiration for Korean people, and the Sulls was multiplied several times.

The only occasion I spent my own money – and Hisook didn't know about it – was for photos. I had several 36 mm film rolls from the last leg of my stay in America, and in Tokyo. I didn't think of getting photos done the previous three days in Seoul as I didn't want Hisook to pay for it – she would have insisted.

It was my last night's stay in the hotel and, by chance, I saw a small photo shop inside the hotel lobby. I casually asked the young man if there was any chance my film rolls could be developed and printed. (Those days there were no digital cameras and phone cameras that don't need films and processing.)

I was pleasantly surprised to know that he would process and print ALL the rolls and by morning everything would be ready for me.

They were ready, and with another pleasant surprise. He told me that he saw one of the very nice photos out of the big collection and he took the liberty to enlarge that for me. He said if I don't want the enlargement, it would be okay. I saw the enlargement and liked it. Thanking him was nothing special but the impression he made on me of a hardworking Korean toiling almost the whole night and not treating it as a mere 'job' but loving it, is lasting.

[Years later when I wrote a book *Korean Experience* I was already an admirer of hard-working Koreans and their enthusiasm for success. That spirit – of course help from the US – has made the divided country one of the largest economies in Asia. In 1972, I had the honor to visit Korea again, thanks to the invitation from the Korean Government delivered to me through my good friend, Ambassador Woonsang Choi, in Cairo.

I knew Choi and his wife when they were in India. Luckily for us (my wife was also with me on that trip.) Choi was Ambassador to Egypt and we immediately connected. Before I left Cairo he was able to get me the confirmation of a 'state' visit to his country for a week or more.

My knowledge about Korea had to be revised and increased and that resulted in that book, *Korean Experience*, in 1979. More about that later.]

Indeed South Korea has come a long way. According to Wikipedia, *South Korea is famous for its spectacular rise from one of the poorest countries in the world to a developed, high-income country in just one generation.* South Korea has now the fourth largest economy in Asia and 11th largest in the world. Wow!]

After my first Korean visit on my way back home, it was Hong Kong, still under the British government, to be returned to China in 1997. It was mainly because of Hong Kong through which China was able to import and export whatever was required and became a powerhouse – both militarily and economically. The British saw their economic gains by allowing China to obtain whatever America denied to it through British hold over its territory for nearly two decades after the Communists came to power.

Hong Kong is still under a limited autonomy though ruled by China under a 'One Country, Two Systems' arrangement, though under strain.

Before leaving for America, Sujata wanted me to bring for her *chabi battee wali motor* (a car with the key and lights). Hong Kong was the place to buy that toy and make Sujata jump with joy. I got exactly the toy she wanted. I bought several other gifts, all affordable in Hong Kong.

Hong Kong even then had a number of Indians, mainly businessmen, big cloth merchants also with their own tailoring departments. The driver of my sightseeing tour van was also Indian; some doormen of big hotels too.

First day of my stay I went to a shopping center and was happy to see an Indian for the first time in weeks. I thought he would also be happy and would ask me about India and the events there. As soon as he saw me, after a quick greeting, he asked me how many suits I wanted; custom-made suits were promised within a day or less. He was only interested in getting my order dampening my enthusiasm and eagerness on seeing an Indian in weeks and talking about India.

I didn't want any suits and moved on.

Later I roamed the streets of Kowloon and ferried to real Hong Kong island – the other part of the territory. I tried to contact my group-friend Brian Cuthbertson but probably he was still traveling, may be to his Australian home and family.

I went to see the night bazaar also, did some shopping and had fun. It was yet another novel experience for me.

The other 'experience' was at the Hong Kong airport where, because of a shorter runway (or was that an excuse?) they weigh everything you carry – including my small camera and a tape recorder. That meant excess baggage and I had to dish out a tidy amount.

That was a big hole in my pocket!

But overall, Hong Kong was exciting. So near the big brother, Communist China, and yet a freer society with flourishing private sector businesses and fashionable ladies on the road, in stores and clubs! A shopping paradise and of course a bristling territory counting its last period before it would be 'devoured' by China. Unlike Taiwan, Hong Kong-Kowloon was joined to China by the 'umbilical cord.'

[Hong Kong also became a transit point for us as our family of four in 1982 stayed there for a couple days for shopping and sight-seeing en route to the United States for Sujata's wedding. Seema was lucky to celebrate her birthday there with a ferry-ride and a camera as her gifts.]

11

Vietnam 'Where the Action Was'

My next stop was Saigon (South Vietnam), now Ho Chi Minh City. It became about a 10-day trip and took me to south of Saigon and to Da Nang, in the north, just near the border at the 17th parallel.

I flew on military helicopters and planes that were not pressurized and even had openings at the back with bucket seats on both the sides; the space between the two rows of seats was for arms etc. The flights were hazardous, full of strong winds, and, of course, without air hostesses or food trays you see on commercial flights.

That's the kind of life the military men and women live and fight for our ideals, our freedoms and our principles to keep us safe and secure and even to ensure our right to blast the armed forces and their members.

The United States lost about 58,000 men and women in the nearly 20-year Vietnam War and also lost face in withdrawal in 1975 with the fall of Saigon to the North Vietnamese army. It was a half-hearted war by the Americans and as my guide, the Colonel, told me that "we are asked to fight with our hands tied at the back." Now you have an idea of *that* war and the main reason America lost.

That was indeed the political mistake of the US government resulting in a disgraceful exit from Vietnam. There was relentless pressure, and military support from the then Soviet Union and China to North Vietnam. Even the general American people turned away from the War and because of the constant psychological propaganda by the left, liberals, 'peaceniks' and the like it had become an 'ugly war,' the price for which the American military and the nation had to pay dearly.

The Vietnamese people also paid a heavy price in destruction, killings and relentless bombings on lush green fields in the country. Hundreds of thousands of refugees from South Vietnam, Laos and Cambodia fled the war-torn country and a bulk of them found home in America.

In several American cities the returning soldiers were jeered, and even spat on, were subjected to insults and ridicule for no fault of theirs. They were following orders by the political authorities. Of course they were humiliated in that war, but not for their lack of courage or fighting capabilities, but by their own government's misreading of the political winds, utter lack of planning an effective strategy and absence of perfectly determined execution of their plans.

However, now things have changed enormously. A unified Vietnam, and the entire Southeast Asia, is with the US fighting Chinese aggressive policies in the region, and expansion in the South China Sea.

My visit to American bases, in 1966, was a revelation to me. In India photography at military bases, and even at civilian airports, is extremely restricted. There in Vietnam, I was freely taking pictures – of the bases, of military choppers flying, huge transport planes carrying troops, rockets firing on the ground, all that I was filming on the ground and also flying on the helicopter. No wonder it was a different kind of war, different kind of strategy resulting in a different kind of ending of that 20-year conflict.

Now this is how my Vietnam visit started:

In Saigon, unlike my arrival in New York for the Project, there was what they call a 'snafu'– something that's really messed up. There was nobody to receive me at the airport and no info as to where I was supposed to go and report, and stay. I was quite confused, had a lot of baggage and nowhere to go in a country engulfed in a war with direct and indirect involvement of major powers.

[At that stage I was thinking of Sadhana – and the kids – who would be anxiously waiting for me and would be doubly worried without any information from me. The only thing I assured myself was two-fold: I have to face the music myself, and, secondly, I knew my Sadhana was capable of handling any problem and challenge, and any unforeseen situation, with courage and patience.]

I was right on both the counts.

The only help I thought could be the American military booth at the airport. I told the staffer there that I was visiting as a guest of the American government. He was helpful and advised me to go to the American embassy and contact an officer there.

I got a taxi-cab, loaded it with lots of luggage I had collected in the last four months in the US and stays at three places (Tokyo, Seoul and Hong Kong), and was off to the US Embassy.

There was a large barricade around the embassy compound and it was impossible to take the taxi right to the entrance of the building.

There were two ways to reach the entrance: leave the cab and leave all the bags unattended at the gate of the barricade or let my luggage be in the cab and let the driver wait for me. I chose the latter risk. I trusted the cab driver with my luggage and marched toward the main door of the embassy. The security officer at the entrance to the barricade allowed me to walk in – must have realized my dilemma.

The staffer at the embassy gate was nice and called the Press Officer who, to my dismay, told me he did not have any information about my trip. He did admit the message might have been sent from America but he had not seen it. However, he was kind to ask me to go to *his* home and stay with him, for now. I got his address and rushed out to the taxi I had left waiting with my luggage.

My trust was not misplaced. The cab, its driver with all my bags intact were still safely there.

Harold Kaplan, the American Public Affairs Officer, did not have his family in Vietnam, only a cook, a maid and a young teacher for giving him language lessons (all Vietnamese). He too had arrived only the last year (and stayed for only two years).

[However, Kaplan was extremely knowledgeable and his comprehensive commentary about everything Vietnamese – the background, the old problem, current situation, policies, the conduct of war, political and military aspects, overall assessment, also the conduct of the Media and the American public, written in 1982, is masterly. I read it much later.]

The Kaplan staff made me feel at home. I had food and waited for him. He came sometime later and told me not to bother about the info from the US; he will eventually sort out the matter. It took quite a few days but meanwhile he chalked out a plan for my stay (at his house), attend briefings and travel outside Saigon.

That was okay for me. There was just one problem – I did not have much money and the US embassy was still sorting out the matter so that payment to me could be authorized. I managed with whatever I had. While in Saigon with Kaplan, I would just have breakfast at his home and would go out meeting people, sightseeing on my own, and attending press briefings at places if not far by walking or taking a cycle-rikshaw.

That was also an experience life throws at you, sometimes. But I was fine and took that in stride.

There were briefings by the Press Chief, Barry Zorthian and the Military Chief, General Westmoreland who was fighting on several fronts: the Communist enemies, the American politicians and the public. Even the American defense department and the military were never on the same page making Gen. Westmoreland's task more difficult. I had a very short time to do extensive research or assessment and do a thorough study on land; but I could get a feel of the situation and observe first hand some of the problems and difficulties. It was a complex war with half-hearted action and limited political support at home.

The situation was made more complex – and grave – by the liberals-leftists-disgruntled-anti-war activists and others who did-not-know-what-else-to-do and journalists who were as confused as the politicians themselves. Too many journalists, too many so-called opinion-makers, and too many know-all writers/commentators/analysts/professors etc. were at hand with their half-knowledge but full-head commentaries.

All these know-all worthies lacked the correct perspective; they did not have the right information and had only partial and superficial assessment of ground realities. There was no long-term vision or perspective. The American military, and ultimately the US government, got a good beating, though undeserved.

But that's politics; those were half-hearted, indecisive and unnecessary policies and also a love-hate relation between the government, public and the media.

[In India it has been rather different. During the war, and generally otherwise on crucial national security issues, the Press did not act as adversary, but as a constructive and cooperative critic. We, generally, went along with the government on national and international issues of importance, if probed methodically, analyzed correctly, and presented sincerely.]

On one of the trips on a military helicopter closely following American troops to be airdropped for 'action' against the North Vietnamese (Viet Congs), I faced imminent danger. The pilot, just after a 10 minute flight, landed the chopper in an area we were not supposed to land. A photographer from The Telegraph of London, and I were the only two civilians with a few American airmen scheduled to follow the troops and see action from close quarters, possibly from the ground.

After a 15-minute halt and close inspection by the pilot and the on-board engineer, we were told that it was a fire-alarm, found to be false. However, they could not ignore it and landed the chopper to thoroughly investigate and check.

That delay meant we had lost contact with the troops we were following. The only thing we could do was to overfly the area of action. We did see rocket firing and skirmishes, retaliatory firing (that I photographed) but not action from close quarters. In any case, that experience was also unusual and also dangerous.

I took it as professional hazard.

One day while in Da Nang, my military guide, the Colonel, took me around and showed me a big column of Patton tanks, the mainstay of land battle.

[A short description about the 'Patton-War' and its 50th anniversary (2015) are worth quoting. This is a part of the report by Avijit Ghosh of *Times of India* News Service (TNN), Aug 30, 2015:

"The brave men who had demolished Pakistan's feared Patton tanks in 1965 are a part of village lore in Asal Uttar, Punjab. Asal Uttar and neighboring villages – Bhura Kuhna, Chima, Amar Kot, Valtoha and Bhura Karimpur – had turned into a battleground for four days. The desperate, do-or-die battle between Pakistan and India began on September 7, 1965.

"The landscape surrounding the memorial of Abdul Hamid is pretty as a picture postcard. Paddy fields sway in the easy breeze and ashen clouds play hide and seek with the sun. It's impossible to imagine that 50 years ago the region was the theatre of one of the most intense and decisive tank battles in history.

"By the time it was over, Pakistan's General Ayub Khan's dream of capturing Amritsar had turned into a nightmare. The combat zone had also become a graveyard for the feared Patton tanks. Pakistan lost 97 tanks in all, including 72 Pattons. Enough to create, for a brief while, an open-air showroom called Patton Nagar *(city)* in nearby Bhikkiwind.

"Of the many supermen who engineered this triumph, one of the most audacious was Company Quarter-Master Havildar Abdul Hamid of 4 Grenadiers, who displaying total contempt for personal safety, destroyed three Patton Tanks with his recoilless gun and was killed going for the fourth. He was posthumously decorated with Param Vir Chakra, the nation's highest gallantry award."

Asal was the name of the village where the main tank-battle was fought; afterwards it was renamed Asal Uttar (Fitting Reply). Very appropriate!]

A few months later at Da Nang, when I was going around and looking at Patton tanks I could not stop smiling, visibly.

Intrigued, the Colonel asked me the reason.

My reply must have shocked and unnerved him. But the experienced man recovered quickly.

I told him the reason of my mocking smile: India, in the just concluded war with Pakistan, had made mincemeat of Patton tanks that America had given to Pakistan. The bunch of Pattons destroyed by India made up a 'Patton Nagar' (city), an outdoor showroom.

The veteran Colonel took only a few seconds to reply: "Those tanks with Pakistan must be quite old, not the most modern."

Both of us had a good laugh.

While in Saigon, I looked for my old friend, Ambassador Do Vang Li, a former envoy of South Vietnam in India. He was the first foreign diplomat we, the local reporters in Delhi, came in contact with. I was then covering only local politics and administration – not Parliament, the federal government and the larger diplomatic world. But Li and his petite wife, were different; they invited us 'locals' too to their parties and became friendly with the reporting crowd.

Vang Li loved India, and also all the other places he was posted to. He told me one of his daughters was named Merdeka (freedom, rich or prosperous), in Indonesian Bhasa (language) as she was born during his posting in Indonesia. He also told me that one of his sons was named Dilliram, as he was born in Delhi (India), also pronounced as Dilli. I don't know if these kids loved their names, especially Dilliram, and/or they retained the names in later life.

I was able to find where Ambassador Li lived. He was put under house arrest by the then South Vietnamese government as he differed on policy matters. When I reached his house there was just one security guard who let me in after I explained to him that I was just visiting from India and knew the ambassador.

I spent some time with Ambassador Li and came out a little wiser about the situation, though he was not sure about the outcome of this absurd and difficult war. I respected his views.

After I returned from Da Nang, Can Tho, Pleiku, Hue, and other places for a final couple days in Saigon, Kaplan informed me that he did receive information about my trip and sanction of funds for me. The only problem was he was expecting another senior journalist from the United States and that he was supposed to play host to him. He suggested to me a nice hotel nearby and I moved to that place profusely thanking him for his hospitality for about a week.

My last two-or-three days were spent visiting an old shrine and to the home of Indian Consul, Thakore Saheb Kotda Sangani, a nice man and the current 'Raja Saheb' of a small princely state in Gujarat. He took me to a diplomatic reception one evening and had a good time. When we came out of the party he seemed a little drunk. I was not. His driver and I helped Raja Saheb to his bedroom. I was dropped at my hotel by the envoy's driver for the next day's flight back home, via Singapore, my last stop before Delhi.

The flight home was not easy – I mean, you could not leave Saigon those days without an Exit Permit. I had never heard of a permit like that. I thought you need a permit – a Visa – only to enter, not exit. But Vietnam was in the midst of a war and things were different. [I don't know if a permit is required in some other countries also.] Of course things were different when I was leaving the US. Here, in Vietnam, nobody was looking after my needs, paperwork etc. And there was none to see me off. In any case, I was not expecting Royal Treatment in a war zone.

At the airport when I checked in I was asked for the Exit Permit. Since I didn't have it I was asked to go get it. I had no choice, booked my luggage and off I went to the appropriate Vietnamese office, fortunately not very far off.

The guy at that office made me fill a form (I don't remember if I paid any fee) and asked me to come in two days to collect the permit. I was in a, kind of, panic, and told him that my flight leaves in about an hour. I don't know about any divine intervention but he just relented and issued me the permit right then. I thanked him and rushed back to the airport to catch the flight in time.

[Later in India, I got a letter from Papa Floyd profusely apologizing for the 'snafu' in Saigon, about my visit to Vietnam and the US Embassy or the Press Office not ready for my 'welcome' and necessary help. It was no big deal. I wrote back and thanked him for the opportunity to see Vietnam and the 'action' first hand.]

Singapore was my last stop before New Delhi. In 1966 Singapore was nowhere near today's flourishing and prosperous city-state but did have the potential. It was an organized place, full of life and activity.

One of the first things I had was the biggest raw coconut at a roadside stall on Ben Kulan street. I like raw coconuts, the soft pulp and the fresh water inside. Every day I had my fill. [A few years later I visited the same road (wide and more organized) and the stall also larger. However, no fresh raw coconut and water – all pre-cut coconuts and the water stored in a large container. I did not relish *that* kind of development.]

Another interesting spectacle was an Indian in a roadside shop/eating place making *chapaties* – flat bread, Indian style. I had my fill with *dal-roti* (lentils and flat bread) and *sabzi* (vegetables) every day for two days.

A fair outing, sightseeing, a little shopping and it was time to depart, now straight to Delhi, home.

However, a little drama always accompanied me everywhere.

With so many stops and quite a fair amount of shopping I had almost exhausted my funds. Per-diem in Vietnam was less than what we got in the United States. So when I reached Singapore airport to take the flight home, I had just $20 left. I didn't mind as it was the last leg of my flight home, though with lots of luggage.

After I checked in I was told that because of excess baggage one of my suitcases could not be included with other bags and would be sent on another flight. This seemed strange but since I did not want to pay extra, this was probably the only solution the airport staff suggested.

I had no choice; I didn't want to part with my $20 currency note, my last American money. Of course I did not carry any Indian money, was not allowed by law to do it. And that was all right for me. Had no choice but to say okay.

But lo and behold: as I was walking to the plane (in those days at almost all airports you would walk from the terminal to the plane) I saw one of the staffers who was helping me to check my luggage. He was cycling toward the plane with my extra suitcase on his head to be put on the same flight. He saw me, smiled and I could only give him a big Thank You. I could not even tip the man as I had my last $20 bill and nothing in smaller currency. The man loaded my suitcase, said good bye and left me admiring the kindness of the man – and Singaporean hospitality.

Thank you Singapore whom I repaid with at least three more visits, on my own, with family and enjoyed the orderly, prosperous city-state with a sizable Indian population and typical Indian markets, and nice places to do sightseeing and shopping.

The flight was routine with no fireworks or anything of note and I was at Delhi airport in about 5½ hours. Of course, the air hostesses were pretty in colorful full-length Malay dresses. They were speaking English with typical accent.

As I mentioned, I had a lot of baggage and was little worried about Indian custom duty and regulations at Delhi airport. Of course, I did not carry gold, wines, guns, cigarettes, or major electronics etc. that required hefty import duty. I was not sure of dutiable items as that was my first oversea visit. I did not want to take chances and so I joined the line for duty-paying passengers for the officers to decide.

My turn came and I opened all my suitcases and told the custom officer to see everything that was dutiable. He had asked me if there was something dutiable. I said I don't know, you can see. He opened some suitcases, saw what was there and said his calculation of the value of my 'imports' was Rs. 600 and I was allowed Rs. 500 worth of items; the rest valued at Rs. 100 would be charged @ 150%, that is a total of Rs. 150.

I thought it was very fair.

[It started a favorably lucky chain where I have not paid any duty for 'importing' items from my several foreign trips while in India. The only custom duty I paid was while I returned from India to the US. There also I was able to get a refund of 50% on the duty *already* paid at the airport; could have got back the entire amount but for lack of continued effort.

But that's okay. I don't 'import' any dutiable or illegal items – no gold, no diamonds, no guns, no drugs etc.]

There was a close family 'reception party' at the airport; unlike these days family and friends could receive you right after the custom and immigration area. I did not have Indian currency – didn't want to pay in US dollars. Indrajit and Sadhana, who were at the airport along with my father and the kids and some other relatives came to my rescue. I was bringing eight times more weight than what I had with me when I left for America. I was loaded with things, most of which I bought in the US, Hong Kong and Singapore. The ones I got in Korea were personal gifts.

Some of them were on demand – and my Sadhana didn't ask for anything at all. I got requests from friends, some other relatives, neighbors and even a friend's wife, but not a single one from my wife. I did buy a few for her and a camera, a portable typewriter and a recorder for myself. I had bought about 120 newly introduced ball-pens for a whole bunch of staffers at my office; some better and pricy gifts for the Editor, Ratan Lal Joshi, and General Manager G.N. Sahi.

All that was assessed by the customs officer and paying Rs. 150, I was out with my family. Seeing my close family, especially my strong and patient wife, I was happy, a little tired but in one piece despite spending about 10 days in Vietnam, a country fighting a treacherous and haphazard war that knew no ending.

[It had to continue for another decade till America pulled out in 1975.]

After missing me for more than four months Sujata took a couple minutes to connect with me but Seema, who was not yet one year-old when I had left, immediately reached out to me and was in my arms.

The two sisters still mention that 'welcome' and that the younger one had scored points over the other.

It was a long trip and meeting my family was the best thing for me and them. There was jubilation and moments of thanksgiving, especially for my dear Sadhana who stood up like a rock to care for and support the family despite hardships and problems of all kinds. She was ecstatic to see me back, healthy and full of stories and experience that we shared for a long time.

My first foreign trip was to visit the US but was extended to many others.

And what a trip it was!

There were hundreds of varied stories and observations, experiences and anecdotes about the trip. It was also the start of a career studded with several other foreign visits – also one extended trip with Sadhana to Europe and to the US later for Sujata's wedding. Thirty years later we were in the country that I visited first and have been here since 1986.

The American trip resulted in immediate rewards. I had not imagined that it would bring big change in my life, in my career and family life. That we will end up living in America for three decades and also see Sadhana pass away here.

That, they say, is God's planning. That is His will. That's destiny.

Back home, Sadhana had so much to talk with me, tell whatever she faced and how she coped with all that. On the contrary, she minimized her challenges, diluted her troubles and took every problem as yet another opportunity to rise to the occasion and come out swinging.

She never complained.

It took me quite a long time to actually know fully what she had encountered and how she solved every problem she faced with courage.

I was impressed by the strength of her character, once again.

[Sadhana was a wonderfully brave and tenacious woman whom nothing could scare and nothing could make her give up. In later years too she proved her mettle and faced every adverse situation with determination and brought something good out of it. There were new challenges there and she came out on top.]

12

Settling Down in the Office and Quick Reward

That was early 1966. I did not take further time off as I was on unpaid leave for the last nearly two months. I reported for duty the very next working day and found surrounded by colleagues eager to hear my stories – and share my gifts. I was the third staff member of the editorial department of *Hindustan,* ever to visit a foreign country. The second one was Editor Mukut Bihari Verma who went on an invitation to Britain, for which I had played an important part to persuade him to accept the invitation. He was a shy man and it took some effort from a bunch of us – beginning with me who, accidentally, had opened the letter and had alerted some of my colleagues to plead with Verma *Ji*.

The first was Chandulal Chandrakar, the Special Correspondent, who was bitten by the travel bug in1952 when – denied permission and vacation – he quit his job to go to Helsinki (Finland) to see the Olympic Games. He was soon re-instated and covered the Games for *Hindustan*. He continued to travel, report and attend the next six or seven Olympic Games. He was not essentially a sports-writer, but was interested in sports – himself used to play club-level tennis, and other sports while in college.

[Chandrakar later became the Chief of Bureau – my immediate boss – and about three years later the Editor when I took over his job as the Bureau Chief.]

A couple days after I joined duty, General Manager G.N. Sahi called me in his office. As a local reporter I had only occasional interaction with him. But now I was 'US-Returned' and 'deserved' a special meeting with the GM, who was the administrative boss of the organization since Devdas Gandhi died.

Mr. Sahi was happy to see me, asked a few questions about the trip and did not waste any time in asking me for *my* preference for immediate promotion – Chief Reporter or Special Correspondent?

My choice was clear – Special Correspondent. Getting the vast playing field to witness and report about the national and international political drama, Parliament, foreign affairs and defense, big business and other important events, was more exciting and rewarding than local reporting.

Second, there was already the local Chief Reporter, Kedar Nath Sharma, and I was, technically, reporting to him as local reporter, accredited to the local Delhi Administration. As Special Correspondent I would be accredited to the Government of India. In that capacity, sky was the limit. And there were unlimited opportunities with wider contacts nationally and internationally – the whole world.

I would be working in the News Bureau with Chandrakar as the Chief.

The task was challenging but who was afraid of it? Sadhana was immensely pleased – my good luck charm played her part ever since I married her in 1961. Four years later I had the invitation from the United States and on my return got the important promotion with more opportunities, more pay and more perks.

I had my reward in ample measure. God's grace, Sadhana's devotion and love, and my hard work all combined to push my luck. For the last 14 years I had been in the same position but working my way up in output, extra contribution to the paper, being more active and had made a place for myself worthy of better things. As a matter of fact, the Editor of our rival paper, who was also a senior friend, told me that he wished me to be with his organization. I was flattered but, inside, I was not inclined to accept the offer if it really came my way.

I had a sense of loyalty.

When I told Sadhana about it she said she felt all along that her husband was capable of impressing even the rivals. However, she totally shared my firm views about loyalty and was certainly not in favor of 'defection,' professionally or politically. I could not move to the rival paper and continue to work *in the same city*, meeting the same set of people and to claim representation for a different organization.

In my profession of journalism, other people changed their papers whenever they got a chance, not me. From *Hindustan* in New Delhi to *Bhaskar* in Indore as Chief Editor was an entirely different situation, some two decades later.

As a Special Correspondent I was first assigned to report the proceedings of Rajya Sabha, the Upper House of Parliament, and other important government ministries such as defense, foreign affairs, railways, and all others which Chandrakar would not directly – or regularly – contact. It worked fine with me as I got a still larger field to explore and report. I was free to report anything else, and interview anyone of importance, even without prior okay from Chandrakar. He knew me well for 14 years and trusted me totally.

I did not waste much time to buy a car (I had a scooter earlier, and before that a motor-bike since 1954). It was not easy to buy a car – or a new scooter – as production did not match the demand and people were in the waiting list for years. As accredited correspondents, we had a Press Quota and priority. But first I bought a used car, as it should be.

After a couple years I bought a new Fiat car from the Press Quota.

Being mobile for many years I had the added advantage to rush anywhere, return quickly and report my stories without loss of time. That enabled me to score over many others, in the big bunch of professional reporters. Newspapers had deadlines, out-of-city editions to catch the train or flight and we had to submit our reports according to the time of the particular edition.

I was in the habit of writing and submitting my stories as soon as the particular event was over – sometimes within half hour. I had to get it done as soon as possible to move on to the other. That's how I scored over many of my colleagues in the profession.

Once an interesting situation arose. General Manager Mr. Sahi called me and said I should have submitted my story about a particular meeting held in the morning, to be printed in time and dispatched a couple hours later as an out-of-city edition to catch the train by early afternoon.

Sahi *Ji* was stunned when I told him that the story is already in the edition sent out, and that I had written-submitted the story before noon.

Since then he had more soft corner for me and never questioned about anything.

Sadhana, when I told her about it, said that she knew her husband would never falter.

That was our relationship. That was our level of confidence and trust for each other. Sadhana also gave ample examples of rising to the occasion and finishing the job she had in her hand *before* time. She was particular about these things and was a perfect complement for me. For her there was a set time for doing particular things, keep everything in an organized manner and stick to schedule to make things easier for everyone else. People could depend on her. Finishing a job even before the expected time and beating the deadline had become a habit for her, and me, both. That made life easier and more organized.

Sadhana was an excellent mother-teacher for the girls. She made sure the kids went to school neatly dressed, with homework done, and prepared to learn more. After school, she would first get them in the shower before they could eat. Later, she would see to it that they finish their homework before they go out and play.

Sujata and Seema had learnt the stirring Martin Luther King Jr. song "We shall overcome," and its apt Hindi translation by the eminent poet-broadcaster, Girija Kumar Mathur, titled *"Hum honge kaamyaab."* Frequently, on special occasions we will ask them to sing the same to the applause and appreciation of the attendees, including at some diplomatic gatherings.

Sometimes the girls would privately react to our frequent demands for the same song, but that's one of the privileges of parents to make their kids obey. They did without any audible murmur; we came to know much later about it.

Love you Sujata and Seema for making us proud on this score also!

I have been reporting activities and developments on many fronts and came across situations when top leaders showed they were not only humans but also full of humor and wit.

There were many instances when hardened politicians and ever-inquisitive journalists would find some relaxing moments even when political maneuverings were all around them.

One such instance was when after Lal Bahadur Shastri's death, Mrs. Indira Gandhi and Morarji Desai were the front runners. Indira was supported by some stalwarts of Congress Party who thought this "not-so-smart and not-so-experienced" woman would be under their control, and so they supported her.

Morarji, being the most experienced politicians among the lot and had vast experience as a minister was the strongest claimant and he stated emphatically that he was the most suitable person to head the government.

Things moved swiftly and the next day the situation had changed. Morarji, talking to us, journalists, conceded that Indira Gandhi would be the leader (Prime Minister) and that he had accepted to be the Deputy Prime Minister.

We recalled what he had said the previous day: "I am the most suitable person..."

Morarji silenced us all with his remark: "Yesterday was yesterday, today is today."

Obviously, the situation had changed and he had accepted the position.

However, Morarji's wit had scored the point.

One of the other memorable events of my career in India was, when during the 1967 election campaign for the Congress, I was on a reporting assignment with Deputy Prime Minister Morarji Desai. A special group of three reporters accompanied Morarji *Bhai* (as he was often addressed). The first day we were on a train with him starting in the morning. He said he does not take lunch, only fruits, nuts and milk. We said fine, we will happily share. He would have only dinner.

After a few hours on the train we toured the dusty and extensive countryside in cars and Morarji *Bhai* addressed half a dozen meetings at various stops. We got basketful of fruits and nuts and downed that with milk and tea that the hosts and organizers offered.

So far so good.

In the evening Morarji took us to a local leader's home for dinner. That was the first regular meal we had in more than 24 hours and so we had our fill.

The small Press group had come down to two by then as we took a short flight from Agra to New Delhi.

And it was then *it* happened, or was *about* to happen.

Because of the very hectic schedule on the dusty and bad roads, irregular and hurried eating followed by a full dinner and then a flight on a six-seater, non-pressurized Beachcraft Bonanza aircraft, things started reacting inside my body. I was feeling nausea and became miserable a few minutes after we took off.

On the plane were the pilot, Morarji *Bhai*, his secretary, another reporter and I. I could not hide my discomfort. Morarji *Bhai* sitting in the front row sensed what was happening – or about to happen. He took out a couple of cloves (a common spice in India) from his pocket and asked me to just chew them and gulp the juice.

Cloves did a miracle. In a few minutes I was okay – no nausea, no throwing up at all. The rest of the short flight was fine and we landed nicely in Delhi.

I was fine but did not want to continue with Morarji *Bhai* the next day as scheduled because of his heavy agenda - and his eating habits.

But he did not give me a chance.

As we landed and got off the plane he asked me how I was feeling. When I said your 'medicine' worked the miracle, he gave me a fistful and said, so we meet tomorrow *(for another round of campaigning.)*

What could I say? I thanked him again and said I will be there.

Of course the next round was also hectic but ended without any problem. In the next three days or so we had covered a large part of Agra, Mathura, Vrindavan and some other parts of the state on more dusty roads of the deep countryside.

Sadhana listened to the whole narrative and thanked God for my 'recovery' and for not making a nasty and embarrassing scene. She also appreciated and thanked Morarji's 'medicine.' It was one of the many stories I brought back from my tours that she attentively listened, thoroughly enjoyed and generously shared with others.

That was my wife, sharing everything and making you feel important, with a loving smile.

Sadhana was thrilled and full of appreciation for me when I used the clove-ing treatment on others. A few days later I was touring another backward and hilly region of Bastar (Madhya Pradesh) and Morarji

133

Bhai's 'medicine' saved the day for a group of passengers on a rickety bus that I was also traveling on.

Since the first encounter with Morarji, I had made a habit of carrying a bunch of cloves with me on tours and gave a couple each to about a dozen passengers whom the bus conductor was reluctant to take on board. They were all paying-passengers but were being harassed.

The conductor told me that passengers like those, would always throw up as the bus would negotiate winding, hilly, and uneven dusty roads. Confident of the 'medicine' in my pocket, I assured him that nothing will happen and that I take full responsibility. I gave a couple cloves to each of the dozen or so men and women passengers and the miracle happened – none got sick on the rough road trip for more than 20 miles. The prosperous-looking lady sitting in the 'Upper Class' with her husband, near the driver, who did not ask, or get, my cloves, was the only one to throw up.

After winning the elections in 1967 and again forming the government, though with a reduced majority, Indira Gandhi began her leftist and socialistic (she called it left-of-center) policies that created a pronounced rift among the people. She forced Morarji to resign and cunningly outmaneuvered 'establishment Congress' and its older leaders. Following the policy of 'divide and rule', Indira Gandhi managed to split the age-old Congress in 1969 and started rapid drift toward 'socialistic' policies.

To muster massive support from the common people, Indira adopted major radical programs such as nationalization of big commercial banks, and later, abolition of the Privy Purses of erstwhile princely rulers of states. This was a clever step to convince the country that she was indeed a 'people's leader' and gave many catching slogans.

This was a sure-shot vote-catching populist strategy. She emerged as the undisputed leader and got a huge majority in the elections of 1971. Her forming a separate Congress party – later officially recognized as the sole Congress Party – (Indian National Congress) had indeed worked.

[Prime Minister Narendra Modi, during the 2017 election campaign, has often mentioned that the opposition Congress Party and its leaders are again trying to divide the people for votes. 'Divide and Rule' is an age-old strategy – adopted by the previous rulers and later by Congress – and continued and encouraged by today's Congress leaders.]

Of course, this is nothing new, for, the Congress itself has been divided a number of times. The last major split was 1969, as I mentioned, when a shrewd and political savvy Indira Gandhi – having herself been expelled by the Party Establishment for 'anti-party conduct' – turned the tables on the opponents.

The many attractive slogans like *Gharibi Hatao* (Eradicate Poverty), and remove inequality (redistribution of wealth, like Barack Obama did in the US) are vote-catchers. Indira Gandhi used these slogans and had made a solid impact in earlier winning support and elections, and also making a come-back in 1980 after a stunning defeat in 1977.

With the policy of dividing people as rich and poor, haves and have-nots, Hindus-Muslims, and now Patidars and Patels and Jats etc. the Congress is still following the same policy of 'Divide and Rule.' It worked for some time, but remember the saying; "You can't fool all the people all the time." The poll results proved that subsequently in the last few years. This trend might continue in future as people have become wiser. Well, time will tell.

[Indira herself had become somewhat disillusioned in the last couple years of her life, though was still the Prime Minister. She was not her old self. Domestic situation and unexpected events weighed heavily on her and that showed when she visited Indore while I was there as Chief Editor of *Dainik Bhaskar* newspaper.

Standing in the receiving line as she walked and met the invitees, she did pause for a second and smiled (as she knew and recognized me) it was clear she was worried and tired.

She was assassinated by her Sikh bodyguards on 31st Oct. 1984, a few months after she ordered military and armed police to flush out militant groups from the Golden Temple, Amritsar (the holiest Sikh Temple) that had been made an armed fortress.]

With Sadhana playing a variety of roles as a wife, mother, teacher, friend, my assistant, writer, broadcaster, painter and house-keeper-homemaker, our life was smooth, happy, and satisfying - though quite hectic. I was busy with my work, also writing books and doing radio and TV programs, going out of state and country on work-assignments and Sadhana doing her various jobs.

In between that hectic life, we would attend parties and special occasions, meetings and celebrations – national and international. These included diplomatic parties, government functions, meeting dignitaries on special occasions and also at the Rashtrapati Bhavan (the President's House) and other big business events.

Looked like, we had 48-hour-day, instead of the usual 24. We had quite a crowded schedule.

Sadhana and I had become quite a popular couple in the social circles. With her elegant Indian sarees – and a dignified demeanor – she was welcomed everywhere. She would play host for a variety of friends and acquaintances at our home for lunches or dinners. We didn't serve alcohol, and only vegetarian food and that was made clear on the invitation cards or orally, and the invitees were too willing to come - and enjoy our hospitality. Sujata and Seema played their assigned roles to make our parties a homely, informal, family affair many missed in a big city with rigid protocol and propriety. The girls were willing servers, and also played games to amuse themselves.

In the midst of all that, we embarked on two projects, our own. One was Deep Features, an enterprise to write and send articles, mainly in Hindi, every week to various newspapers all over India. The second, a monthly magazine in English titled TRAVIANA – on tourism, aviation and adventure. Sujata helped in proof-reading some of the articles we sent out. As a reward, I gave her the 'exalted' title of Assistant Editor, though not printed or shown anywhere in the magazine.

Sorry about that Sujata!

These two ventures required constant hard work. Both Sadhana and I handled these projects with passion and dedication while also sticking to our own separate roles – she looking after the home and kids, articles, poems and radio talks; I working diligently for my newspaper, and also doing a lot of radio and TV programs.

Reflecting on the time gone by, I can't imagine how we could do all those things and still remain loving, caring, stress-free, most of the time.

We were made for each other. We did have challenges and problems and we faced them together with understanding, ingenuity and responsibility. And we were always on top of things and never neglected our family, our other relatives, friends and old and new neighbors.

Sadhana took care of the kids' education and upbringing. She would take them for swimming lessons, outings, visits to friends and relatives and shopping too. Whenever possible, I would join them, pick them up or drop them and be a part of Sadhana's plans. If not, Sadhana would manage everything on her own.

I would be off on some major assignments out of the city and state, sometimes out of the country. Sadhana was always supportive and would bid a loving send off to me with prayers and smiles. Her consistent support and encouragement gave me all the energy and sustenance during all those hectic trips and quick reporting.

My reward would always be waiting for me with hugs and smiles and her sigh of relief. Needless to say, tasty dishes were always there. I would also try to bring some small gifts for Sadhana and the kids, sometimes for relatives and neighbors too. That gave me pleasure and Sadhana would wholeheartedly share it with me.

Many of my trips away from home were for reporting special occasions involving the Army, Navy and Air Force, Border Security Force and Coast Guard, business enterprises, big development projects, top political meetings and election campaigns with top leaders, or independently, special functions in different states for their special occasions and projects.

During my career I had the opportunity to see India from East to West, from North to South and also the southern-most parts of India some six hundred miles from the mainland – the sprawling Andaman and Nicobar group of islands. I visited Nagaland in the East, Gujarat in the West, Jammu & Kashmir in the North and Kerala/Tamil Nadu in the deep South, besides several other states in-between.

Not many on our staff liked to go out – and disrupt their own schedule. Some only followed a set routine – home-to-office and office-to-home.

For me news, comments, interviews, first-hand stories had to be managed entirely differently. Office visits were only for writing and submitting stories. Some breaking news was reported on the phone. For me a journalist's life was not confined to the four walls of the office and gossip with other colleagues. It included going out of the office and logging miles wherever the news took you. It was not that I was not a part of the office parties and the like. I would be there for everyone.

Each trip and coverage was a different kind of experience and I would bring back memories – sweet, sour, exciting, encouraging, thrilling and what have you. I would frequently share my 'reports' with Sadhana as she was always my strength, my confidant and my support – often my captive audience but with a willing ear – and also useful feedback.

[For every trip out of Delhi, if I had to spend even one night away from home, Sadhana would pack my bag. She would, invariably, slip a note also with her prayers and good wishes (sometimes instructions about my food and health) duly stamped with her kisses. Opening the bag I would look for the note and put it first to my lips. My Sadhana was unique.

I don't know if other wives did that or do that now, if not, they better start doing it. It makes your man feel great, feel loved – and your love story goes on, as mine did.]

I have often mentioned about Sadhana's culinary skills in providing tasty food. My mother was a good cook but for decades I had not had the opportunity to enjoy her cooking. I was not living with her, and she passed away early, in 1953. Sadhana not only matched her skill but outdid her in many things. The result: I love eating – of course Sadhana had raised the bar, so be careful if you want to compete.

I maintain and confirm that 'the way to a man's heart is through his stomach.' Feed him well and win him over.

I have added a proverb – as I often do – to the English language, twisting the earlier one a little bit:

'The way to a woman's stomach is through her heart.'

You figure out what I mean.

13

More Changes and the Caravan Went on

Our moving to Rajori garden also made another change in our lives. There were many more trips abroad and one with Sadhana – when Sujata and Seema were just 9 and 8. It was a 40-day trip leaving the kids in the care of *Mataji*, their *Nani* (Sadhana's mother who was then 87) and our good neighbors. We moved to Rajori Garden from Ramesh Nagar in 1969. Here we had a four-room independent house with our own terrace and a small backyard. It had a hand-pump (underground source of water) also and a guava tree with insignificant amount of small fruit crop.

The hand-pump water has an advantage – getting a little warm water in winter, cooler in summer. Very clean and potable water.

The small guava tree was a challenge for Sadhana who worked around it. The next season it gave bigger and sweeter fruit with a bumper crop. Sadhana changed it completely with her recipe: add water to the just emptied milk bottle or pot and water the tree with that 'concoction' – milky water or watery milk.

The miracle was seen and tasted to be believed. It worked wonders.

I had taken a wise decision to buy a used car at first. I had not quite driven a car all by myself till then but it did not take me long to learn. After a couple months with the learner's license, I got the regular driver license. It was easy as I was a member of the Automobile Association of Upper India (like AAA here). It was a quick driving test; the officer at the AAUI told me to meet him at the United Coffee House in Connaught Place, New Delhi (not far from my office). He followed and watched my driving. We met at the designated spot and he asked me to go back to the AAUI office and wait for him. He again followed and watched me drive.

We reached his office, parked, and once inside his office it took him a few minutes to hand over the license to me.

I had passed the test.

In India getting a car was one, expensive, and two, not easy to get.

India used to produce only three types of cars: Hindustan Ambassador; Fiat (Indian version but very good) and Standard. The production was much smaller than demand and so it was years of waiting after you register and pay a fixed amount. The Italian Fiat was in big demand, as it was the best. Its production was less than the more roomy Ambassador, and so the waiting period was longer.

Fortunately, as accredited correspondent, I got the new Fiat car within a year of buying the used one. Getting a car loan from a bank was easy and soon we had a car number DHB 6092. I would always tell friends that I may retire at 60 and die at the age of 92.

I did not retire at age 60; the other thing is - I am still running at 88 despite losing my companion a year earlier. That's how God's system works, I don't know why, and I don't agree with His plans.

[That car was with us till 1985 when we left Indore. The loan was all paid off, and as things were then in India, the re-sale value of the car was higher. I got more than I had paid for after driving it for about 15 years.]

Just after we moved to Rajori Garden and made acquaintances with our neighbors on all directions there was a near-tragedy that was averted by Sadhana who never hesitated in helping others.

Two of our neighbors, just opposite our home, were senior officers of India's premier bank, State Bank of India. We had introduced ourselves and met them casually a couple times. Ram K Gupta and his wife Savita had two sons, Ashish and Paul. The other, Harbans Lal Sawhney and his wife Geeta had three kids, the youngest girl, nicknamed Billa, was about three, and probably had seen Sadhana not more than once or twice.

One day there was panic in the neighborhood. Billa was missing and her mother standing at their gate was crying inconsolably. Sadhana heard it all, ran to Geeta, asked her to stop crying and describe the dress Billa was wearing.

Like an expert, Sadhana organized the search. The neighbors were sent in different directions and the search began instead of crying and panic all around. Sadhana herself briskly walked in one direction and started asking every passerby and shopkeeper on both the sides about a 'lost' girl wearing that particular dress of a particular color – and might be crying.

That was a near fool-proof search operation.

The quick, systematic search brought good news. One shopkeeper told her about seeing a man with a little crying girl going in a particular direction. Sadhana did not miss any minute, briskly ran and soon caught up with the man who asked her if she was the mother. As soon as Billa saw Sadhana, she stopped crying and extended her arms toward her. The man immediately handed over Billa to Sadhana and walked away but not before giving an advice to the 'mother' to be more careful.

Seeing Sadhana, and Billa in her arms, Geeta and the worried neighbors heaved a big sigh of relief and praised Sadhana's quick thinking and initiative. Geeta said, from today you are also Billa's mother.

What a nice, and sincere, compliment, fully deserved. We became closer.

As long as we were in Rajori Garden we and the Gupta family also were quite close. Later both our families moved to other places. We continued our close relations with Ram-Savita family since 1969 and met them several times when they visited America and when we went to India. [Sadly, Ram *Bhai* passed away in 2014, just a short while after they both visited us in San Francisco area where we lived with Sujata-Mujtaba.]

Whenever possible, we went on a family vacation. Sometimes things happen without your planning. One such occasion was when General T.N. Raina, the Chief of Army Staff, asked me to bring my family to Ranikhet, the home of Kumaon Regimental Center and the Naga Regiment. A few months earlier he had taken me to Ranikhet on the occasion of Dussehra, the most important festival, 20 days before Diwali.

[Ranikhet (Queen's Meadow) is a small but beautiful and picturesque hill station in the state of Uttarakhand (then it was a part of big Uttar Pradesh state), 6,132 feet above sea level, within sight of the western peaks of the mighty Himalayas.]

Sadhana, Sujata and Seema were excited. We were housed in a villa shared by a senior officer, Col. Issar and his family. A little further was Gen. Raina's villa; Sadhana would not leave chances like that and made a sketch of the General's villa.

We had a good time and the girls got more excited when a bunch of young army cadets and officers engaged them in conversation. (Probably, they had not seen their mothers and sisters and friends for months.) Sujata-Seema always had a high regard and respect for soldiers, and

141

police people. And so they all had a good time chatting and giggling. It was real fun for them.

[After Gen. Raina retired from the Army he was appointed High Commissioner (ambassador) to Canada. On a chilly early morning in Delhi's winter he was leaving for Canada. Guess who also were at Delhi airport to see him off?

Sadhana and I.

The General and his close aide, Brigadier Kapoor, who also knew us well, were pleasantly surprised to see us that early in the morning. They were more surprised when Sadhana took out the sketch she had made of Gen. Raina's Ranikhet villa and presented it to him.

It was a scene worth recording, but we did not plan for any photo or video session and indulge in these luxuries, then.]

Rajori Garden also had another close family, happened to be a distant relative of ours – also a Bhatnagar. It was a big family with five children but one, the oldest daughter Sucheta, nicknamed Guddo, became the closest and was extremely helpful. She was about 16 years.

She was the one who took care of Sujata (9 years) and Seema (not yet 8) while we were away for 40 days. Of course *Mataji* was there but Guddo would do many chores for us. She would get the kids ready for the school and also help them in after-school tasks. She was also a great help for respected *Mataji* who had come from Dehradun.

We had ample faith in her.

But before our 1972 trip to Europe, I visited three more countries, (then) East Germany, Prague, the Capital of (then) Czechoslovakia and Egypt (Cairo, Aswan and Abu Simbel temples, five hours away from Aswan.) I had an overnight stop-over in Cairo on my way to America in 1965. So, technically, that was my second visit to Cairo (Egypt). Adding to the number is not bad.

Germany was then divided between East (Communist), a part of the Soviet controlled states, and West Germany (part of the 'Free World.').

The three-state visit was in 1969. That year was significant for two more reasons, the death of President Dr. Zakir Husain, whom I met several times and who had given an award to Sujata at a Children's function.

And the second was the death of D.K. Tyagi, one of my dear friends and the brother of VK Sharma, one of my closest friends.

[President Husain was also the Chief Patron of Chitra Kala Sangam and had attended a few of our functions.]

Something significant about Tyagi:

He was my colleague in *Janasatta* newspaper in 1952. Later he started Raj Features which was passed on to VK Sharma.

DK took up a job with the government of India and in just a few years rose to the senior post of Director and handled family planning projects. He took the Family Planning campaign to incredible heights of popularity and acceptance. He was the one who 'invented' the *Lal Tikon* (Red Triangle) – the symbol of Family Planning in India. He also gave the slogan, *Do Ya Teen Bachche Hote Hain Ghar Mein Achchhe* (two or three kids are best in a home). Later the slogan became *Hum Do Hamare Do* (we two, ours two).

These slogans did miracles in creating awareness among the villagers and the common people of India about the importance of a planned, small and happy family.

Sadly, my friend Tyagi fell victim of Cancer and passed away at the young age of 41.

Himself unmarried, he was very much dedicated to the cause of 'limited family' in over-populated India that while in the hospital, he wrote in his will about how he should be cremated: No traditional chanting of *'Ram Naam Satya Hai'* (Ram – God – is the eternal truth) at the funeral procession and no flowers/wreathes, only Red Triangles made of anything – paper, cloth or the like, and the family planning song he helped compose to be sung/played at the last rites.

These were his wishes, clearly written in his will finalized in the hospital.

They were carried out faithfully.

Sadhana made a beautiful garland of red beads in the shape of a triangle tucked on a silk cloth that we put on his body.

The news of Tyagi's death and his unique funeral procession and tributes were widely reported by newspapers. His mission got a boost.

I was out of India during part of his stay in the hospital but was back before he passed away. While in New Delhi, I would visit him every evening returning from my office and also to pick up his mother and drop her at Tyagi's home.

[It was unfortunate that a few years later his mother and a sister also fell victims to Cancer. What a tragedy! My close friend VK is also no more. His son, Vishal Sharma is in California with his family but we are hardly in touch.]

I have been going on various assignments out of Delhi and one memorable visit was to Nagaland, the small Northeastern state of India carved out of a larger state of Assam during Nehru's time.

The visit to Nagaland was an eye-opener for me. The state was created with 'help' that the small group of armed Christian rebels, propped up by the active Christian missionaries. Actually the missionaries were in the forefront of 'talks, mediation, contacts and agreements' with the federal government of India.

Nehru finally agreed to carve out the small state of Nagaland much to the heartburn of neighboring Manipuris, Assamese and others who were relegated, especially the Manipuris. Assam remained a state despite a part given to Nagaland but Manipur (which once was a princely state) was sidelined and ignored, and Nagaland elevated to full statehood. That resentment still persists in Manipur.

There was another state, Sikkim, that became a full state, and an integral part of India following confusion as the British left in 1947. The Chogyal (prince) later was reported to be scheming to remain fully independent. However, a popular non-violent public agitation resulted in intervention by the federal government following a referendum.

I was associated with both Nagaland and Sikkim, with Nagaland as a witness to some injustices and helping to create history. Similarly, I helped to create history in changing the status of Sikkim.

Sadhana saw me interview the then Prime Minister of Sikkim, Kazi Lhendup Dorji on India's TV, in 1975. He vehemently denounced the Chogyal in no uncertain terms. I did not interrupt him, rather kept probing and encouraging him to speak freely. He urged the federal government to help the Sikkimese people and accept the full statehood for Sikkim. This was after a popular referendum overwhelmingly opposed the Chogyal-rule and demanded total democratic independence and merger with India.

The government acceded to the people's will, deposed the Chogyal and made Sikkim an integral part of India as a separate state.

Kazi Dorji paid a return visit to New Delhi and asked the Ministry to invite me to interview him again.

That I did happily. It was, kind of, a 'Thanksgiving' appearance for the 'Prime Minister' who had fallen in line with other states and had become the Chief Minister.

After that I asked Sadhana how my interviews were going. She not only applauded them but also helped me polish my appearance. She would select the shirt or suit that I would wear for an interview. More importantly, as my most loved but keen critic, she advised me, 'no moistening of lips by the tongue.' Since that correction, I was a better interviewer controlling the movement of my tongue.

Lips were better taken care of at home.

Indeed Sadhana was my best friend and the best constructive critic.

Another memorable TV interview was with Lalit Narayan Mishra, the Railway Minister, and one of the closest Ministers in Indira Gandhi's cabinet, around the time of the big railway agitation. It was sharp and crisp; controversial questions were answered expertly by the Minister.

Afterward LN Mishra was all praise for me and specifically asked me to treat him as a friend. Actually he told me he would talk to the owner (KK Birla) of *Hindustan* (my employer), as he came to know of sheer injustice being done to me. When I politely declined the offer, he remarked: What are friends for?

I didn't want any political interference as I have always considered it being temporary; it could change with the political changes. I was right.

[Sadly my sincere friend Mishra died in 1975, in a bomb blast, on a train, under mysterious circumstances.]

There were several memorable and interesting interviews/press conferences in my long career. One was addressed by the then 'His Imperial Majesty, Aryamehr, Shahanshah', the Shah of Iran.

[I had reported a part of his earlier visit when he came to India with his second wife, Soraya and attended – a part of their busy program – an exquisite display of Torchlight Tattoo, by the Delhi Police. I was not far from the royal couple, just two rows away from where I could see both the distinguished guests.

After the show, I had a closer view of the couple, one an exceedingly beautiful half-German, half-Iranian Soraya and the other, Shah, once reported to be the most handsome man in the world. He grew up among a host of women led by his mother and was extremely fond of women, especially tall Europeans.]

Apart from that, the Shah on his second visit addressed a press conference at the famous Vigyan Bhavan, in New Delhi.

As happened many times, I set the ball rolling with a question, a little provoking: "What are your views on the question of abolition of Privy Purses of Indian Maharajas?"

[Privy Purses were the amount settled between the Government of India and the Princely states that agreed to merge with other states and became an integral part of India after Partition. It was a solemn agreement between the Government and the rulers as the amount of compensation for giving up their royal rights. Prime Minister Indira Gandhi wanted to assert her ideological preference for 'socialism' by abolishing that agreement and discontinue paying the agreed amount to the rulers.]

The Shah seemed a little confused and that showed. He said: I don't know as I don't know any Maharajas.

My first question had elicited some interest and subdued smiles but the next – the supplementary – had something more.

I pointed to the Minister- in-Attendance *(the one who is usually assigned to accompany a King or the equivalent dignitary on his India visit)*: The Maharaja of Jammu & Kashmir (Dr. Karan Singh) is sitting near you.

Anyway, that question-answer was not *that* relevant and the matter was closed with laughter all around.

Another 'encounter' out of many more, was with Prime Minister Indira Gandhi. She was accompanied by her close aide, and the Minister of State for Information and Broadcasting, Mrs. Nandini Satpathy. *[Mrs. Gandhi herself had the overall charge of I & B, at that time.]*

I asked about a campaign by the I & B Ministry to which Mrs. Gandhi replied: "Ask the Minister for Information and Broadcasting about it."

I was quick to remark: "But *you are* the Minister of Information and Broadcasting."

There was big laughter in the hall.

I would always bring home these interesting stories to share with my dear Sadhana as she eagerly awaited them, knowing fully well there had to be some juicy ones to go around when, for her husband it was all-in-a-day's-work all the time.

Sadhana and I had become quite popular in many other circles. There was this organization, set up under National Discipline Scheme (NDS – later named Nehru Yuvak Kendra.) It was directly under the Central Government for providing physical education instructors to hundreds of Central schools all over India.

We both got more interested – and also involved – in that scheme. It had its Headquarters at Silisedh in Alwar district of Rajasthan. It was the brain child of one of the stalwarts of freedom struggle under Netaji Subhas Bose and his Indian National Army (INA.). That man was Major General J.K. Bhonsle, Netaji's Chief of Staff. He was one of the *very few* people of INA that Jawaharlal Nehru 'rewarded' with respectable positions in the Government, after independence.

The other was Shah Nawaz Khan. Incidentally, Khan was junior to Bhonsle in INA, but was made a Minister of State by Nehru. Bhonsle was appointed a Deputy Minister.

Both had fought the election and had won as Congress candidates. Their campaign was mainly based on their association with Netaji Bose and the Indian National Army (Azad Hind Fauj) that fought the British for India's freedom in 1942-45.

I gave a lot of publicity to Bhonsle's NDS and even visited the HQ in Alwar when Dr. Rajendra Prasad, the first President of India, paid a visit to the Center and saw what a wonderful training center it was. Young men and women from ordinary families made spirited groups of motivated instructors by their tough training – physically, mentally, and spiritually based on ardent sense of nationalism and passionate pride for ancient Indian history, culture, heritage and glory.

Bhonsle liked me and wanted me to again visit the Center with Sadhana when Nehru was scheduled to visit. That was Bhonsle's dream to show the Prime Minister what could be achieved with dedication and also without huge funds. NDS was run on a meager budget but was producing dedicated instructors.

While the plans for Nehru's visit were being finalized I moved to Ramesh Nagar from Jore Bagh, a second time. As I mentioned earlier, phone-transfer was not easy or quick and I was without a home phone for several days. I missed Bhonsle's calls – for some reason he didn't want to call my office – and I did not know of the plans for the Prime minister's visit to the Center.

[Meanwhile, tragedy had struck. Bhonsle had a heart attack the night before Nehru's visit. He was only 57. His body was kept at the Center when Nehru visited and the officers and instructor-trainees decided that The Show Must Go On.

Nehru saw a thrilling display of physical fitness and other items by the trainees – they had teary eyes while performing.

Bhonsle was cremated with full honors by a tearful and grateful group of young men and women.

One of the then trainee-instructors, Avdhesh Kaushal, a senior official with the renamed organization – now Nehru Yuvak Kendra – was quite active in social and cultural fields also. He got in touch with me at *Hindustan*, and later became like a close member of our family and addressed us as *Mama Ji* and *Mami Ji*. He was posted in Dehradun – my Sadhana's city.

Kaushal told Sadhana and I about a traditional, but cruel practice, kind of a ritual, in the hilly region, especially at a place called Lakhamandal, some 80 miles from the city of Dehradun.

On the occasion of Dashhara (or Dussehra), a Hindu festival celebrating the victory of Shree Ram over demon King Ravan, the villagers in Lakhamandal made a bull run while they attacked it with sticks, swords, spears and stones until the poor animal dropped dead.

This was the cruel practice. Then the animal was left for the smaller animals or the birds for their meal.

Sadhana and I decided to help end this cruelty.

We accepted the invitation of Avdhesh, and with half a dozen young volunteer men and women took a bus ride to Lakhamandal. The moment the young fellows saw us, their enthusiasm for an adventurous project virtually vanished. [We could guess that.] They thought their 'picnic' was spoiled with the presence of an older, married couple.

Within minutes they realized their mistake and from then till eternity we were their loved and respected *Mama Ji* and *Mami Ji* (uncle and aunty.) By our loving, caring and jolly nature, Sadhana and I had put them at ease and made them our dear children and young friends.

It rained on the way and we had to face a landslide also. The bus was old, and so were the roads – narrow, winding and without any kind of fencing along most of the way.

After the first landslide, big and small boulders blocked our path. The driver said he will send someone several miles down the road to arrange for a road-repair gang of the concerned government department. That, he said, might take hours, or days.

I was in no mood to resign to our fate and remain stranded, dependent on somebody else, and uncertain of when we would be 'rescued' and resume our perilous journey.

I got down the bus, did a quick survey and started clearing the road by first throwing smaller stones, down the hill.

Quickly all our team-mates joined in the task. I let Sadhana remain on the bus to keep a watch on our team's carry-on bags.

The initial reaction of other passengers was to mock and deride our efforts by their laughter and comments. They took us to be a bunch of fools who were either showing off or had undertaken an impossible task.

Looking at what we were fast accomplishing, half the people on the bus got down and enthusiastically joined our effort. They had realized that the task was doable, not impossible. Big boulders were pushed by more than one, smaller ones were no match for single volunteers.

It took us not more than an hour to clear a substantial part of the road. In the midst of our efforts, more boulders started to fall. I deputed one person to keep a watch and warn us. This joint effort continued for more than one hour till we made a reasonably clear path for the bus to move.

149

It was then that our group – first the small and later the bigger – got hearty applause from everyone. We had accomplished something that was unthinkable just a few hours back.

By the time we arrived at the spot for river-crossing to finally reach Lakhamandal, it was raining quite enough to prevent our attempt to try and cross the turbulent river and proceed that very evening. The river had no bridge – only a rope connection. You sit on a plank hanging by a rope, and the rope pulled from the other side.

It was not easy. It was scary. It was dangerous too.

There was this turbulent river along its mountainous route with waters flowing at a high speed over boulders and winding path.

We had to cross but we decided to put it off till the next morning as it was getting late and dark; and there was no electricity around.

The place for river-crossing had just a couple of shops for nearby residents. There was a tea-shop and a, kind of, grocery store, with a small apology of a warehouse. There were not many customers, especially at that hour.

We asked the tea-stall owner to take a break – we will prepare whatever we needed, tea, snacks or anything else. He was glad to know his stuff would be used – sold – and he would not have to do anything, just watch.

Sadhana took charge of the 'kitchen.' It was just a small space with a hearth using coal and firewood. We got all the ingredients we needed from the neighboring shop and to begin with, Sadhana, made some heavenly delicious *pakoras* with *besan* (gram flour.) We had never tasted anything like that before, especially in those circumstances.

[That day, October 6, happened to be our younger daughter Seema's birthday and we took it as the celebration. Seema sometimes had birthdays at odd times, odd places, and sometimes not even present – like that day. But she is a sport.]

Our luggage (including some sheets and small mattresses) put on top of the bus was soaked in rainwater and had become, somewhat a liability. However, we managed to huddle together and spend the night at the warehouse. There was no bathroom and in any emergency, we had to venture out in darkness and drizzle.

Morning came and we got ready somehow, with minimum of facility and convenience.

Then there was a revelation – last night's *pakoras* were made with *besan* that had given 'sanctuary' to some illegal immigrants. They could not be detected under a dimly lit stall that just had a small kerosene lamp. The solid evidence was there in the left-over *besan*.

The reaction of our team-mates was hilarious. Some said the *pakoras* were real tasty – they tasted divine under the circumstances.

One went further. This was Gyan Gupta who said, with a mischievous smile that whatever it was, it cured his constipation, and this morning he had enough for the next two days.

We all had a great laugh and hailed the discovery of the merits of worm-ed *besan* we used for our *pakoras*. Maybe the worms had crawled in after the first round of *pakoras* last night.

Our group had four more young persons – Sunil Pant, Rohini, Sudha and Asha beside Avdesh, Sadhana and I.

In the morning we crossed the river's fast moving waters one by one, via the hand-pulled rope.

It looked very scary but I volunteered to go first. While you are being pulled you feel that you are fast going upstream. Scary, but it was an adventure and you, kind of, enjoy and feel happy you *did* it. I waved to everyone on the other side constantly to put them at ease.

Thanks to the man, Nain Singh Rana, who was pulling the rope.

Next was, my constant partner Sadhana. After three quarters of the 'pulling adventure' she noticed the rope giving way. She must have been worried but did not panic; it would have been futile as she was some 20 feet away from the shore.

As soon as she put her foot on the shore, the rope snapped. She was anticipating it and was careful while landing. But Rana and others, on both the shores, were startled. Rana was totally shocked, but heaved a sigh of relief to see Sadhana safe and unhurt.

Rana thanked God and told us that he had pulled at least 150 people during the last few days and if something tragic happened that day breaking his 'safety record,' he would never have forgiven himself.

It took some persistent cajoling for the others – especially two girls – to cross the same way after the ropes were fixed and checked thoroughly.

Once everyone made it to this side of the river we trekked the hilly track and reached the village of Lakhamandal.

The welcoming party had the village elders, some other residents and their wives – some had multiple wives - very young and beautiful.

The place had a very old big building, half burnt and damaged. Village elders enthusiastically described it as Lakshagrih (the House of Lac – the highly inflammable material). It was supposed to be the 5000 year-old palace built by *Mahabharat's* ambitious Kaurav prince Duryodhan to burn down, and get rid of his cousins, the Pandavas.

The excavation and historical evidence-seekers had not reached the place till the day our group reached Lakhamandal.

The next day was the important event of immense brutality and we did witness it in all its ghastly details. The big crowd of villagers from nearby area had flocked to this traditional 'festival' but most of the women we saw had closed or covered their eyes than see the cruelty to the animal. Women, though reluctant to witness the cruelty, were asked by the 'elders' to be present as it's *the traditional event*.

We returned with a heavy heart that such practices were still prevalent. But we were determined to do something positive about it.

I wrote in my paper about it and kind of, started a campaign against it. Nehru Yuvak Kendra's young members and Lakhamandal's reform-minded activists joined their supporters in Dehradun. The momentum was created and by next year the authorities had ensured a clean, cruelty-free festival with music-dance and distribution of sweets to replace bull-chasing and killing.

[However, the happy outcome had taken the precious life of one young man who became the victim of 'hard-liners' wrath. But his sacrifice did not go in vain.]

Kaushal remained with the Kendra for a number of years working for social causes. He was selected for a visit to Japan and met with youth and welfare activists there.

A return visit by Japanese children's delegation (sponsored by their Prime Minister's office) was warmly welcomed by Dehradun's Nehru Yuvak Kendra and also in Delhi.

I arranged a meeting and photo-op with Prime Minister Indira Gandhi at her official residence in New Delhi for the Japanese children and their leader, who were all praise for me and my help.

14

More Trips Abroad and New Friends

Coming back to the magazine and our 1972 joint trip abroad. That trip was our own though a part of the airfare was covered by our magazine TRAVIANA that used to get advertisements from companies, including airlines. Most of the tickets were already used by our partner in the publication, JK Jain and his wife Nirmal, on their trip; a small part was left for us. We financed a big part of the trip that somehow, for some unforeseen circumstances became ill-organized and had to be curtailed leaving the later legs totally uncovered and abandoned.

It was more than a challenge but it showed our determination, our ability to face anything in life together. It also brought out the real Sadhana in all her courage, patience, and indomitable spirit. She was compelled to return to India alone, without me, and fight with the Reserve Bank of India to bring me back home.

More about those 'Two Tourists, 40 Days' story later.

Both of us being active everywhere brought us new friends – both Indian and foreign – and newer adventures. That included more foreign trips for me and more staying alone and caring for the kids for Sadhana. As usual, she never complained and was always supportive of me. She never hesitated in playing host to friends and relatives. The relatives sometimes came from outside Delhi, from Jaipur and Dehradun, but also from far-flung cities and states all over India.

Among my very old friends were two classmates, Mr. Uddhav (Udho) Daga and Miss Swaran Gulati. Udho was with me for five years from 1941 to 1946 when we graduated from Marwari Vidyalaya High School, in Bombay. He was my oldest school friend – the class of 1946.

Swaran was with me and sister Lata for a year in college in 1946-47. I left Bombay in 1947; Lata continued for another year and then enrolled in medical college in Agra. Swaran continued for a couple years more and completed her BSc.

Years later we were re-united. Both Udho and Swaran with their families had moved to Delhi. They did not know each other earlier. Swaran had married Baldev and become Mrs. Gambhir. Both the families were dear to me and Sadhana and our kids were very friendly with theirs.

All were welcome at our home. Swaran came with her family and so did Udho. With Udho it was special. We shared birth day and birth year. He would sometimes call around midnight to tell us they are on their way and we all would go out for midnight tea and snacks. Our favorite was Ashok Hotel, just a few hundred yards from our place, but around 10 miles from his. But among friends it was alright.

When we were in India, Udho would organize 'full moon night-long' picnics, mostly at Surajkund, in the state of Haryana, an hour's drive from our home in Chanakyapuri. 20-30 family-friends and relatives would gather for a night-long feast, music and fun.

Ah, those good old days!

[Sadhana and I visited India in 2007 after nine years and wanted to re-connect with them. We didn't have the phone number of Udho – phone directories had become history and everyone was using cell (mobile) phones. It took us four days to find the number. Sadhana called – Udho had died a couple days before.

It was devastating for us, both. We went to his house and wept bitterly, loudly. Udho and his family were very close to Sadhana and me. And so were the kids.

It was extremely painful for Sadhana and me.

We were not destined to see our friend. We attended his *chautha* (the fourth day) and paid our respects and mourned this tragic loss. Sadhana had extreme difficulty in climbing the stairs and she had to go up three floors. But she did for our dear departed friend and to share the loss with his wife, son and daughters and, Rathi *Ji* and other relatives.

We were able to visit with Swaran and Baldev. I don't know how they are as, again, I have lost contact with them.]

Now back to our routine.

We had started TRAVIANA and the magazine had a special place in the field. We would write and report about flying, new planes, travel and tourism, hotel industry and so on. The adventure part was also not forgotten. Various states and regions were also given exposure with their specialty in music, dance and food, sports and traditions. JK Jain looked after sales and advertisements and I handled all the editorial content. Sadhana would manage other things to produce the magazine regularly.

In addition, our Deep Features was also functioning. Sadhana addressed me as Deep (I had given her many names such as Ashi, Ashu, Paru and so on.) and so we named the venture, Deep Features.

Deep Features was actually some kind of rebellion against the Editor, Ratan Lal Joshi. Joshi *Ji*, otherwise an okay editor, did not give me ample scope to write articles – and I was interested in tackling subjects of varied colors and hues and with regularity. I had always been prolific with news, views, commentaries, features, poems (though did not publish many). This was beyond Joshi *Ji*, for reasons I have not figured out as yet, and so Deep Features was my answer.

With Sujata as Assistant Editor to do proof reading for me and Sadhana, in any case, my overall associate, also handled the shipping department with the help of our younger daughter, Seema. Deep Features articles and reports would go to dozens of newspapers all over India, mainly Hindi language papers, and to some embassies too and therefore had frequent articles in English also. TRAVIANA was one of the ventures of our many-sided activities that kept me and my wife – also the family – busy and happy.

Joshi *Ji* used to visit many other cities such as Varanasi, Calcutta (now Kolkata), Bombay (now Mumbai), Patna etc. Whenever he visited a city, he would see the local paper with my article. Sometimes Deep Features would carry my articles in other pen-names. I had many such names that I used for writing as and when needed. TRAVIANA also had articles/reports under many of my pseudonyms. I was happy in what I was doing and couldn't care less for anyone as long as I didn't neglect my primary obligation to *Hindustan*. I never did that.

These two ventures got me satisfaction as well as some extra money. I used to subscribe regularly to several papers outside of Delhi that I sent our articles to. A number of local newspapers were allowed to me free by my employers as I was special correspondent and then the Chief of News Bureau. In any case, I was interested in happenings and opinions in various regions of India and the world and would regularly go through dozens of publications.

Sadhana would religiously keep clippings of items that I would mark on papers I read – for future reading or reference.

The amount of papers ordered and delivered to our home was incredible. In India used papers were sold (here they are recycled by somebody else that doesn't pay you anything.) Our newspaper stacks were so big that Nebhraj *Ji*, the man who came regularly to buy from us, became a member of our family. He would quietly go to the corner, weigh the stacks and pay us at the current rate – sometimes the rates would go up and he would himself pay the higher price.

We visited Nebhraj-family whose business had flourished so much (partly because of our big stacks of papers, I suppose) that he bought an auto-rikshaw and stopped using his bicycle. His wife Savitri Devi, a trained nurse, had opened a small hospital in Patel Nagar area of New Delhi and employed a doctor and a couple of other help. Their children also became successful in business.

This was all Sadhana's caring and friendly nature. I remember when Nebhraj *Ji* first came to our home, the kids shouted: *"Raddiwala aa gaya"* (the scrap-dealer/newspaper-buyer has come.) Sadhana scolded them and said: He is older than you, address him with respect as Uncle. Since that day Nebhraj Uncle became a member of our family. He, on his part, was always there for us when needed.

These were the qualities my dear Sadhana had in ample measure. These were also automatically handed down to our children and followed by them, in letter and spirit, willingly.

There was another stranger who, with her family, became our family.

Sadhana was 'at work' again.

One day a group of men and women came to our home. They were going house-to-house to persuade people to open accounts with their bank – Syndicate Bank – in our neighborhood.

Sadhana invited the group inside and treated everybody nicely and offered them tea and snacks. She did open an account also (though we had accounts in two other major banks.) Sadhana thought it impolite to refuse a new account to those who came. That started a close family friendship with the main member of the group, Anju Bhatia, whose kids Dimpy (Sandeep) and Minky (Prashant) then grew up with Sujata and

Seema as they lived not far from us. Family visits became regular; Anju's husband, Vijay Bhatia, was equally friendly and jolly.

As it happens often, tragedy struck; the younger son, Minky fell victim to a rabid dog bite. We were devastated as a family.

Our relations were so close that when we had moved to Indore and Anju became very sick, Sadhana flew to New Delhi to be with her for a few days and take care of her.

We are still in touch with the Bhatia family. [Sandeep's wife, Sunita is a sweet *bahu* (daughter in-law.) We loved her when we met her in 2007.

Sadhana had been more active in 'extending' our family. Anyone who came in contact with her was treated kindly, nicely and went with a unique impression.

This happened with the swimming coach of Sujata and Seema. Luckily the pool was just opposite our home in Chanakyapuri (where we moved in 1974) and Sadhana took them every day. The award-winning coach, Mr. Chatterji, a Bengali gentleman commonly addressed as *Dada* (brother) was persuaded by Sadhana to wind up his day with sharing a cup of tea with us, every day. Soon his family became our family.

Sadhana would take the kids to the pool daily and watch them learn. One day she thought, why am I wasting that hour, why not learn? So she enrolled and started taking lessons from Dada.

She did not need to buy a swim-suit. She, an expert in sewing, made a one-piece swim-suit for herself the very next day and surprised Dada and the girls at the pool.

After a couple days, it so happened that nobody was around and she lost her footing and balance and found herself drowning. For a couple minutes she thought she was lost but just at that moment a young swimmer held her hand and directed her to the safe corner.

She was, naturally, shaken. Dada was apologetic; probably he was busy with others and felt bad about it.

That night when I returned from work she narrated that incident and I heaved a sigh of relief. Then I asked what's she going to do the next day?

I heard what I had expected. My confident wife told me that she was not giving up, she would continue.

I felt proud of her, again.

Sadhana practiced and learnt swimming – all the strokes and floating etc. She became a fairly good swimmer.

My Sadhana had got another 'medal of merit' from me, and other well-wishers. Her 'never-give up' spirit had prevailed.

In the list of strangers becoming close friends, and family, my insurance agent, A.S. Nakra, became close right from the day he sold me a life insurance policy.

His 'entry' was interesting.

One day he knocked and as we opened the door, he said: I am A.S. Nakra, I am an insurance agent and if you allow me, I will come inside.

Once inside, he convinced Sadhana and I about the benefits of taking a life insurance policy, the particular policy that suited us. He also announced: I enter as insurance agent, but if you get a policy from me, I will become your friend.

Nakra *Ji* became our close family friend. A few years later as I got a substantial raise, he sold me another policy that paid me at least twice a sizable amount, at a few years interval and, on maturity, paid the full amount insured. Annual bonuses and interest amount were regularly added to the principal amount. In all, I got much more than what I had insured for. The *total* life insurance amount was paid to me, that too without me dying, just at maturity. In the US, on maturity, we got nothing at all.

That was the beauty of India's life insurance schemes. And that was the result of my insurance agent-turned close friend A.S. Nakra and his sound advice.

He would see to it that my premiums were paid in a timely manner, a luxury I did not have when I took my first policy from somebody else that expired after a couple years for irregular payment/no payment.

Nakra *Ji* had also successfully persuaded many of my colleagues in the office to get life insurance policies from him. He was excellent at his job and a good friend.

He also tried to sell me the idea of having our own home and assured me that he would get it constructed without any extra burden on me. His idea was, probably, to borrow money from my life insurance amount. I did not change my stand on not owning a house; and Nakra *Ji* gave up.

I still cannot figure out exactly if I was right or wrong. But who cares?

[I don't know where Mr. Nakra is now. He must be my age and I am 88 years and six months. The last time, many years back, I roamed about the area where he lived, I didn't have his address handy, and so I could not locate him. May God grant him a long life; his wife had already gone many years back.]

Among many good friends of the journalistic fraternity were VP Ramachandran and Virendra Mohan of the United News of India. From All India Radio were the prominent news-readers, Devki Nandan Pande, Ashok Bajpayee and Shiv Sagar Mishra. From India's official TV, Doordarshan, Director NL Chawla often himself planned and also watched my talks and interviews.

My first TV program's producer was Swadesh Kumar (PP Saxena), who, in 1948, was the first to print my humorous article in the reputed magazine, *Sarita,* when he was the senior editor there.

VP, Virendra Mohan and I would frequently meet on our beats and press briefings. Mohan's wife, Nalini, was among Sadhana's friends and we sometimes exchanged visits.

Literary figures and political leaders I was meeting quite often were numerous to mention, it will fill a separate book. To recall a few, were Banarasi Das Chaturvedi, first President of the Indian Federation of Working Journalists and an eminent activist-writer (nominated to Rajya Sabha for 12 years, (also a friend of my father), Seth Govind Das (for 50 years, a member of Parliament – a record), renowned poets/writers such as Maithili Sharan Gupt, Balkrishna Sharma 'Naveen', Ramdhari Singh Dinkar, Neeraj, Devraj Dinesh, Virendra Mishra and many other top poets from the 50s to 80s.

Sadhana also had met many of these luminaries and we shared the same admiration for them and their contribution.

15

The War in 1971,
Birth of a Nation, Books

India, since independence, had to face catastrophic situations not once or twice but on several occasions. The year 1971 was no exception. And again it was the neighbor, Pakistan, once a dear and vibrant part of our own Motherland.

The extraordinary situation created by Pakistan in its Eastern part saw the two countries at war just six years after the war of 1965. The result was also extraordinary with heavy losses for Pakistan and also loss of a big chunk of its possession – the Eastern part of Pakistan became a separate and independent country.

The whole of India was affected by those developments, our family too as I became professionally and emotionally involved in the conflict. Sadhana too could not keep herself aloof and played her part enthusiastically and passionately.

A product of Partition of India, the former part, Pakistan, was also divided between East and West Pakistan right at its birth. These two parts of Pakistan were poles apart in everything but religion. The separation of the Eastern part of Pakistan into an independent nation of Bangladesh proved the point once again that ONLY religion cannot be a binding force for countries.

Several other factors play more important part than religion.

East Pakistan was entirely different from West Pakistan in language, culture, and history. The divide was exacerbated by the strict, superiority complex of the West Pakistani Punjabi-Pathan military complex that dominated Pakistan's government, business and the ruling elite. East Pakistanis (Bengalis) were treated as second class citizens and dealt with disdain and indifference.

The Bengalis constantly faced a lot of discrimination, neglect and indifference from the ruling elite that was functioning from afar. Despite

East Pakistan's larger population, West was getting a bigger chunk of budget and attention. Bengal was under-represented and ignored, and Bengalis discriminated against.

The result: unrest and disaffection, heartburn and alienation, and the rise of Bengali nationalism.

The 1970 elections resulted in a majority held by the Eastern part and the leader Mujibur Rahman staked his claim for Prime Minister's post. The dominating West replied by massacres, intimidation, and suppression. Torture and rapes were rampant; Hindu minorities were relentlessly attacked, harassed and killed. Muslim Bengalis were not spared either.

Armed action in various parts of East Pakistan, widespread torture and arrests resulted in over 10 million Bengalis fleeing to neighboring India upsetting the people and the government there. The results of the elections were annulled and Mujib and thousands of others were arrested. A systematic elimination of nationalists and intellectuals was carried out by the military. Mass murders and deportation were resorted brutally.

In March of 1971 Pakistani Army let loose a reign of terror and genocide. Some 30 million Bengalis were uprooted, internally. Universities, students, intelligentsia were specifically targeted by military strikes and air raids.

The Bengalis rose in revolt, formed a Mukti Bahini (Liberation Army) and pleaded with India for help. The East Pakistani military regiments, para military and nationalist civilians became the liberation force and revolted against Pakistan. The provisional government of Bangladesh was formed that made its temporary headquarters in the neighboring Indian city of Calcutta (now Kolkata) as government-in-exile. Thousands of Bengali officials, diplomats and other civilians defected and joined the provisional Bangladeshi government and started functioning inside and outside Bengal.

The military operations by Pakistan were widely condemned – worldwide. India, as the closest neighbor, and terribly affected by the Bengali influx and other problems, had to act. New Delhi decided to offer its diplomatic, economic and military support to the emerging free nation, Bangladesh.

Pakistan's military dictator Gen. Yahya Khan was banking on the American support as the then President Richard Nixon had a soft corner for him. He even threatened to send the US 7th fleet to the region. Nixon was roundly criticized by the American people. Democratic Senator Ted Kennedy, and even American diplomats stationed in East Pakistan's capital, Dacca, expressed stiff opposition to Nixon's pro-Yahya stand. Kennedy led a spirited campaign in the American Congress against Pakistani atrocities on Bangla soil.

In this context it must be remembered that India was, finally, forced to actively join the conflict after Pakistan launched a pre-emptive air strike on North Indian cities. India had to fight on two fronts – East and West, but soon established its air superiority in the East joining the war there on December 3, 1971.

The combined Indian military forces and Bangladesh's Mukti Bahini moved swiftly and within 13 days changed history and geography. Pakistani military was outmaneuvered and their commander, Lt. Gen Niazi, surrendered on 16 December in Dacca. A new nation of Bangladesh was finally born to change the geopolitical landscape of South Asia.

Soon a majority of member-countries of the United Nations recognized Bangladesh as an independent country.

In addition to capturing a sizable chunk of Pakistani territory in the West, India had also got over 93,000 Pakistani troops as Prisoners of War. India treated them with internationally accepted hospitality and care. Left to them, many would have opted to stay in India but the protocol did not permit it. They were repatriated after just a few months following India-Pakistan agreement signed in the Indian city of Shimla. The captured land was also vacated by India.

The reason I mentioned Bangladesh Liberation War and the emergence of a new country in some detail was that Sadhana and I were closely involved in it. I covered the War extensively for my paper and radio/TV by actively keeping in touch with the planning and execution of the whole operation, attending important high-level briefings and talking to the principal military and civilian leaders in New Delhi. Top military officers would daily – sometimes twice daily – brief us about the progress of war and the resultant arrangements.

I had made all the preparations to go to the war front (including getting an olive green military uniform quickly stitched.) However the war was over earlier than expected. We had exclusive representation in both the sectors, East and West (Punjab-Rajasthan-Gujarat) where major operations took place.

Another reason for my delay in going to the Front was that I was in touch with some of the Bangladeshi diplomats in India and visiting Bengali leaders whom I was constantly interviewing. One prominent writer even stayed with us as Sadhana and I got more closely involved with the publicity of the freedom movement.

In addition, the entire Indian intelligentsia was involved in the Liberation War by arranging meetings, demonstrations, seminars, poetic recitals and publications during, and after the War.

Incidentally, some of the prominent British, Indian and American musicians organized the world's first benefit concert in New York City to support the suffering Bangladeshis.

Sadhana, meanwhile, had started collecting poems and compiling a book on Bangladesh and its liberation. She also wrote one poem, and I did the same in our book – *Kranti ke Swar*.

That was also the time when I had my first book published. This was the first book about Bangladesh written by one man (a couple were collection of reports/articles by several persons). This 350-page, hard cover book came out much before the formal surrender by Pakistan and total liberation of Bangladesh in December, in 1971.

I wrote *Bangladesh, Birth of a Nation* and got it printed/published in June taking the declaration of a Free Bangladesh and setting up of a provisional government of Bangladesh, in exile in April, 1971, as the *birth of the nation*.

M. Hossain Ali, then Head of the Bangladeshi diplomatic Mission (based in Calcutta) wrote the foreword mentioning that the book will help promote an understanding of the struggle of the people of Bangladesh. He also added some more significant words saying, "I hope the book will find a wide readership and thus contribute to rousing the moribund conscience of mankind."

Moving words from the representative of a suffering people!

My book was released by the then Defense Minister Jagjivan Ram in the packed hall of the Press Club of India, in New Delhi. Sadhana and the kids were there. Babuji, as he was fondly and respectfully addressed, spoke about Bangladesh's struggle, India's grave concern and about the book, and praised my efforts.

He was gracious – and I must add, one of the most knowledgeable and efficient Defense Ministers India ever had.

[I can't help mentioning an amusing anecdote at the reception that followed the book release and speeches. Sadhana offered a plate to *Babuji* with a couple pieces of *barfi* (Indian sweet) and *pakoras* (salty vegetable fritters.)

Sujata and Seema were also there and Babuji offered a piece of *barfi* to cute little 6-year-old Seema but she refused. Babuji insisted and she still said, no thanks. I squeezed her arm indicating that she better accept it but Seema did not budge from her stand. Finally, Jagjivan *Babu* got out of that embarrassing situation (for himself and Sadhana and me too) by saying that the girl is conscious of her figure even at this tender age (*avoiding sweets*).

Later at home we asked Seema why was she so adamant and not accept *burfi* when such an eminent leader – and our honored guest – was offering it affectionately.

She came up with an answer: he had hair on his ears.

Whether she really noticed his hair or just made up some excuse for her stubbornness, we don't know, but the answer was hilarious. We often still remind her about the incident and she continues to stand by the 'convincing' reason for her refusal.]

I did not stop there. Within less than three months another of my books, another first, *Mujib, the Architect of Bangladesh* was in the market. There was no news about the arrested leader of the Bangladesh revolution – whether he was alive and where – and not much information about the man and his struggle. I did whatever I could gather from reading scattered accounts and meeting with people who knew something. Sadhana helped me with both the books, and so did her *Rakhi*-brother Brij Mohan Chhibber.

[We got the sad news of Brij passing away as I was writing *this* book. A great unassuming guy, quiet, selfless, loving, caring and dedicated to us, always there for us all whenever we needed him at any time of day or night, without any notice, or very short notice. I guess, the passing away of his sister, Sadhana, just a year back also contributed to his declining health, among other reasons.

Dear Brij, you will always be remembered. You were, and will always remain, a part of our family and our lives. May you now rest in peace.]

I was fortunate to get the Foreword for the Mujib book by none other than, Syed Nazrul Islam, the Acting President of the newly-formed Bangladesh government in exile. He was gracious and praised the earlier book *Bangla Desh, Birth of a Nation* also mentioning that "the biography of Bangabandhu Mujibur Rahman is far wider in its scope and will certainly call for much deeper understanding of the hopes and aspirations of the people of Bangladesh." Then he heaped praise on Mujib in some details and wrote that "the life of Shaikh Mujibur Rahman is a saga of struggle, sufferings and sacrifice. He is the torch-bearer of Bengali nationalism."

Syed Islam ended his message with words that still echo and have become more meaningful after the tragic assassination of the leader: "So long the people of Bangladesh will exist, Mujib will be loved, respected and remembered as the most beloved son of the soil."

What a tribute from the leader to adorn my book on Mujibur Rahman!

While I had already two books about Bangladesh published, I was roped into a third. Sadhana had collected and compiled a book of poems in Hindi about Bangladesh and I joined her in getting it also printed about the time Bangladesh was formally liberated. We both wrote a poem each and also translated a few. It was printed with our names, with our journalist-friend JK Jain mentioned as the publisher.

"Kranti Ke Swar" (the voice of revolution) was the collection of beautiful, inspiring and nationalistic poems by nearly 60 poets. The first poem was *"Amar Sonar Bangla"* (My Golden Bengal), written in 1905, by the celebrated Indian poet, the 1913 Nobel Prize winner, Rabindranath Tagore. The poem became the National Anthem of Bangladesh, the birth of which he never witnessed. Of course, Tagore also did not see his 'Sonar Bangla' being divided in 1947 as India was partitioned by the British government.

Tagore has the rare distinction that two countries have his poems as their National Anthems – India's *"Jana Gana Mana"* is also by Tagore though he died six years before, in 1941, sadly,without witnessing the spectacle of India's independence.

16

Release of Mujib, Welcome in Delhi

While we had the three books ready and in the market, Mujib was in a Pakistani prison probably waiting for his death. However, following the liberation of Bangladesh and the resignation of dictator Gen. Yahya Khan, an ever ambitious Zulfikar Ali Bhutto took over control of Pakistani government and then things changed.

Responding to strong international pressure, Bhutto had to release Mujib on January 8, 1972, after about nine months of incarceration, but sent him to London (instead of New Delhi or Dacca). Mujib was given a warm welcome by British Prime Minister Edward Heath. Mujib also addressed international media in London and was then sent on a Royal Air Force plane to New Delhi, January 10.

Delhi and the airport were given a festive look to welcome the great leader of Bangladesh.

I was one of the thousands at Delhi airport that day to greet Mujib. He was warmly welcomed by India's President V.V. Giri and Prime Minister Indira Gandhi whom the Bengali leader thanked profusely for helping to liberate Bangladesh.

The entire Indian cabinet, scores of members of Parliament and the chiefs of India's armed forces were also present. After a short while and a spirited address, Mujib was rushed to the nearby Garrison Grounds where half a million people had gathered to hear him speak. He again profusely thanked India and its government and briefly spoke about his vision for the liberated Bangladesh.

A towering personality and an impressive speaker, Mujib mesmerized his large audience. After an hour or so he arrived back at the Delhi airport to continue the flight to Dacca where a million people were waiting for the leader of the liberation movement to give him a befitting welcome. I was at the Delhi airport again, when Prime Minister Indira Gandhi, several cabinet ministers and MPs and a handful of reporters were present to give him a hearty send off.

I was in the second row of VIPs present to see Mujib off to Dacca. I was 'armed' with all the three books we had published about Bangladesh and wanted to present them to Mujib. I stole the opportunity when Mujib was taking leave of the small crowd, followed by Indira Gandhi. I looked to Mrs. Gandhi, she smilingly nodded and I blurted out, Sir, as Mujib passed in front of the line behind which I was – in the second line.

Mujib and everyone moving paused and I went forward with the books. I said, Sir, we didn't know where you were in the last few months, but here are three books we have brought out about Bangladesh.

Mujib took all the three from my hand, turned a few pages and said: I hope you have put everything here.

I replied, I have tried to do my best.

That was a short encounter with the man, the leader and the liberator – all before the most elite audience in India, headed by the important liberator of Bangladesh, Mrs. Indira Gandhi.

I felt very happy and honored. I thanked him and Indira Gandhi. Mujib boarded the Royal Air Force flight to Dacca that was waiting for his historic and triumphant arrival after nine months of nightmare for him and the country.

Our story with Mujib and Bangladesh did not end there at Delhi airport.

A couple months later, I was in Dacca, again armed with copies of the same three books – my passport to Bangladesh and Mujib. I had no appointment fixed.

However, it didn't take much time to get an appointment with the leader as, I presumed, his staff knew of the books and my connections with Bangladesh struggle. The Bangladeshi diplomats in India and their messages might have mentioned something about me.

I was led into Shaikh Mujibur Rahman's modestly furnished office and he greeted me affectionately.

Not sure if he remembered me, I held the three books in my hand and said, Sir, you might not remember me but probably you remember these books I wrote about Bangladesh.

Mujib was quick to reply with a smile, in his familiar booming voice: I remember, you gave me these books at Palam airport in Delhi.

I felt flattered. The great man remembered me. He invited me to sit with him on a sofa and we started to talk.

In a few minutes, an assistant walked in and said something to Mujib in a soft voice.

Bangabandhu looked at me, and said, sorry, *I* have to deal with all these things that come up.

He was signing some papers – even some checks as, I guessed, then he was the only one authorized to sign. I kept marveling at the man. He had just taken up the responsibility of managing the newly emerged independent developing nation with bad economy, unorganized and inadequate infra-structure, and a myriad of problems with expectant people hoping for miracles.

As we talked on the current tasks there was another interruption. Mujib had to attend to another task with yet another assistant.

These things continued for nearly 45 minutes, in between our talks. Mujib did not talk much about where he was kept in Pakistani prison and how he was treated but spoke about his vision for Bangladesh.

The 45 minutes or so passed quickly and I had to stop as Bangabandhu Mujib was scheduled to go to a high-level meeting. He was very down-to-earth and very popular leader; he apologized for not been able to give exclusive, uninterrupted time to me and hoped to meet me next time I came to Dacca or he visited India.

But before we parted, he did not forget one thing – he quickly called for his official photographer and posed with me for the historic photo. He thanked me again and left.

I asked the photographer when and how could I have a copy? He assured me that he would definitely send one to my hotel the same day, if not, the very next day.

I am still waiting for that historic photograph. Normally, I don't like to push myself for pictures with leaders – I could have thousands in my career – but a photo with Mujib could be my prized possession.

I did not meet him again. Also for various reasons, some unfortunate, I could not update the biography of Mujib and add chapters after his return to Dacca and taking up top posts and his assassination – the final chapters in a long saga of struggle for the rights of Bengalis, declaration of independence and triumphant return and his vision of making Bangladesh a progressive and secular country.

You do have regrets in your life. This is one of them.

[Three years later Mujib and his entire family, save two daughters, were killed in a treacherous plot by disgruntled and ambitious politicians – some from his own party – some junior army officers, and other anti-Mujib and pro-Pakistan elements.

The daughters were in Germany and escaped assassination. One of them, Hasina, is currently Prime Minister for the third time. Sadly, she was not allowed to enter the country for about six years following the assassination of her father on August 15, 1975, when anti-Mujib band was ruling.

The killers had exploited the worsening economic and social conditions and failure of the government on many fronts. Nobody cared for the fact that Bangladesh was liberated just four years back and there was a huge backlog of problems that would test any government. Mujib did not get reasonably minimum time required to make a dent, and was, tragically, eliminated.]

Bangladesh has since hovered between regular/secular rule of Hasina and more Islamist government of Khaleda Zia – widow of one-time a strong Mujib associate, Army Commander, opposition leader, and later president, Ziaur Rahman.

Zia began Islamization of the country and was joined by his close associate, another Army officer, later Lt. Gen. Hussein Muhammad Ershad (who himself led a bloodless coup and gained power). Zia pardoned many of the assassins of Mujib and gave them high diplomatic posts. However, Zia was himself assassinated in a military coup in 1981 as the country drifted more towards Islam and away from socialism, secularism and democracy.

Ershad was also ousted from power and forced to resign because of popular opposition to his rule. For a change, both Hasina and Khaleda Zia led the opposition to Ershad. He remains an active politician with his own party, Jatiyo Sangshad.

Bangladesh has been under military rule and democratically elected government intermittently. So have been Sheikh Hasina and Khaleda Zia, alternating as Prime Ministers. Awami League (AL) of Sheikh Hasina is center-left secular, while Khaleda Zia's Bangladesh Nationalist Party (BNP) is center-right-Islamist. These two have dominated Bangladesh politics for a long time but now both are depending on coalitions of like-minded parties. Hasina has been the head of AL, her father Mujib's party, since 1981 when she returned from her exile.

BNP was founded by President Zia in 1978 when he consolidated power.

Both Hasina and Khaleda have been alternately in power since 1991 and are popularly known as "Battling Begums."

India and Bangladesh have had tumultuous relations since alternating between cooperation and controversies – especially with the influx of refugees and illegal migrants in large numbers and Islamic extremism in Bangladesh. Internally, Bangladesh has been unstable and full of coups, controversies and conflicts. But with Hasina in power things are a little under control as she, of all the current politicians, remembers fully Indian help that liberated her country.

I, on my part, have not been able to keep up with the same emotional association with Bangladesh, partly because of the political-social-religious upheavals in that country during the last three decades since I left India, and partly the distance – in miles and also emotions.

It was right in the same year 1972, the fight for Bangladesh was well over and things had changed. Indira Gandhi had already gained a huge majority in the previous year's elections with 351 seats in the all-important Lok Sabha (the Lower House of Parliament.) That had given added strength and confidence to Indira Gandhi to take a tough stand about Bangladesh liberation. She had already added to her popularity due to her role in the liberation of Bangladesh and defeat of Pakistan.

However, several problems remained. Why didn't the Prime Minister pursue two main issues: Get the Kashmir issue settled once for all and reclaim the land from Pakistan's illegal occupation when that country was humiliated and down? The second, India could have 'fixed' a confusing and disturbing part of the border with Bangladesh when the time was best suited for it.

The advantage of a victory in the 1971 war and having over 93,000 Pakistani soldiers as prisoners had given a tremendous opportunity to

India for a tough bargain with Pakistan. However, the opportunity was badly missed.

Critics would always argue that you don't take advantage when the other side is down as there could be adverse reaction from the international community and big countries such as America and the then Soviet Union.

The answer is, these outside apprehensions were already there when Indira Gandhi decided to support the liberation war for Bangladesh and took the opportunity to strike when Pakistan launched an unprovoked war on India. It was clearly hesitancy and miscalculation by Indira Gandhi and lack of appropriate advice from her advisors. She missed a big opportunity for a final solution to the 'Kashmir problem.' Everything would have been fine with sporadic adverse comments, internationally. That's all. They would have died a natural death.

However, that's that and these problems would continue before someone shrewd and tough, calculating and decisive would take the reins in India. Currently Prime Minister Narendra Modi is definitely doing a better job and one hopes in due course, some of the problems would reach an acceptable solution.

17

Two Tourists, 40 Days

Back to our world, after 1972. I immersed myself with work as we completed 11 years of our marriage. In addition to my US-Japan-Korea-Hong Kong-Vietnam-Singapore trip, I had already visited East Germany (then divided Germany), Prague (then Czechoslovakia), and Cairo. Sadhana had not had any foreign trip till then. It was overdue and I made sure it happened, howsoever badly planned it was.

It was also a tough decision to leave the kids with *Mataji* and the neighbors (though Indrajit's family was also in Delhi but was a little far away.) We were sure that the kids would be well taken care of and since it had become a prestige issue, Sadhana and I decided to make the trip, come what may.

The itinerary we chose (also depending on the airline tickets we had and the amount of foreign money sanctioned by the Reserve Bank of India) we thought New Delhi-Cairo-Rome-Paris-London-Frankfurt-Hamburg-Munich-Prague-Warsaw-Moscow-Tashkent-Kabul and back home would be a nice and not-so-expensive tour full of adventure and education.

Little did we know that it would turn into a challenging tour requiring innovative ideas, improvisation, patience, last-minute changes, frugality, adventure, and new experience in foreign lands. We would also bear the irreplaceable loss of valuable works of art, will have to make desperate attempts to solve unexpected problems, cut short the trip and make changes in our plan. That was not all; we had to do the unthinkable - Sadhana returning to India alone and me waiting in Cairo for special efforts and arrangements in New Delhi by her, for my return.

It turned out to be not-so-wisely-and-adequately planned trip. So what!

We tripped – or made to trip – as our planning came to naught right at our first stop in Egypt. We had to accept it as a new phase of adventure and challenge. Both Sadhana and I faced the problems head-on and despite everything, made the best of the opportunities that came our way. With all that happening, Sadhana did some beautiful sketches of various places we visited, picked up a few things and gained experience. We did fairly extensive sightseeing on a limited budget and faced all the challenges with courage and lots of smiles.

Our trip resulted in a host of memories to last a lifetime. That included experience of people's behavior – good and bad both. We came to know of how lousy the French police was, how unsympathetic the French journalists were and how some Swiss workers at an eating house at the railway station – and the tourist police posted there – behaved. The cab driver was no better.

Of course, there were extremely nice people also at many places we visited. There was this nice family with kids who helped us with our bags when we were leaving their Bed-and-breakfast home, called Pension, in Berlin. There are many other pensions in several cities in Germany.

There were fellow passengers in a Prague tram car who did not allow us to pay the fare and one even got down to show us the place we were visiting, only to get back on the tram car after helping us.

Also there was a family of Indians with whom we stayed in London that took us sightseeing and insisted we extend our stay for a few days more. The lady of the house, Mrs. Sethi, wished Sadhana would stay on in London (of course with me) and open a day-care center like the one she was running.

[While staying with the Sethis, Sadhana had helped the lady take care of the kids and taught them some new games and songs. Their parents who came to pick them up were happy to know that a 'new assistant' had joined Mrs. Sethi and who had become popular with their kids in just a couple days.

That was my Sadhana who was always much sought after and loved by those who came in contact with her even just for a few days.]

More about our UK visit, later.

18

Egypt, Hospitality and Where the Problem Began

O ur first stop was Cairo (Egypt), my second visit, and the country I loved for more reasons than one. We had some good Egyptian diplomat friends in India; been to their homes and many of them visited us in ours.

There was a new concept for promoting friendship and cooperation between countries without aligning with any of the two major power blocks led by the United States and the (then) Soviet Union. Though the Non Aligned Movement (NAM) was often perceived to be favorably inclined toward the Soviet Block (USSR) it still remained non-aligned to a large extent and had a strong voice at the United Nations.

[I was fortunate to have covered some parts of the visits of the important NAM leaders to India, including Nasser of Egypt (then United Arab Republic), Tito of Yugoslavia, Soekarno of Indonesia and many others. I had attended Nasser's important press conference in Cairo also.]

On our visit, Sadhana and I were lucky to have enjoyed the hospitality of an Indian family – and a Bhatnagar for that matter – in Cairo. Mr. Bhatnagar was an engineer working for a UN project and lived there with his wife Prem (also my older sister's name) and a teenage son. They also happened to be our distant relatives we had never met. Another distant relative in Delhi had suggested we stay with the Bhatnagars in Cairo.

This family was extremely nice, hospitable and generous.

Our hosts had a domestic help, an Arab woman named Mabrooka. She was quite young, probably in her early 30s but had eight children already. They produce at a high rate, everywhere, and she was still quite young. She was nice, caring and respectful and got along with us, especially Sadhana, well.

We had good time with the Bhatnagars. They took us around the city and on some major sightseeing trips. I can never forget their love and hospitality. Later in India, I was in touch with Mr. Bhatnagar's mother who lived in Allahabad.

It's a pity we lost contact with them.

We did some sightseeing on our own and also enjoyed a camel-ride. That's just a little scary, especially when the tall animal sits down to let the riders disembark.

Our camel ride at the Pyramids had an interesting story. I had met a man who claimed to be a guide and said he would get us a car (cab) but what he got was a camel cart.

When confronted he replied: Yes, this is a car, a sand car.

We laughed the matter away and 'enjoyed' the camel-ride.

Our plans were to travel from Egypt to Italy by ship. When contacted, a travel agent in Cairo assured us of a cabin on a Greek ship that was due in about four days. We were advised to go to Alexandria to catch the ship. We did that but in Alexandria were told that we would have to share a cabin. Reluctantly, we agreed as there was no option. But we were asked to wait for a couple days more.

On a day before the arrival of the ship, finalization of our accommodation and payment of the fare (the agent was postponing the deal for obvious reasons, I think) the agent burst the bubble and told us unashamedly that there was not even the shared cabin for us on that Greek ship. He also told us that there was no other ship for the next 10 days or so.

I have not yet figured out whether I was totally naïve or the agent was absolutely a big fraud. I am inclined to vote for the first, but the agent is not much behind.

We had to return to Cairo and again stayed with the Bhatnagars for a couple days more to make plans and book seats on the flight to Rome. We didn't have air tickets for this leg. That totally upset our limited budget as airfare was much higher.

And that was the beginning of our problems. Little did I realize that not getting on the boat would make things *that* bad.

There was a bright side also: First, continued hospitality of the Bhatnagar family. Second, our good friend, the Korean ambassador to India was in

Egypt at his new post, and our contact with him continued to pay rich dividends for us.

Ambassador Woonsang Choi had come to know of our visiting Alexandria to catch the ship and insisted that we stay with his family that happened to be in that port city. We could not say no. Perhaps that was destiny otherwise we had to dish out extra money for our forced extended stay in Alexandria waiting for the ship that we never got on.

In Alexandria Mrs. Choi and their kids were, as usual, very sweet and kind. We were with them and also spent time at the private (Mamura) beach and resort of the former King Farouk of Egypt. That place had become a place for the elite. Shah Farouk was ousted as the Egyptian revolution led by Gen. Naguib and Nasser succeeded. Later Nasser prevailed and Naguib was totally sidelined, lost power and put under house arrest. Nasser had become a symbol of Arab resurgence, secularism, socialistic policies, nationalism and anti-imperialism.

[Farouk's sister Fawzia was Shah Iran's first wife.]

He died two years before we visited Egypt.

While in Cairo, Sadhana and I were invited to meet, speak and recite our poems at the Writers House, a place set up at Nasser's initiative, I was told, for writers and journalists to meet regularly.

[I had visited Egypt earlier and had been to Aswan and also had a chance to see the world-famous Abu Simbel temples, the monument built by Pharaoh (King) Ramesses II in the 13th century BC, as a magnificent and a lasting monument to himself and his queen Nefertari, to commemorate his victory at the Battle of Kadesh.

Their huge rock relief figures have become iconic.

The Egyptian Pharaohs were Sun-worshippers, just like the Hindus. Of course Hindus worship Moon also and all other planets, as they regard the whole Solar System, the stars, the galaxies and all the planets, created by God Himself.

Abu Simbel temple's entrance and the King's throne were placed in a beautifully conceived, astronomically and architecturally perfect manner where the first rays of the Sun directly reached the throne.

That was something astonishing and measured to perfection some 3500 years back.

The main temple was saved from the waters of the sprawling Lake Nasser when the Aswan High Dam was constructed by cutting the huge statues part by part and rejoined beautifully some 80 meters high up. United Nations Educational, Scientific and Cultural Organization (UNESCO) spearheaded the restoration project with help from dozens of countries, worldwide, including India. They are some of the important Heritage sites and preserved.

I had also written a poem about Abu Simbel: I recited it at the Writers house in Cairo.

[I also knew Mama Loubna –pen name of Notaila (Natilla) Rashid, a writer and editor of Dar Al Hilal publishing house of children's books. Loubna was the name of her daughter. I met Notaila in East Berlin in 1969 and renewed my friendship with her later in Cairo.]

In 1972 when both of us were in Cairo, we met Notaila, her daughter Loubna and son Hisham. Sadly we lost contact with her too and recently read that both Mama Loubna and her husband died a few years back. I don't know if Loubna is still in Egypt and what she is doing. This is life; we are like passengers on a train or bus or on a flight. We become friends for a limited time and seldom able to continue our contacts after our journey is over.

Sadhana made a few sketches while we were in Egypt. One was at Khan Khalili, a market, where Sadhana put her sketch pad on the hood of a parked car and drew. She did one sitting along the famous river Nile.

In Cairo we also met two of our old Arab friends whom we knew in India. One was Mr. Hamad, a senior diplomat in the Egyptian Embassy. (We also knew Galal Rashidi, the Press Officer of Egypt, in New Delhi.) Another was the Chief of Arab League in India, Mohammed Wahbi. Both Hamad and Wahbi were posted in Cairo. We were invited by Mr. Hamad and met his family, had a good dinner and spent a few hours at his place.

Ambassador Choi arranged a party for us and also invited some of my friends that helped enlarge his circle of Arab friends.

It was a nice re-union with old friends. This was one of the rare occasions you find your foreign friends in two different countries, re-connect with them and recall old times.

The travel problems had started in Egypt but we took things positively. We decided to make the best of everything. We thought whatever good we saw, whatever hospitality we were given and whatever made us happy we should enjoy thoroughly and cherish. We did that in plenty forgetting our problems. We had some wonderful and unforgettable experience the memories of which will never fade away.

On my previous visit in 1969 I lost two pens, one was an expensive golden Parker pen, the most popular and costly pen those days. My front coat pocket was picked in a style I had not imagined before. This happened on a street with nice shops and a diverse clientele.

Walking on the sidewalk (we call that Footpath) of one of the main roads in downtown Cairo named Qasr al-Aini, a tall man with a small box full of handkerchiefs came rushing to me with the sales pitch, "five piasters, five piasters" and brushed against me while I said no, I don't want any.

As I continued to walk he came back with the same box and the same sales pitch, "five piasters, five piasters" and again brushed against me. Annoyed with this I told him, this time rather harshly, that I don't want any and I have told you before also.

He went away and I continued my walk toward my hotel.

Once inside my room as I was taking off my jacket I noticed my two pens in the upper pocket were missing – including that prized golden Parker.

It was one of the gifts from my Korean friend, Hisook and now it was gone forever.

I realized the man selling kerchiefs had employed this trick – come rushing, brush against my jacket and with the sharp ends of the tin box, snatch my pens. Probably at his first attempt he got the not-so-expensive pen. His next attempt yielded the costly one.

I couldn't think of doing anything but to feel sad at this loss, an expensive pen and that too a gift. I generally didn't carry that pen in India, but thought in a nice and safe place in Cairo my prized possessions would be safe.

Sadly, I was mistaken.

Two days later I was talking to the press chief and casually mentioned the robbery. To my astonishment – and regret – he said, why didn't you let me know as soon as it happened. We know where these costly things are sold and we might have recovered your costly pen.

Well, the robbery had happened and I didn't react quickly. A lesson learnt, used later but sadly, that yielded no result. But that's another story, later.]

I didn't have the opportunity to visit Egypt after that but what I read now makes me think twice before planning to visit one of my favorite places. There life is much more dreadful with uprising, shootings, arrests and unrest of all kinds, change of governments, rise of fanaticism, jihadi terrorism, and much more.

A country that used to get millions of tourists has become one of the hotbeds of extremism and non-Muslims are harassed, and killed. This was not the Egypt that I saw, stayed and admired. This is not the Egypt during Shah Farouk's regime or when President Nasser was at the helm of affairs. Whatever you may say even during Hosni Mubarak's presidency things were much better for two decades.

Now I don't know if the extremists would allow the new regime of President el-Sisi to function in a peaceful, secular and orderly manner. I hope and wish, but I am not absolutely sure.

Wish things change for the better and stability returns sooner than I fear.

19

Beautiful Rome and Geneva Adventure

Our budget was already upset as we had to take a flight instead of the boat, but under the circumstances there was no other option. We adopted an attitude of *dekha jayega* (we shall see.)

The flight from Cairo to Rome was otherwise uneventful except that the Al Italia plane was built to accommodate more passengers – with less leg room but more money.

We were warned to be extra careful in Rome and that your pockets might be picked and handbags snatched. We had become extra careful but nothing like that happened in our three-day stay.

In Rome several roads are narrow and most of the cars quite small. Roadside parking was almost bumper to bumper but the steering system enabled cars to be safely maneuvered in small spaces. This was something interesting and ingenuous and an appropriate solution to parking problems.

We took sightseeing tours to the Colosseum and The Vatican, St. Peter's, Sistine Chapel, the Dome, the Pieta, the famous ceiling and so on by the world famous Michelangelo. This genius painter, sculptor – and also a poet – was born in 1475 and was acclaimed as the greatest artist of his age while still in his teens.

According to reidsitaly.com "Michelangelo Buonarotti was the greatest of all Renaissance masters. Supremely talented, divinely inspired, both a great craftsman and insightful innovator, seemingly able to master effortlessly any artistic pursuit he attempted, he would become the High Renaissance's greatest painter and sculptor, and renowned architect, and trusted military engineer."

Yes, his paintings, frescoes, and sculptures in the Italian capital are superb by any standard.

We were keen to see all these masterly works. My talented artist wife was more interested in them and we both were charmed beyond words.

[Incidentally our guide on the most important sightseeing tour was a noted historian, a lady of great knowledge and excellent English. We thoroughly enjoyed the tour and her commentary/explanations.]

We also visited the world famous Trevi Fountain, 86 feet high, 161.3 feet wide. Several movies have featured this fountain, one of which is the eponymous *Three Coins in the Fountain.*

The fountain is also popular for people putting coins in it and making a wish. We both wished (later revealed) for our lasting love and for earnest wish to walk life's road together, hand-in-hand, till eternity.

Some wishes do come true – some remain unfulfilled because that's God's planning. *Kabhi kisi ko mukammal jahaan naheen milta* (you don't get everything you want.) All wishes don't come true. We were happy to make our wishes, though.

We were fascinated by Rome and made the most of our three-day stay, without losing anything, except a part of our hearts.

The trip to Switzerland with all the visions of a beautiful country and its legendary neutrality, the great watches, popular cheese, and greater Swiss banks with trillions of world's 'black money' and so on was fascinating.

We decided to stop in Geneva and spend some time there.

However, like some of the other parts of our ill-organized tour, we found ourselves with a problem at the Geneva airport itself. As we landed and went to the required immigration counter we were asked for our Swiss visa – we didn't have one. I had presumed that for a neutral country and tourists' paradise travelers like us would not need a visa.

I was shocked at my naiveté again.

However, there was a silver lining. The immigration officer asked us about our stay and I said – under the circumstances – just one day.

He was kind – or was that the rule – he saw our tickets, passports etc. and kept everything with him and gave us the permission to spend 24 hours visa-free and told us to get our things back for our outward flight, the next day.

Happy at this turn of events I told Sadhana, here we come and enjoy what we have. She was game for everything.

Depositing our luggage in the airport lockers off we went to paint the city red, green, white, orange or what have you.

We did not know what was in store for us.

The first thing was to find a place to stay. Looking for a pension-like place (bed-and breakfast) we took a taxi cab and told the driver to look for one which he said he knew. As we started I checked the meter and thought the starting amount to be a little high. When I asked the driver how much does the meter show at the start, he seemed very upset.

I explained to him that I was just asking a simple question. Either he did not know English, or had a fight with his wife, or the previous passenger did not give him a tip, whatever, he became more aggressive and even said he would call the police.

After the polite and considerate immigration officer, the second Swiss was different. We said we don't want to go further. We paid him off and after a few minutes found another cab and found the place we were looking for.

The story had another turn.

We didn't like the place and decided to go to the railway station and have something to eat.

More was to come.

At the station we went to a small eating joint and finding not much for us vegetarians in the menu, asked the man for two veggie sandwiches, telling specifically, no meat, no fish, no chicken, only veg.

What came was sandwich with ham in it.

We protested and reminded him about our veg order. He obligingly took out the piece of ham from the sandwiches and said, okay, take it.

Shocked and upset at this, we protested but he stuck to his point, I have taken out ham, you can eat your Veggie sandwich now.

When we argued, his stock answer was, no English, speak no English.

An officer with a 'Tourist Police' badge was at hand but was absolutely unhelpful. The restaurant neither replaced our sandwich, nor even returned our money.

We were shocked further and upset that even a Tourist Police officer was there just in name. What kind of Swiss hospitality it was, we wondered!

We had to seek another place and managed with something resembling toast and fries to fill our tummies.

Well, our spirits were down but still we went to see the surrounding area, the shops and the market without bothering to look for other landmarks for which we had no appetite left. We just had to pass the remaining few hours till the next morning.

We did go to a nearby hotel and found that a night's stay would cost us – without food – 45 Swiss Francs.

We did some window-shopping and also went inside a jewelry store to look for something Sadhana had seen with someone, sometime back. I knew that – it was a ring-watch. A lid opens and you have the watch. Close the lid and wear it as a ring. It was real good one and we found one at one of the stores we visited.

The price was exactly 45 Francs.

Sadhana had liked that but never asked me for it; she was always thinking for others. Of course she loved sarees, purses, shoes, shawls and jewelry too, but would always keep the family finances in mind – always balance the budget.

On this trip everything was not going well but we were still managing and still enjoying the adventure. Geneva was one such place, of course with a difference.

After we had our 'window shopping' trip we managed to get something to eat. It was now the time to decide where to stay the night. But before that we thought we could watch a late night movie – the theater was also very near, at walking distance from the station – and then go straight to the airport for our early morning flight.

Something struck me. I asked Sadhana to wait for me at the theater gate and made a quick trip to the same jewelry store and bought the 45 Franc ring-watch. I was very happy.

Returning from the store I put the ring watch on my dear wife's finger and watched her reaction – happy, yet curiously surprising smile and a loving look for me to enjoy the moment. I couldn't think of a better gift for Sadhana at that time, and thought, hell with the hotel room just for a few hours. No, no.

We settled for some more adventure.

We had become familiar with our surroundings around the railway station. As in India, that Swiss railway station also had hundreds of waiting passengers on the platforms – some sleeping on the benches, some loitering. We also managed to settle on one of the benches and tried to take a nap.

Things were much orderly, peaceful and crime-free those days.

At dead of night there was an announcement for us, some 200 passengers on the platform, to clear the benches and leave the platform. No rounding up of us, stray passengers and loitering dozens. It was just for the routine clean-up with water hoses and we were free to come back in a couple hours when the clean-up was done.

You could see the happy, singing, cheering crowd of adventurous passengers – including us – roaming about the nearby streets of Geneva, enjoying the beautiful night singing and joining others, late night (almost 2 in the morning) stroll. There was a big group of people, but none rowdy or unduly boisterous. It was sheer fun.

Around four the whole group returned to the clean and tidy station for a quick nap. We did the same and by the first rays of the Sun we were on our way to the airport. The rest rooms were waiting for us; we freshened up, had our simple and inexpensive breakfast of toast and tea and got ready for the flight.

Everything at the airport was as we left them. We got our bags, tickets and passports thanked the officer before boarding the flight to Paris.

The enchanting city of Paris was waiting for us. The capital of France has fascinated the world. We were not the exceptions. We looked forward to our three-day stay in Paris, regarded as the Cultural Capital of Europe with all its fashion, history and glory.

20

The Memories of Paris, a Bad Dream

Paris is loved by millions, and for the right reasons I guess. Our excitement was also natural. It's a city of joy, for art-lovers, for its history and culture and so on.

We were in Paris around the national day – July 14th, Storming of the Bastille – the right time and occasion to be in Paris. The record says that "on 14 July 1789, a state prison on the east side of Paris, known as the Bastille, was attacked by an angry and aggressive mob. The prison had become a symbol of the monarchy's dictatorial rule, and the event became one of the defining moments in the Revolution that followed," (*Wikipedia*).

We took a taxi cab at the Charles de Gaulle airport and reached the hotel. Got our bags out and checked at the reception. And just at that moment it struck me that a rolled bundle of Sadhana's paintings, mostly water color on paper, some on canvas, was left behind our seats in the cab.

Our hearts sank.

These paintings were invaluable to Sadhana and me. Many were done before our marriage and so were cherished even more. We had displayed them in Cairo, at the Writers House – could not do it in Rome. In Cairo there were offers from admirers to purchase them – at attractive price. We were not selling them and planned to have mini exhibitions on our stops, all over Europe and elsewhere.

The loss was devastating, but I thought there was hope.

Fortunately, I remembered the logo on a small flag atop the cab hood – Slota Company.

The hotel receptionist was nice and connected me to the company's office. They acknowledged that a cab had picked us up from the airport and dropped us at the hotel. They also said that after dropping us the driver returned to the office, deposited (parked) the cab at the office parking lot but has gone on vacation.

There was no mention of the bundle of paintings but we were assured that when the driver returns on duty they will ask him about our paintings and get back to us.

That day didn't come. There was no contact for three days.

As an additional precaution we went to the nearest police station and lodged a complaint with some details. We were assured that French Police would be on the case and will locate the driver and get back to us.

That day also did not come.

The French Police might still be trying to locate *us*, not the driver. Or some police officers have retired, some promoted, and some.....

[We didn't want to give up. We called the Paris police station from London but got no helpful or positive response. The driver would have returned to his duty, or he also quit, retired, moved elsewhere or....]

An additional shock was the attitude of French journalists. We also went to the office of France-Soir, a popular and highly circulated newspaper, hoping to meet with sympathetic and helpful fellow-journalists. We were disappointed, shocked and got no sympathy, no help. On top of it we heard a remark that the French are art-lovers, you can hope to get back a packet of diamonds but art... that's different.

I told Sadhana and she agreed – that if a French tourist had faced a similar situation in India and had approached me – or any newspaper staffer – he/she would be immediately helped to get lost things back. I, or my other colleagues, would contact the Police, personally speak to the officer-in-charge – or even the top official – and the cab company, and pursue the case till things were restored to the rightful owner, the complainant.

But Paris and its officials broke our hearts. Our three-day Paris stay was totally ruined. We were devastated. Sadhana was heartbroken. Her water colors with Indian themes were precious and she had devoted weeks and months to complete them. Oil paintings, to her, were easier and quicker to make but water colors were different. We were sad, disappointed and also mad. We hated Paris, hated France.

The last day of our stay, the third day, and time to depart! We had not done any sightseeing – no museum, no visit to the world famous art museum Louvre which, on any other day, Sadhana would not have missed for anything. All those were pointless for us, out of our wish-list. The only thing I could think of, and wanted for Sadhana, was to at least visit the impressive Eiffel Tower.

I persuaded Sadhana to see The Tower, if not anything else. We should at least have something else to tell our friends and kids about our stay in France apart from the terrible loss.

The Eiffel Tower is undoubtedly an impressive monument of engineering miracle, towering above the city this is a world famous tourist center. It's a symbol of Paris, of France. We did go up on The Tower, but our spirits were still down.

After the brief visit it was time to dash to the airport to catch a flight to London. The traffic was heavy with returning holiday crowds but our eyes were, kind of, looking for the cab that was the key to our lost paintings.

We were not destined to see them again, though I still hope against hope that someday, somewhere on my unlikely visit to Paris, I might see some of Sadhana's art work in a shop, a home or a museum.

They have got to be in France and someone might have laid his or her hands on them, and might still be enjoying and appreciating.

So be it.

They were indeed beautifully done, passionately preserved, heartily admired by those who saw them, but lost by *me* not being adequately alert on that fateful day in the capital city of France.

This regret still haunts me. Sadhana lost interest in painting and sketching for quite some time. It was difficult to forgive myself for the lapse. It was not possible to get over this loss for Sadhana. She did not paint for years after that terrible loss.

It was a superhuman effort when Sadhana put aside this terrible loss and did some *sketches* in London, Berlin and Prague that we visited after the Paris disaster.

21

London, Germany and Unforgettable Prague

Visiting London was a different experience. The capital city of England that ruled over India for some two hundred years and left in our lifetime was, in a way, the center of the world. London has history, old relations, particularly with India and Indians. During the British rule, London was the most visited city and England the most visited country for Indians. Anyone going out of India would go to London, England. Students, politicians, business people, writers in English language, all were attracted to England. Such was the 'charm' of London, England.

While staying in Ramesh Nagar one of our favorite cloth merchants in the nearby market was one Mr. Sethi. Even when we moved to Rajori Garden, Sadhana and the kids would often go shopping and meeting with the Sethis. Basic Indian culture was – still is, by and large – to treat others as members of our own family. The young or old people we knew were either our brothers or sisters, sons or daughters, uncles and aunties and *Bhais* (brothers) and *Bhabhis* (sisters-in-law).

The Sethis also were like family. They had an older brother living in London and when our friend came to know about our plans he made sure that we stay with his brother. He would not listen to any excuse, we did not offer many.

In London, therefore, we were treated as family of the senior Sethi and his wife whom we had not seen before in India. This is the depth of family relations and traditional hospitality among the traditional Indians.

The Sethis were traditional, though living in England for ages, and were British citizens.

Mrs. Sethi ran a day-care facility at home; Mr. Sethi worked at Heathrow, the world's busiest Airport.

We had quite a few days stay with the Sethis and Sadhana soon had endeared herself to everyone in that home and in the neighborhood. The kids told their parents how a new 'Ma'am' took care of them, how she taught them new songs and entertained them. So much so that Mrs. Sethi asked Sadhana many times to manage to stay on in London and help her to expand her day-care facility where she could earn a lot of money; or better, open her own day-care.

Sadhana thanked her profusely but we had other plans.

Our efforts to get any information from the French Police on our complaint about lost paintings did not yield any results. We decided to make the best of our stay in London with visits to Hyde Park, see the Crown Jewels, including the famous Koh-i-Noor diamond (on the Queen's crown), 'gifted' by a hapless Indian Maharaja to the British. We also toured the city to see the other landmarks and Sadhana took time to sketch Buckingham Palace sitting on the grass across from the historic home of the Queen. She also did the Big Ben and the Parliament House.

[I still have the original sketches though I have been seriously thinking of sending them to the Queen. I am sure Sadhana would have approved and liked the idea.]

While in London we had to rethink about our plans for continuing with the trip. We met one of our 'adopted' brothers, Ratan (who also went with my party to Dehradun and had attended our wedding.) He was staying and working in London.

However he wasn't much help in re-setting our trip or our messed up budget. But that was okay. People have their own priorities and demands. We had set out on our own and were determined to continue the trip on a shoe-string budget, cut down the expenses where we could, and make it enjoyable to the extent possible.

Of course there was no other option.

The trips to German cities of Frankfurt, Hamburg, Berlin and Munich were intact and we enjoyed our stay in either Pensions or smaller hotels. Pensions were a unique experience for us staying with families who provided their spare rooms and breakfast at affordable rates. You get to know how a typical middle class German family lived, and we were happy about it. At one such pension two small kids even helped us with loading our bags in the cab when we were leaving. Of course, not all pensions are similar, some good, some not so good as we saw in Geneva.

We went sightseeing and Sadhana mustered some inner strength to do sketches – I dutifully, and happily, carried her sketch-book and pens. It was my love for her, my appreciation for her, and my contribution to her endeavor coupled with her own determination that the *Show Must Go On.*

We also visited the Munich Olympic stadium where a month later, at the 1972 Olympic Games, a group of Palestinian terrorists did a horrible and shameless act of violence. The German security was not extra tight, probably because an attack on the Olympic Village was unheard of, and never expected. Taking advantage, the Arab terrorists sneaked into the living quarters of Israeli athletes, took 11 of them hostage and following a failed rescue effort by the German police, killed them all.

It was the first such attack on athletes at the Olympics and was condemned worldwide.

Olympic Games are cherished events when the youth of the world come together in friendship and amity to peacefully, and happily, though vigorously, compete with each other in sports, win medals, make life-long friends and depart with lasting memories. The viewers at the site, and worldwide on TV also, enjoy and cherish the unique meeting of sportsmen and women from 150 plus nations to showcase their talent and hard-work in a spirit of friendship and healthy rivalry.

Only deranged, crazy, selfish, hateful, vile, despicable and devilish, utterly brainwashed and fanatic thugs following extremist teachings would do those horrendous crimes against humanity.

[Sadly, the civilized world did not have the will to take on the terrorists and take decisive action to see that it did not face such acts in future. The killings, taking hostages and destroying indiscriminately continued and escalated. That trend has resulted in more killings and more destruction.

Even (New York) Twin Towers destruction and killings, the Mumbai Massacre and thousands of other incidents since then, worldwide, have shown that the initial hesitation, inaction and indecisiveness paved the way for more disasters. The civilized, peace-loving world failed to act together and rid the world of the scourge of Jihadi terror. Terrorism has grown to horrendous proportions with attacks, killings, infiltration of millions of 'refugees' and unsettling of nations worldwide.]

Back to our trip. We did a lot of sightseeing in Germany and Sadhana made sketches, though she was not very enthusiastic about doing that after the Paris fiasco. But, as I have always maintained, she was a fighter, a doer and a strong person set to face challenges and losses and rise again, like a Sphinx.

I have always been very proud of my dear Sadhana.

[We didn't have much time to extensively tour Germany and meet some people I wanted very much to meet. One was Professor Anita Bose, the daughter of Netaji Subhas Bose, my hero of India's freedom struggle. I had met and interviewed Anita in New Delhi and wanted to renew my contact. Then there was my other hero, Dr. Lohia's Humboldt University, where he did his Ph.D., I liked to visit.

I could not do all that. And in life, you seldom get a second chance.

I have been a rarity: I got many chances of visiting Cairo; same for Seoul and also Prague. But there are many more places I have been missing with no hope of ever visiting those places, meetings those people. Again, that's life.]

Our next destination was Prague, the Czechoslovak capital. The country, its people, my admiration for and friendship with many, had attracted me again, this time with Sadhana. She was not disappointed. Though we could not see many of our friends we made in India, we managed to meet with one couple, but not before another round of adventure as we crossed the border into Czechoslovakia (now the Czech Republic).

We had planned to take a train from Frankfurt to Prague, the most convenient and cheaper method. We decided on the night train to avoid another night's stay in a hotel. We reached the station to catch the train a little past midnight that will take us to Prague the following morning.

We had a few hours to spend and we made ourselves as comfortable as we could on the station bench. As at other stations this one was also crowded with many sleeping on the floor. One next to our bench had too much beer – it's said that the Germans and the Australians drink so much beer in a year that can drown their countries. And that's a lot of beer.

Good, we do not contribute to the possible drowning of these two great countries though thousands of miles from each other.

Of course we couldn't ignore the man sleeping dead drunk on the floor next to us. He didn't know anything about what was happening with him, the streams that could have drowned him – well not really – but succeeded in soaking him wet.

192

That was some experience but that's not abnormal when you are at the railway station saving hotel charges.

Our train came around 2 A.M. and just a few passengers alighted at somewhat deserted – but safe – station, and probably, we were the only ones to board it.

Nothing significant happened till the train stopped at the German-Czech border station for immigration and customs officers to board and check papers and do all the other formalities. It was a half-hour or so stop for doing all the formalities.

We were not worried as in this case we had a four-day visa for our visit.

A smart young officer boarded our compartment, saluted us (the normal, welcome-courtesy we don't see on Indian railways.) He checked our passports and visa and asked us to pay $32, four dollars per person for four days stay. This was the rule to, probably, guarantee that we were bringing, and would use, legitimate money. We had paid the Czech embassy no fee in New Delhi for our visas and I could not figure out the necessity to pay anything at the border, especially with the state of our fast depleting funds.

But obviously that *was* the rule, the *law* and it was *clearly mentioned on our visa*. The officer showed it and insisted that we paid, and paid right then and there.

I refused. My point was that India and Czechoslovakia had a Rupee Agreement and all the transactions/payments would be only in Rupees and not dollars or pounds, or any other foreign currency. I would change my Rupees into Czech Crowns in Prague, officially, I told him.

The officer disagreed and on my refusal warned me of action and got out to bring a senior officer.

In came the senior officer (a uniformed officer like the other one, with more stars) and curtly asked me to take our luggage and get down from the train, immediately.

I stood my ground. I explained to him about the Rupee Agreement but he insisted that we take down our bags and detrain or we would be arrested since we were not paying 32 dollars, the required fee.

Sadhana must have felt a little uneasy but she had full faith in what I was doing and confident that what I was doing was right. And I was right about the Rupee Agreement between the two countries.

[The officers did not know my weak point and I was not in a mood to let them know.]

The argument continued and I told him with a resolute straight face that he was free to take down our luggage and throw us in jail. I also warned him that when we come out of the jail we will raise a hue and cry and launch a vigorous protest as the two governments are legally bound by the Rupee Agreement.

I was not going to pay in dollars.

Seeing my tough stand the senior officer thought he might land in trouble for violating *the Agreement*. But he had to save his skin also and said: In that case will you change your Rupees in the local currency *through a bank* in the city?

[There might be unauthorized transactions and I thought he wanted to ensure that my transactions would be authorized through a bank, not from a roadside money-exchanger, if there was any]

I did not have any objection to that and the matter was settled. Sadhana heaved a sigh of relief and looked at me with loving and admiring glances for putting up a fight on a foreign land and winning the battle. Fellow passengers also seemed to be quite impressed and the train was on its final short journey to Prague station.

[I admitted to Sadhana, and I can now admit to all, that *my weak point* was that I did not have *even the Indian Rupees to convert*, if that officer had asked for them. The Rupee permit - with the sanctioned amount – was *not* in my hand. It was mailed to me care of Indian Embassy in Prague, and was supposed to be waiting for me there, when I was arguing with the officer at the border.]

We reached Prague on a Saturday; that meant the Embassy was closed, only to be opened on Monday. We had a full Saturday and Sunday to stay in Prague, eat and see the city sights – without any local currency. We had dollars that we were clinging to in case of Emergency only (like if the officer at the border was adamant and had not accepted my Rupee Agreement point, I had to dish out 32 dollars.)

Despite having no local money, and our reluctance to spend dollars, the beautiful experience of our stay in Prague was free of problems, unbelievably sweet and absolutely memorable.

For two days and nights we had best of breakfast, lunch and dinners; we went sightseeing by bus and sometimes by taxi with the local money – Koruna or Crowns – that we did not change with Rupees, *but were given by the hotel*.

We did not ask for it.

That was something unexpected and that needs some explanation.

I had stayed in 1969 on my first visit to Prague at the same Crown Hotel. I/we checked into the same hotel again, in 1972. Earlier the room-rate included breakfast. Now with the higher room-rate you got breakfast, lunch and dinner.

[The hotel has since changed its name to Hotel Crown Plaza.]

The other advantage of this hotel was that rates were quite less if you didn't insist on an attached bath. Who needs a 'separate, exclusive' bath as most of the time you are out and you need the bathroom only in the morning or at night. We found this arrangement very convenient and opted for it. The unattached (common) bathroom, just four steps away from our room, was always at our disposal as our waking time was different from the other guests.

This also helped us immensely with our limited budget.

Now another beautiful, interesting and especially valuable part:

As soon as we checked-in we were given coupons for 24 meals (three meals, each day for two people for four days). Each meal-coupon had a certain money- value. That's how the Hotel planned to make more money because the guests would not eat out and would like to come back and eat in-house. If they don't return and eat out, too bad, they lose that money.

Since we were vegetarians our meals were less costly and so when we gave coupons to pay for our breakfast, lunch and dinner, we got the *difference - in cash, in the local currency - Crown*.

So, for those meals we kept on getting back cash in local currency. It was enough for our bus or taxi ride in the city for two full days till Monday when we got our Rupee permit packet, fortunately, waiting at the Indian Embassy. Of course, the hotel meal coupons-cash back continued as we made it a point to return to the Hotel for food as far as possible. Hurrah!

We took that as the compensation for our problems and difficulties encountered earlier on this trip – and laughed. We were adventure-loving couple who would find laughter amid tears and strength in the face of any problems – come what may.

That nature also helped us all along the journey of life, everywhere.

I will not forgive myself if I don't mention the hotel restaurant's waiter (sorry pal, I don't remember your name, probably Sadhana would) who was the first to wait upon us as we went for breakfast soon after we checked-in and freshened up.

Finding us a little confused with the menu items – and telling him that we were vegetarians – he said he could get us something satisfying if we would wait for 15 minutes. What he brought was a delight and remained our main dish throughout our stay at the hotel.

Picture this: before us a plate of two, baked, crisp, vegetable cutlets with stuffed potatoes, little rice, and some other vegs, and as you cut it open a small piece of butter, still not fully melted, looking at you with inviting eyes! The shape was great, cooked and warm just right and the taste, out of this world. Sadhana and I agreed that they were the best vegetable cutlets we had ever eaten anywhere.

And they were quite filling too.

Thank you my waiter friend. Many thanks to you, Crown Hotel's main restaurant in Prague!

Sorry, I wasn't able to visit you again since those memorable trips in 1969 and 1972.

In Prague there is so much to see, the Prague Castle, the Museum, Charles Bridge and the Old Town Square, Wenceslas square, the famous Big Clock where hundreds gather at every hour to see and hear something spectacular. At the stroke of the hour, a door on the face of the clock opens, a figure pops up there, another one appears elsewhere, and yet another figure shows up at another place – all on the clock. It is a beautiful and memorable sight for a few minutes till the hour-bells stop ringing. This is repeated every hour.

[Our visit to Prague is also full of memories that after 44 years could put a smile on the face of my sick wife when a physical therapist came to help her and I told her that she is from Prague. Sadhana's face lit up with sweet memories of the beautiful city and its pretty nice people. Those memories helped Sadhana to happily and willingly respond and do whatever Pavla Gould, the PT lady, wanted her to do.

This happened just a few days before she was taken to the hospital, never to come out alive. It was Sadhana's last PT with Pavla. Sadhana gave her a hug and smile and got the same from Gould. Sujata had made a video of Sadhana's exercises and had given it to Pavla to show that to her supervisor. We also showed it to the doctors, to prove that Sadhana was capable of doing that and was gaining strength.

Alas, PT was for a fixed duration and could not continue because of the government rules.

Thank you Prague, thank you Pavla Gould from Prague. You put, probably, the last smiles on Sadhana's face before she said final good bye to all of us.]

When I visited Prague in 1969 I wanted to see Alexander Dubcek who had led the 'Spring Revolution' in 1968 against the occupation by the then Soviet Union. The USSR had sent tanks, replaced and arrested Dubcek and planted their own man, Gustav Husak, as the President.

I was advised against trying to contact Dubcek as that would further make his life miserable. The same was with my friend, the senior most diplomat (acting Ambassador Smysl in New Delhi who was recalled and fired, and probably sent to a factory as ordinary worker, after the Spring uprising was suppressed.

The theaters in 1969 were still showing a quick history-reminder, just a momentary flick with the dates (1938-1968) on their screens. It was to remind the viewers of Hitler's invasion and annexation in 1938 and later of the Soviet's invasion and suppression in 1968.

In 1972, Sadhana and I were, similarly, advised not to seek out and meet Mrs. Smysl and their two kids whom we had welcomed in New Delhi and I had managed to meet during my visit in 1969, a few months after the uprising and suppression in 1968. I had admired the spirit of the people then. Sadhana and I fell in love with the country and its people, again, in 1972.

The only contact with like-minded couple I managed to locate was with Marie Hlavachkova and her husband. Marie was working for the official radio and she and her husband fully shared our views about freedom and democracy, human rights and opposition to Soviet hegemony.

They took us to a restaurant quite far away from the city where we spent some time talking freely and having a nice outing and lunch. On the same outing we saw the famous Tatra (or Tatri) mountains. Sadhana made a partial, hurried, sketch and completed the oil painting of the Mountain when she was back in India. We still have the original with us – only a few out of dozens of beautiful originals.

Alas, I have had no contact with any of those nice friends even after the dissolution of the Soviet Empire in 1993 and emergence of a free Czech Republic, and the Slovak Republic. In the Embassy in India there were some from both the regions.

[In 1969 when I managed to get a visa and visited Prague (returning from a week-long visit to East Germany on the government's invitation) I had managed to meet with Mrs. Smysl at her home.

As was natural, we took some fifteen minutes to assess the other sides' views on the current situation (the Soviet re-assertion of overlordship and imminent firing of my friend, acting ambassador Mr. Smysl (in India). Soon we connected and then for quite a long time talked about the current situation and the future.

Mrs. Smysl was sad and gloomy. I cheered her up with a positive stand and, kind of, clear prediction. When she expressed her pessimism and asked in a resigned demeanor: "Mr. Bhatnagar, will we ever be free?"

I could read clearly how disheartened and disappointed she was with the situation but I, as usual, keeping up the spirits, told her my prediction, with conviction: "My friend, 10 or 20 years are nothing in the life of a nation. You will be free."

Some prophecy that was!

The Soviet Union started to disintegrate in 1989, exactly 20 years after my 'prediction.' The process took two more years to complete and the 15 countries became fully independent, free of Soviet domination. The Union of Soviet Socialist Republics was reduced to the Russian federation, or simply, Russia.

The 'Velvet Revolution' in Czechoslovakia in 1991 was followed by the 'Velvet Divorce' in another two years. The country split into two, the Czech Republic and the Slovak Republic. This was the first Partition/ Division without any bloodshed; it was done peacefully with the consent of the people and the political parties.]

Back to 1972: Our stay in beautiful Prague was coming to an end; days had passed quickly.

Sadhana had a ticket right up to New Delhi but I had no ticket from Cairo to New Delhi. What was left with me was Prague-Cairo ticket only. According to our original plans, we were supposed to go from Prague to Warsaw (Poland) and then on to Moscow, Tashkent, Kabul and back to India. We planned to spend our own money and travel by train to some of these places and then back in India – without using Sadhana's Cairo-Delhi air ticket.

Now, that was not possible with the original plan failing right in the beginning, and right from Cairo, thanks to the Egyptian agent messing up with the Greek ship. A better planning right from Delhi could have averted all that mess, but that's life. You slip up, make mistakes, and face the challenges, and continue.

We did all that. We did our best, and we still enjoyed the adventure and never allowed the situation and problems to overwhelm us.

And we were still young and healthy. Not once we had any health problem traveling thousands of miles, sleeping and not sleeping, walking miles, eating different things and sometimes not eating enough. But that was a part of our adventure, a beautiful part of our being together and sharing whatever we were offered, with loving smiles and loud laughter. *Dekha jayega* (we shall see) was fine, our *Mantra*, our inspiration to make the best of a bad bargain.

22

Trouble, Air India's Help in Prague, Geneva

Not having my return ticket to Delhi became quite a serious problem. We rescheduled our trips and dropped Warsaw, Tashkent and Kabul part and started thinking about returning to Cairo and back to Delhi. There was no direct Prague-Delhi Air India flight. We managed Prague-Cairo but the problem was till I got permission from New Delhi – and a Cairo-Delhi ticket - I would be stranded in Cairo. It could be a couple days or couple weeks, we didn't know, and of course, our treasury was getting empty at a rate faster than…well you know.

I contacted Air India office in Prague (luckily they had one) and met extremely helpful staff – and beautiful Czech women working there – who did their best continuously for a couple days to sort things out and obtain a ticket for me. As things turned out, nobody in India, not even the Minister of Tourism and Civil Aviation, Dr. (Maharaja) Karan Singh could, or would, help. I knew the Minister personally and thought it should be a piece of cake for him to get me an Air India ticket on deferred payment or could make some other suitable arrangement.

I still don't know what really was lacking and was required of me to obtain a Cairo-Delhi ticket while in Prague or Cairo? Was it bureaucracy, or inefficiency in India, or strict rules? I don't know but they posed a big problem for me.

It was left to Sadhana and her determination to fight the odds and get me back in India, within a few days.

We got back to Cairo but before that yet another piece of adventure awaited us and, for a change, this was a pleasant one without us paying anything anywhere.

The flight we took from Prague to Cairo, (paid by us) was via Geneva, for some strange reason. I don't remember exactly why and how that happened, but as they say, everything happens for a reason. After these many years (1972-2017) some memories do fade.

On the Prague-Geneva flight we met two Indians. One was a serving military officer, Major General Williams, and the other a senior Defense Ministry official, Mr. Jain, a Joint Secretary. In Indian system a Joint Secretary is a big boss, head of a wing of a department, something like an assistant under secretary in UK, or an officer in the senior executive Service in the US. He is like a CEO of a wing of a department. There are several Joint Secretaries but Jain must be more important to have been included in the delegation to Moscow.

[All this I mention for a reason.]

Both were returning from Moscow where they were part of the official Indian Defense Ministry delegation headed by Jagjivan Ram, the Minister. After the Moscow meeting the duo decided to spend a couple days elsewhere before returning home. The Minister returned on a direct flight to Delhi.

Williams was a lively and knowledgeable person, quite opposite of Jain. We started talking and became friendly. I was sitting with the Army officer while Sadhana was with Mr. Jain, who she thought was a little boring for a senior officer.

Williams and I got along well and discussed things. We had a few hours to reach and then the better part of the day to spend at the airport to catch the next flight to Delhi via Cairo where I had to break journey and Sadhana had to proceed.

Major General Williams and I were unhappy about the unnecessary idle hours at Geneva airport. We thought about a plan and Williams took the initiative. He talked to Air India Manager at the airport. We were to catch an Air India flight and entitled to some perks, we thought. Williams used his charmingly effective conversational skill and convinced Air India official to arrange for us – all four of us – a short tour of the city to utilize the idle time.

The fact that the two officers were on an official government visit and returning to India, and the way Williams must have talked, resulted in us getting a cab and a short tour of the city - courtesy Air India.

[I wish Major General Williams was the Chief Negotiator with enemies; we would not have to wage wars to settle disputes.]

It was, for us, the second part of our Geneva trip and Sadhana and I enjoyed it thoroughly. The driver seemed a perfectly knowledgeable tour guide and described important places, buildings etc. and their role in national and international events in the past, and their use in the present.

Geneva also has a sizable United Nations presence with offices and big staff. It's actually the second biggest UN center after the one in New York, USA, with many specialized agencies and program headquarters. The driver described in details about various important conferences held there. We stopped at some places, and parks, to do some walking also – though Jain *Sahab* was not much enthusiastic about that.

Williams told me about some civilians in the Defense Ministry who, by virtue of their seniority, were at higher posts but did not know much about how the armed forces worked or what their needs were. Probably those people were exceptions; the people I have encountered in India's various government departments have been, by and large, extremely knowledgeable and quite efficient in their jobs.

Of course, exceptions are always there.

Williams gave me the example of a senior officer who wondered why the army units need to conduct periodic training in various parts of the country – and even abroad. He naively asked: "Are our soldiers untrained?"

He had to be educated that troops need to be updated with new equipment, new methods, new tactics, new terrains and new strategies and frequently; and that they have to be trained in varying seasons and at particular places. It's a constant exercise, all the time.

The military has to be kept always battle-fit. That's what training is – a must for every country.

There was another who wondered why the equipment being sent with the troops for a certain mission to a certain post included a dentist's chair?

The answer was that a soldier will not be fighting-fit if he had a bad toothache. The dentist would not be able to do his work properly without the special chair.

It was education for those less-than-expert officers – and also for us – directly from a senior military officer with considerable experience.

The flight to Cairo was otherwise uneventful only that Mr. Jain would not stop talking and would not allow Sadhana to take a nap. Some time she pretended to be sleeping, and let him also doze off. Otherwise Jain was also a nice person, only a little naïve and, probably, was on his first foreign trip.

It was the first for Sadhana also but she never showed it.

At Cairo airport I had to deplane leaving almost all the bags for Sadhana to take to Delhi. I did not know how long I had to stay in Cairo and I didn't want to have more bags than I thought I could handle. I asked Mr. Jain to help Sadhana if she needed it in taking her baggage, and going through custom-immigration formalities, in Delhi.

Sadhana gave me a report of that 'help' when I was back in India. She told me that as soon as the flight landed at Delhi airport and passengers started lining up for immigration - custom and so on, Jain *Sahab* was nowhere to be seen.

Actually at one point before all that, Mr. Jain had even asked Sadhana to carry one of his bags, and she obliged.

With no one to help, Sadhana managed everything herself.

It took Sadhana quite a few days to get the permission and ticket for me. She went to the Reserve Bank of India for the required P form and had to forcefully argue with the officer about it. She didn't want money, only a piece of paper. She told him point blank: You want an Indian citizen to be stranded in a foreign country indefinitely and you would do nothing? That's not acceptable to me.

She finally got the papers signed and managed to arrange a ticket for me.

Meanwhile in Cairo, though I did contact our host, the Bhatnagar family, who graciously invited me to stay with them but I did not feel I should do that. I made some excuses and thanked them profusely for their kindness and consideration.

I opted to stay in my familiar hotel near the famous Tahrir Square in central Cairo city.

I had many more things to do. That time proved to be reassuring and also unexpected results followed.

My Egyptian friend, Mama Loubna (Notaila Rashid) was kind enough to meet me again and invite me to her home where I was able to meet her charming teenage daughter – Loubna – and son Hisham, again. Her politician-writer husband was away on tour and I missed him, again.

The second and unexpected, but welcome news came from my friend, Ambassador Woonsang Choi.

He conveyed to me the invitation from his government for a week's official visit to Korea. And the added advantage was that my travel to Seoul would be taken as a continuation of my Cairo-Delhi flight and that I was just getting a layover in Delhi (India). This way I did not have to get fresh permission from Reserve Bank of India and go through all the formalities of a foreign government's invitation re-routing through the government of India.

The result was that upon arrival in Delhi I was booked into Ashoka Hotel to spend the day and catch the earliest flight the next day for Seoul.

[Something good, sometimes, comes out of a difficult situation.]

This was some fun – meeting Sadhana and the family in Ashoka hotel and exchanging notes there. Added bonus was that there was no direct flight from Delhi to Seoul and I was booked to Kathmandu (Nepal) for a day and scheduled to board a flight to Bangkok next day on Korean Airline, everything included.

That meant a day of sightseeing in Kathmandu which I absolutely enjoyed. India and Nepal had extremely close and cordial relations so much so that there was no visa requirement for Indian and Nepali citizens. On top of it, traditionally, the Nepali Chief of Army Staff was deemed to be an honorary Chief of Indian Army, and vice versa.

[There was another close connection between Nepal and India. Nepal's Prime Ministers have been from the famous Rana families who in turn were reported to be connected to 16th century Rana rulers of Mewar, a princely state in present Rajasthan state of India. Mewar's ruler, Maharana Pratap, bravely fought against Akbar, the then powerful Mughal ruler of India. Pratap didn't accept defeat and did not surrender. He fled into forests and continued the guerilla struggle and finally was able to recapture his state.]

The next day I took the flight to Bangkok and from there the connecting flight on Korean Air. As soon as I checked-in a polite Korean staffer told me that I was upgraded to First Class – the first time for me. Charming cabin crew extended appropriate hospitality and offered the choicest wines. I did not drink and so did not avail of this 'top hospitality.' I preferred extra fruit and chocolates.

Those days, as I have mentioned earlier, airlines used to employ beautiful young women and handsome young men as cabin crew. Probably all the airlines had a policy to hire unmarried and presentable staff and Korean Air was no exception. I, as a First Class passenger and also a government guest was showered with extra hospitality with high quality cushions and blankets to make my journey as comfortable as possible.

Thank you Korean Air, and thank you Ambassador Choi for enabling me to make another visit to the land that has become one of my favorites for several reasons. I had Korean friends; I saw how hardworking and hospitable Koreans that have made their country the fourth largest economy in Asia. Korea and Indian Army had close connection during and after the Korean War of 1950-53.

All that later resulted in my book, *Korean Experience.*

23

In Korea on a 'State Visit'

My second visit to Korea - in those days Korea, generally, meant South Korea as that part of the Korean Peninsula was more active diplomatically and economically. While in India I had met with North Korean diplomats also in my professional career, but South Korea was more pro-active.

South Korea was fast forging closer relations with India and the government in New Delhi. It was more open and encouraged more contacts and interaction. [Diplomatically, the Indian government had similar relations with both Koreas.]

No wonder I was invited by the government of (South) Korea for an official visit. I had already been to Korea for three days in 1966 but that was a private visit and then hospitality was provided by my friends Sull Wonshik and his wife Hisook.

The visit six years later was all paid for by the Korean government and it was for a week traveling extensively. I was well taken care of and also stayed at the same Bando hotel as in 1966. There was an interpreter also and when I went out right up to the North-South border, Panmunjom, and deep south to Pusan I also had another guide. In Seoul, I attended top intelligence briefings and government parties, and was also taken to prominent entertainment centers and interviewed.

There was a special demonstration of martial arts, Taekwondo, in my honor, by children from 5 to 15 years. It was unbelievably thrilling, and an eye- opener. Till then I had not known about or seen any Taekwondo demonstration anywhere. In India Judo-Karate was known but this form, typical of Korea, was comparatively unknown, to my knowledge.

The boys and girls put up an impressive show worthy of wholehearted admiration, also made memorable for yet another reason.

After the show ended, I was asked to say a few words. Praising the performance wholeheartedly I said, seeing this demonstration, I wish at least one of my two girls would learn it.

[Little did I imagine that about two decades later in America, Seema, and her son Arjun, both, would learn the art and science of Taekwondo in the city of St. Louis, where they were living at the time. Both got black belt, one of the higher levels of the martial arts.

Seema invited me and I flew from California to Missouri to witness the historic event. I spoke about it and told the very talented, highly decorated coach about it. Both Seema among the adults and Arjun (in his own age group) broke wooden and concrete slabs and gave a thrilling demonstration to the delight of their coach, other classmates – and me.]

I was overwhelmed. Thanks to the Korean government and the host officers who gave me this opportunity to witness the show and pass the message of its total usefulness on to my kids.

I am proud of both of them.

My trips outside capital Seoul took me to the border that was heavily militarized and was still tense even after so many years since 1950-53 conflict. The South Korean government under President Park Chung Hee had made tremendous strides toward military and economic strength, with far-sight and creativity, hard work and dedication.

India and Korea have very long history of cooperation and interaction since about the fourth century when an Indian Buddhist missionary visited Korean peninsula, comprising both North and South Korea.

Yet another bond is that both the countries celebrate their Independence Day on August 15. Interestingly, North Korea also celebrates that special Victory Day as a unified Korea was liberated by the Allies, from the Japanese stranglehold in 1945. The allies then included both America and the Soviet Union (Russia).

They later divided Korea between their own spheres of influence.

Five years later North Korea invaded South Korea and the Cold War became hot pitting America and its 20 allies against the Soviet Union and its allies in support of their area of influence.

India had not actively and militarily participated in the Korean War but its support and sympathies were with the South. India sent a Field Ambulance unit as a token of support and handled almost everything after the War in peacekeeping and repatriation of Korean soldiers on both sides. Top Indian Army officers such as Thimayya (who later became

India's Chief of Army Staff) and Thorat played a significant role that was praised by all sides and the United Nations.

The peacekeeping operations by the Indian contingent under the United Nations Command then became connected, in a way, with me in 1972.

Toward the south, in Korea, there is a grave and a small memorial for Col. Unni Nair of the Indian Army set up who died during the Korean War. His memorial is in a small city of Taegu on the way to Pusan in deep South. I had read about Nair and decided to stop and pay my respects to the man and his indomitable courage as a Military-man and Press relations person who sacrificed his life.

[Sadhana was moved by the story of Col. Nair when, back in India, I told her about my visit and her reaction was natural. She said something like: I am happy you made it a point to visit the *Samadhi* (memorial) of a man who was associated with both the Armed Forces (which you admire) and the Press (you work for.)

That was my Sadhana, totally in tune with me.]

There was yet another memorable connection I established on my second Korean visit – I got another daughter.

I mentioned about the Indian peacekeeping group in Korea earlier. With Gen. Thimayya and Maj. Gen. Thorat was another officer, Col. D.A. Mahadkar, a distinguished and a knowledgeable member of the team.

Rewind a little: my friend the Korean Ambassador in Cairo had told me that while in Seoul I should look for and meet a girl who was voted Miss Delhi and was now studying Korean language and doing her Ph.D. I was intrigued, who was this beauty with brains, and an Indian? I was anxious to meet this girl both because she was Miss Delhi (my city), and also because the ambassador mentioned about her.

I did not know which university she was studying and where she lived. To my surprise, my Korean guide, Kim Hwa Il (there are more Kims in Korea than Patels in America or Sharmas in India), located Alka in a particular university for foreign students and also arranged a meeting the very next day in my hotel.

Kim had a little complaint: He was looking for a girl named Miss Delhi, not Miss Alka, but finally found that Miss Delhi was Miss Alka.

It was hilarious.

Once Kim brought Alka to my hotel, I found that she was the daughter of Col. Mahadkar, of the Indian Peacekeeping operations. Not only that, Alka was doing her research and writing her thesis on the same subject – The Role of Indian Peacekeeping Operations in Korea.

What a coincidence! And since that day she joined my Daughters' Club.

Alka was not only a very smart girl academically, she was very good in dancing and dramatics. She presented a dance-drama in aid of the victims of recent floods in Korea. Her performance and achievements were admired and President Park Chung Hee invited her and her troupe to his home and felicitated them.

Alka also topped foreign students studying Korean language.

[She later, acted as guide and advisor to the world famous Little Angels troupe of Korea when it visited India. I had seen their breath-taking performance and was mesmerized by these little girls – from five to fifteen – displaying their skill in incredible music-dance-drama shows.]

I felt proud of this girl, my newly acquired daughter. Of course, more had to come concerning her, my family, her family, my friend and her marriage – in India.

[Back in India, I wrote an article about Alka in one of India's largest newspapers, Indian Express (Sunday edition) that brought her father, Col. Mahadkar close to me. He wrote a letter praising my article and we clicked instantly. We met in Delhi several times and also in Bombay where Alka got married. With Sadhana, Sujata and Seema, all four of us were the only non-family people invited for the wedding in Bombay.]

Col. Mahadkar was just like my big brother and we all got along well. Whenever he visited Delhi, he insisted on taking us to a movie. The nearest theater was Chanakya and it so happened a couple times that we went there, settled in our seats, the movie started, and Mahadkar *Bhaisahab* would be in la la land, dozing off. For him it was the best time to relax. However, he was fun and we enjoyed his company. He was also a sincere and loving friend, so was *bhabhi,* his wife, whom we met a couple times in Bombay.

The Mahadkar family is closely connected with the famous 17th century Maratha Warrior-King Chhatrapati Shivaji Maharaj and the Kolhapur princely family.

Col. Mahadkar's son, also named Shivaji, was himself an Army Officer, commissioned in the world famous Gorkha Regiment, one of India's finest fighting units that boasted of two officers who became the country's Army Chiefs. The first, Field Marshal Sam Manekshaw, had once said: "If a man says he's not afraid of death, he's either lying or he's a Gorkha." (The other was Gen. Dalbir Singh Suhag, who retired in December 2016.)

Shivaji, after leaving the Army, took to business. His son, Vishal Mahadkar, worked with the ace film producer-director, Mahesh Bhatt and has now himself become a new-age movie producer and director.

My Korean visit was about to end but I had many more friends to meet – a few had been with the Korean diplomatic mission in New Delhi, a few were with me in the US. A couple of them were out of Korea but I was able to meet with Kim Do Yon and Hong Yong Ki at their homes with their families. It was very informal, very nice.

The Korean government hosts took me around sightseeing and entertainment centers. I was able to see more of Korean dances and hospitality, meet with more people, students and journalists and others. I traveled on the remarkable 428 km (about 266 miles) long road, I called The Prosperity Road, one of the first important highways that opened up the country for quick transportation and distant markets for increased business – farms to markets.

Now South Korea has many more important highways linking the entire countryside with metropolitan areas. That is one major reason for Korea's strong economy and flourishing businesses.

A week seemed to pass quickly. I returned to India with more sweet memories of my Korean visit and connections.

There was the Annual General meeting of the Press Club of India, of which, I was the Treasurer. I was happy to be back in time for the important meeting.

The Press Club was different from the Press Association (I had also been Secretary of that body of accredited correspondents), and Delhi Union of Journalists (I was the General Secretary for many years). The Press Club was the hub of non-union activities, meetings and fun-events. It could boast of having successive Prime Ministers coming to address us and being felicitated.

In 1971 after the Bangladesh war was over we had the unique distinction of hosting all the three Chiefs of India's armed forces – General Manekshaw, Air Chief Marshal PC Lal and Admiral SM Nanda *together* to commemorate the event. Normally, all the three Chiefs do not attend a civilian function at one place and we had to take special permission from the Defense Minister for that meeting.

This helped us immensely, as we did not have to arrange for security ourselves. It was all done by the military itself. It was a memorable meeting, a very informal get-together.

Press Club also organized events, movies and other interesting shows for the families to participate and enjoy. Our family often attended such events. I would join whenever possible, if couldn't, no problem, my ever dependable Sadhana would take care of everything – bring the kids and take them back home, safely.

[I can't help but write about my several personal 'encounters' with General Manekshaw (later elevated to Field Marshal after he retired) in Delhi and also in Bombay. He belonged to a Parsi family – the highly educated and accomplished but very, very small and becoming smaller speedily. (Sadhana was with me at some of the places and met the General. She was also impressed by the informal air about him and his infectious humor.)

One of the first meetings with Manekshaw was when a small group of us, pressmen, met the General, informally and he talked about his childhood – and claimed to be a Punjabi. He told us that his father took his medical degree in England and tried to start his medical practice in Bombay but because of tough competition decided to go with his bride to distant Punjab (undivided India.) As soon as their train stopped at Amritsar (in Punjab) and the young lady saw tall, hefty bearded Sikhs, and was told there would be many more everywhere, she refused to go further. The General's father and his wife detrained at Amritsar and there the new doctor's practice started and thrived.

Manekshaw said growing up in Amritsar, we saw disorganized life, filth and diseases all around and felt disgusted and wanted to return to

Bombay. However, father told us: This is your bread and butter – more sick people, more money coming.

That was Manekshaw, also the funny man.

More about my own separate 'encounters.'

After the Bangladesh liberation war, and Manekshaw's brilliant leadership, we met several times. I started writing a book about the impressive personality and completed a few chapters. I wanted a couple of exclusive sittings with the General to know more on his own personal and family life, and more about his early years growing up.

I approached Manekshaw and told him about my project. He first displayed his modesty and tried to dissuade me but when I told him that I am well set with several chapters ready, and just wanted a couple of sittings with him to complete the project, he agreed. However, he said that he was going to Coonoor (Nilgiri Hills, in South India) and would see me after he returned to Delhi. I said, if you want, I could see you in Coonoor. He said no, no, I would give you time in Delhi, call me in two weeks positively.

I called him and he asked me to contact him in a week.

After a week he gave me time. I went to where he was staying in the military compound in Delhi Cantonment area, but he was nowhere. I waited for a half hour and then saw him coming. He said sorry he had to go for an urgent meeting and would have no time even then for my project. He again promised me and again the same thing happened, he ditched me.

Finally, at the Western Naval Command in Bombay where I had gone for reporting Indian Naval exercises, I saw him at the Navy Ball. He was the Chief Guest there. I accosted him and again he made excuses. He said he would be going to England to see his daughter and would give me time in two weeks. At that point I asked him point blank: General, are you writing your own book? In any case, even if I write a hundred books about you, your book will still sell.

He said, no, no it's not like that, I am not writing a book. I just don't find time. I am going to England to see my daughter.

He asked me to contact him in a few weeks.

I did not and instead decided to abandon that project altogether. I still do not know what his reason was. [He passed away at the age of 94 leaving a great legacy behind.]

I still have half the manuscript, but as of today, have no intention of completing it. (This was sometime in 1972-73 and to my knowledge, then there was no book on him. Much later a few were out.)

I still am an ardent admirer of the brilliant Army Chief and on many occasions, earlier, came to know what a fine and funny man he was. I have many humorous stories on him, some his own funny comments.

Sadhana was with me when we shared some memorable moments with 'Sam Bahadur,' as he was popularly and respectfully addressed. (We would attend military functions, annual parades and receptions etc. and meet the Chiefs and others.) She, as my partner, was also disappointed with no progress about the book and our giving up the project.

24

Back to India and 'Vinolka'

While in India and back to my job I got very busy, reporting the Parliament of India, and important Ministries such as Defense, External Affairs, Railways, Civil Aviation and Tourism, Petroleum and Chemicals and so on. As Chief of News Bureau, I was responsible for ALL the important national and international news, activities of ALL the important leaders, political parties and foreign embassies. That kept me very, very busy. Besides, there were other pursuits and hobbies such as Chitra Kala Sangam, TRAVIANA, the Press Club of India, Press Association and Deep Features.

[We discontinued TRAVIANA after some time but the other activities still continued.]

Sadhana continued to be an integral part of my activities and also busy with her own – raising two girls, doing her radio programs, writing and continuing to be a good host for everyone.

At one of the parties hosted by us at our home (we were still in Rajori Garden), we specially invited two persons and indirectly played cupid for them. One was my young journalist friend, Vinod Gupta and the other our new daughter, Alka Mahadkar, who had finished her studies and had returned to the capital city of Delhi.

They clicked instantly. They continued to connect and within a short time became quite close and planned a wedding. Vinod and Alka had some common interests, both were linguists. Vinod had learnt German at Max Mueller Bhavan, German Embassy's cultural center, in New Delhi. Alka, already a Korean language expert later learnt German and Vinod probably did the same with Korean, [and I presume some Japanese when they were in Japan for some time after their marriage.]

Alka-Vinod's relations became a little interesting in our family. Alka, as our daughter, was *Didi* (sister) to Sujata and Seema. Vinod, my friend and journalist-colleague, was Uncle for the girls. Now that confusion and strange relationship, in the eyes of Sujata and Seema continued. Vinod Uncle and Alka *Didi* continued to confuse and delight all of us. They were also known as Vinolka – Vinod and Alka, a very sweet couple and very talented duo.

Vinod was a fun Uncle for Sujata and Seema who always looked forward to his funny stories, riddles and tongue-twisters, one involving a camel, its hump and its high tail.

That added to our sweet relations.

[I met Vinod and Alka, and Vinod's younger brother Atul, in Cologne (Germany) – also written as 'Koln' in German. I was returning from Mexico City and was on my way back to India. In Mexico I was on a UN fellowship to attend and report a United Nations Conference.

As usual this family, very close both from Alka's side and Vinod's side, was most hospitable. Vinod was then working for the German Radio, Deutsche Welle and interviewed me for its overseas program. Alka and Vinod then worked in Korea and Japan and, years later, returned to India and settled down in Bombay. Alka taught visiting Korean youngsters Indian dances. Vinod, active as usual, wrote for some foreign newspapers for quite a few years.

Atul, the youngest of five brothers had migrated to Germany and lives there with his family. The three middle brothers, Girish, Shyam and Rakesh and their families are in New Delhi and keep in touch with some of us occasionally. [The last time Sadhana and I met them was in 2007 when we went to India from the US where we had settled down in 1986.]

The Gupta families have been very close to us for years. Seema keeps in touch with them more frequently. Girish had persistently asked us to stay at their farmhouse near Delhi whenever we visit. Sadly, Sadhana and I did not have more time in 2007 – and that was our last visit to India together. Sadhana gradually became more and more inactive and after her surgery in 2012 in Houston was confined to wheelchair and we gave up the idea of traveling long distance.

Sadly, Vinod passed away in 2011, in Bombay (Mumbai).]

Back to 1972 and in the capital city of India so many things kept happening that made our lives more busy. However, I enjoyed and was very happy and satisfied with my work. So was Sadhana, all the time busy with the kids, or neighbors, other relations or hosting parties at our home and also attending parties by government, private organizations, diplomats and others.

Our circle of friends continued to grow. We were frequently invited to top-level lunches, dinners, receptions by the New Delhi elite. We were also frequently honored by attending Presidential banquets and special receptions for visiting dignitaries at Rashtrapati Bhavan, the Presidential House. The 26 January Republic Day parade was a unique occasion when Sujata and Seema regularly, and sometimes some other close relatives and friends also, accompanied us to witness the grand military and Police parade and civilian march on the grand Raj Path in New Delhi. There would be elephants and horses and weapons. We would be in the special Press enclosure, right in front of the President's VIP section and had the absolute best view

The civilian sections in the parade included citizen heroes honored by the President, school children, National Cadet Corps, folk dancers and tableaus from various states and many other top class demonstrations of skill and hard work by both the armed forces and civilians.

The R-Day celebrations would wind up a couple days later with the spectacular Beating of Retreat – the grand musical show by the Indian armed forces band. Held in Vijay Chowk, right near the Parliament House and Raj Path, it is a magnificent show with select military marching bands from various corners of India presenting their skill with their musical instruments, drums of various shapes and sizes, bagpipes, flutes, and so on in delightful formations.

We would also meet with top civil and military leaders from India and the world at these grand functions, and also at receptions at the sprawling and beautiful Mughal Gardens of Rashtrapati Bhavan.

We also met the great American boxer, Muhammad Ali (Cassius Clay Jr.), on a visit to India with his beautiful, second wife, Veronica. He was virtually mobbed at the reception. Ali never said 'no' to anyone wanting his autograph – we also got his autographs for both Sujata and Seema on their autograph books that we thoughtfully carried to America with us.

25

Visit to Pakistan and 'the Connection'

I continued with my work and writing and traveling all over India and abroad. In 1973 I was a member of the press group accompanying the official Indian delegation to Pakistan headed by P.N. Haksar (one time Prime Minister Indira Gandhi's Principal Secretary). He was leading the Indian delegation with the rank of a Minister of State. The delegation also had Foreign Secretary Kewal Singh and joint Secretary Ashok. These were the first direct talks with Pakistan after the historic Simla Agreement of 1972 between Indira Gandhi and President Bhutto of Pakistan following the liberation of Bangladesh.

[Simla is now written as Shimla.]

Bhutto was keen to get back 93,000 Pakistani troops under Indian custody and India wanted Bhutto to agree to maintain peace and give diplomatic recognition to Bangladesh. So, much more had to be discussed and decided between the two nations but no headway was seen and relations were at a standstill.

After several rounds of informal contacts finally, both the sides agreed to initiate direct talks at the level of Ministers of State. Pakistan delegation was led by Aziz Ahmed, their Minister of State, therefore Haksar was also given the same status.

[An interesting story I can't – and don't want to - forget is about my then editor, Ratan Lal Joshi. This visit was again, suggested and approved for me by the Ministry of External Affairs of the Indian Government and Joshi *Ji* could not do much about it – unless he put his foot down and said NO to me, which he did not. It would have been awful.

I told him that the Ministry wanted me to join. He asked me about the leader and I told him about Mr. (Parameshwar Narayan) Haksar. He showed he was happy and said very well, I will talk to him. He proceeded to dial a number, and after a few moments the talks, in Hindi, were something like this (fair translation) though I could hear only *his* side:

Hello Parameshwar *Ji*, how are you. I hear that you are leading a delegation to Pakistan. I wish you all the best; it's going to be rather tough but you can handle all that. Yes, my correspondent Yatindra *Ji* will also be with you. Take care of him.

After he hung up he told me that Haksar was happy that *Hindustan* is sending a representative and that, given the situation, the delegation would do its best.

I never, for a moment, believed that Joshi *Ji* was talking to Mr. Haksar.

Yet another anecdote about my Editor, Mr. Joshi, was after he visited America (a couple years after I did) and on return told us, the staffers, that he had purchased many gifts for us and they were on their way on board a ship. As things happen, that shipload of gifts never reached India, New Delhi, and us, staffers - and Joshi *Ji* retired a few years later.

Don't know if the shock of not been able to give us those gifts hastened his retirement.

Sadhana was amused but also disgusted with the Editor and wondered what kept him to that post. I might shed some light on it, later.

[Joshi *Ji* was, otherwise, a soft-spoken man with pleasing personality; he had a very nice, homely wife and, I think, three pretty daughters.]

Joshi *Ji* did not stop there. He knew he could not nail me on anything, but after all, he was The Editor. His next step was sheer favoritism; he wanted an upstart, newly appointed, much too junior young man, promoted and given the title of Political Correspondent. I opposed the move. He said since he reports on political issues he was a political correspondent.

I replied: Even a local reporter does that for local politics, but that doesn't mean he can be a Political Correspondent. This title denotes a very senior and experienced political analyst/reporter, not a newcomer. And with that specialized reporting and being the Bureau Chief, *I* am also The Political Correspondent, none else.

Joshi *Ji* then devised a new scheme, I thought.

He wanted me to be out for a few days to report a political conference in Goa – far away, between 940 and 1250 miles by air or train (your choice). I was not in a mood to go, knowing what he would do in my absence. He somehow, hesitated to do it when I was in Delhi. Probably it needs guts to do a wrong thing.

His peon brought me a handwritten letter on the official letter-head asking me to proceed to Goa, first thing the next morning.

I read it, smiled and let the man go.

The letter itself presented me with an escape route I could have never imagined in a million years.

I did not leave for Goa next day and was present in the office doing my regular job.

The Editor didn't expect it. He had no guts to summon me and sent the same peon to ask me about his order.

I told him that I *did not receive any order from the Editor to go.*

He was shocked and reminded me that he had given me a letter the previous day from the Editor.

I admitted that he *did give me a letter*, and that saved *his* skin. However, I told him to confine himself with just the fact that he had given me *a* letter. That's it, nothing else as to what the 'order' was and why I did not comply with it.

It was okay with him.

Joshi *Ji* could not do anything about his so-called order and elevation of the favorite. (The rumor was that he was planning to forge a family relation with the young man and wanted him to be promoted.)

Years later I called the same peon to set that matter straight, and explained to him why I 'flouted the Editor's order,' as that was *no order*. (He might still be taking me to be a crook who told a lie).

I showed him that letter: Yes, it was on the official letter-head, but written by the *peon himself in his own handwriting* – obviously on the *instructions of Joshi Ji* - and on top of it, *was unsigned.*

That was my solid defense – *there was no order by the Editor.*

Poor fellow! He saw my point. He had to agree.

(Of course, I had not gone to the Editor to get a clarification. I thought why should I? For me, it was NO letter from the Editor, NO order from the Editor. Period!)

For Sadhana, that was hilarious and she marveled at my strategy and jugglery – also was amused at the naiveté of Joshi *Ji*.

[I have written at length about Ratan Lal Joshi because he did not impress me. I have worked with many outstanding editors with their knowledge, integrity, contribution, inspiration and the ability to nurture their staff to rise to greater heights of excellence and achievements. Joshi *Ji* was not a role model for me, that I could learn something to better myself, take my career forward and to better serve my paper. What I did achieve was despite him. Later when I was Chief Editor of *Bhaskar*, I asked for and printed several of his articles and paid top remuneration to him.

Now my perceived notion about how he managed to stay in his post.

He, somehow, managed to gain access to the Big Birla – Ghanshyam Das, the patriarch of the House of Birlas. I didn't know and had no desire to find out, just guess work – sycophancy, and exaggerated account of his own ability.

His solid contribution? He changed the family name of the Boss – from Bidla to Birla. Even the Big Boss would write his name (in Hindi) as Bidla. Joshi *Ji* persuaded him to change and from then onward we were writing Birla and not Bidla. What a solid, life-changing achievement!]

Back to my Pakistan visit: There were about half a dozen of us journalists staying along with the Indian delegation at the Inter-Continental hotel in Islamabad. Every day the two sides would meet and disperse without any agreement on anything. On the final day of the week-long futile discussions there was a courtesy call on Bhutto by the Indian delegation and thereafter we had to leave.

There were two interesting events where I was involved; one, the official dinner by Haksar for Aziz at our hotel where only I and another journalist, Dharmavir Gandhi sat with leaders of the two delegations, Haksar and Aziz, on their table.

And what an official dinner where no political discussion took place!

Enough had already been discussed and concluded without reaching any solution.

As a part of dessert, finest mangoes were served – uncut mangoes. On a formal dinner, cutting mangoes on the table was a little uncomfortable. Gandhi looked at me and I hesitated a little bit and then took the knife and started cutting one. It looked a little clumsy and Mr. Haksar joked to the laughter from our table. He remarked: *"Aap to ise jibah kar rahe hain* (you are executing it).

All of us had a good laugh, though Aziz was a little subdued, for obvious reasons, I guess.

We were also treated to a floor show in the hotel's grand ball room with a charming young woman beautifully rendering the famous song *"Dama dum must kalandar."* That was the first for me, subsequently I heard it a hundred times and have enjoyed it every time someone sang, including our daughter, Sujata. One of the other famous singers to present *Dama Dum* is Runa Laila from Bangladesh.

She is phenomenal.

In the hotel we had been given an entire floor, probably for security reasons. We were about 25 people – officials, press correspondents from newspapers, and radio-TV people from the government setup. India's TV – Doordarshan – had started a couple years back with limited programs and limited timings. Pakistan was starved of Indian movies and songs as their import was banned. This happened with Pakistan on and off though people liked Indian movies and other TV programs. Indians also liked several Pakistani dramas.

[After all, we are the same people sharing crops grown on the same soil, shared the same Sun and the Moon, the same summer and winter, same spring and rains, drank the same water and breathed the same air on the same land, living side by side for thousands of years.]

Our friends from the Indian radio and TV were more friendly, and imaginative, and treated Pakistani journalists and the entire hotel staff to choicest movie songs. Our people had carried cassettes of the songs and played them almost non-stop in our part of the hotel floor. The whole day, and part of the late evening, the Hotel staff and their friends would come and listen to the songs.

The favorite was *Pakeezah*, the cult classic movie with top stars such as Meena Kumari, Raj Kumar, Ashok Kumar, Veena, Nadira and others.

[A little bit about *Pakeezah*, one of Sadhana's and my all-time favorite Hindi movies:

The movie was released just a few months back. It was directed by Kamal Amrohi, the husband of Meena Kumari, and the ace director. He wrote the touching story of Lucknow city's nautch-girl yearning for love but not allowed to.

However, the shooting of *Pakeezah* was a history of delays, separation of the couple, and sickness of the heroine. Meena Kumari was critically ill with Cirrhosis of the liver, a terminal illness and died less than two months after the film was released. She had collapsed on the set doing one of the last scenes and a double (Padma Khanna) completed the dance sequence beautifully.

There were more problems: Music Director Ghulam Mohammed and the Director of Photography Josef Wirsching died when the film was still incomplete. Amrohi then signed Naushad Ali (for the remaining songs and background score); a dozen ace photographers in the industry in Bombay pitched in to help complete the shooting.

For Kamal and Meena it was a love story, a poem on celluloid and a dream come true. After separation with husband Amrohi for more than five years, Meena agreed to complete the movie but accepted only one *Ginny* (one UK Pound) for it.

It had taken sixteen years to complete the love-story and finish the project. It was India's first color film in Cinemascope for which MGM of America was involved with their camera lens loaned on payment of royalty. (It turned out that the lens was a little defective; MGM corrected the flaws, waived the royalty payment and even gifted the lens to Amrohi.)

The songs of *Pakeezah* were an instant hit. Lyrics were by some of the celebrated writers such as Kaifi Azmi, Majrooh Sultanpuri, Kaif Bhopali and Kamal Amrohi himself. The lilting melodies were sung by prominent singers like Lata Mangeshkar, Mohammad Rafi, Vani Jairam, Rajkumari, Parveen Sultana, Shamshad Begum, and Naseem Bano Chopra. The sets and costumes of the movie were fantastic. Chandeliers were imported from Belgium and money spent lavishly on carpets used for captivating *mujras* (classical dance performance by courtesans.)

The sets and costumes chosen by Meena Kumari and Kamal Amrohi themselves were out of this world. That meant a big-budget movie and an audience all over the world for an Indian movie on *that* story and about *that* history.]

At the Islamabad Intercontinental hotel there were any number of listeners for the captivating songs of *Pakeezah*, the cassettes our team had brought. That also made us – Indians and Pakistanis – come closer and both sides liked that.

Many journalists and other Pakistanis we met on the trip, privately admitted that we were much better living together in one country – even if like quarrelling brothers – than in two separate entities constantly at each other's throats.

The other memory *I* carried with *me* to India was *my* meetings and interaction with Pakistani correspondents who were quite friendly and displayed no animosity at all – just like all of us. We frequently invited them for lunch or dinner, time permitting, and would talk about mostly families and the good old days when two countries were one. It was a pleasant surprise – I am sure for the Pakistanis also – that we got along very well without any malice or rancor.

The Indian Press party, on our 'day off', was escorted on a visit to Taxila, the 3000-year-old world famous ancient seat of learning in undivided India. Taxila or Takshashila is now in ruins. Excavations were done and later, in 1980 it was declared a United Nations (UNESCO) World Heritage Site. This is about 25 miles from Islamabad (Rawalpindi).

Sadhana's father (my father-in-law, Ishar Das Jaggi) had vast property in Rawalpindi area, in undivided India. They had to leave everything, including their newer home, a huge complex of residential quarters, personal office, warehouse and rooms for girls school and so on, in Abbottabad, about 2½ hour drive (about 70 miles) from Rawalpindi.

While in Islamabad (the new capital city of Pakistan carved out of some suburban and forest areas of old Rawalpindi) I met with, among others, a journalist from Abbottabad – my in-laws' big home-city. We became good friends – even 'relatives' – when I told him my wife had a home in that city (decades later became 'famous' for Osama bin Laden and his killing by American commandoes.)

This journalist from Abbottabad had no hesitation in accepting this new 'relation' with me. He happily said, that makes you my *Jeeja* (brother-in-law.) Traditionally, all girls and boys in the same village, small towns, are regarded as brothers and sisters. The same with friends of parents – they become uncles and aunts of the kids. They, naturally, care for all the kids in the neighborhood as their own.

What a beautiful tradition that enabled communities to come closer! In bigger cities and modern culture that kind of relation – and closeness – is sadly missing.

That actually summed up the outcome of the week-long talks and our stay in the capital of Pakistan with no agreements both sides knew would not be coming. Anyway, that rounded off our visit to Islamabad. The top members of the delegation had already made a farewell call on President Zulfikar Ali Bhutto.

The last day I was talking to Ashok as the main delegation returned from final round of, kind of, farewell talks, with their Pakistani counter-parts and he mentioned to me that it's time we pack up. I got the hint and with a few more comments, I took a cab to the telegraph office to dash off the breaking news story for my paper.

In the next few hours we were back in New Delhi, around late evening full of memories of our own informal meetings and contacts with our counterparts but with no political solution to any of the problems at government level.

That's politics and we were free to write about our own reports.

The agreements would come later.

26

To Chanakyapuri, the 'Home' of Diplomats

Soon after independence, the government's External Affairs Ministry started expanding at a faster rate. That meant India's expanding relations with more and more countries and also more countries opening their embassies in New Delhi.

For that, land was required and a mini city to be created. In the fifties that was seriously taken up and a whole area was developed to become Diplomatic Enclave – Chanakyapuri, named after Chanakya, the astute Prime Minister and Chief Advisor to the great King Chandragupta Maurya in the 3rd century BC.

It became one of the finest areas of the city with well laid out plans, parks, small shopping areas, hotels and even a movie theater.

Along with various embassy buildings put up by foreign countries, the government's building department constructed homes for senior government officials and Members of Parliament, a few were reserved for accredited press correspondents.

It was designed to be an affluent and posh area and I was lucky to get one of the homes right along one of the main roads – Vinay Marg with the five star Ashoka Hotel on one side, and Akbar Hotel on the other. Right in front of our home was the sprawling Nehru Park with a swimming pool and a small, old temple. It was allotted to me as a senior journalist when I reached the top of the waiting list of accredited correspondents.

The then Minister of State for Housing, Om Mehta, himself saw the list and sanctioned the house to me. I met Mehta along with Radha Nath Chaturvedi, who was also my old friend working for Mehta as his Ministry's Information Officer.

[Here I have to mention a little bit about Radhanath whom I knew since about 1945-46 from Bombay when he stayed with us and became a family. And more importantly, it was because of him that I became a journalist and my career was set. Then sky was the limit for me to grow.

Radhanath was a few years older to me and so became my older brother.

It was my first year in the college and when the summer vacations started I had nothing more to do than play, and read books. Radhanath had come from Allahabad, in UP state and joined *Vishwamitra*, a Hindi daily newspaper. After just a few weeks in the job he got the info about his mother's illness. He asked his Editor for leave but was refused as he was a newly-hired staffer. But the Editor, Pundit Karuna Shankar Pandya, was a kind man; he asked Radhanath if he could get him a replacement for the duration of his absence, he could go on leave.

Radhanath thought of me and persuaded me to meet the Editor. In those days most of the national and international news was transmitted on agency teleprinters, in English to various newspaper offices. The editorial staff's main job was translation into Hindi. Pandya *Ji* gave me a couple of news items to translate and what he found was satisfying. He put me on the job and Radhanath happily went on vacation to see his mother.

Either his mother took a lot more time to recover, or Radhanath wasn't in any mood to hurry back. I continued working for *Vishwamitra* for more than 20 days. When he finally rejoined, Pandya *Ji* asked him to ask me if I wanted to continue working. I felt happy that my work was worth something and, as I had nothing else to do, I accepted the offer.

That was the beginning of my long career as journalist-writer-poet-author that has continued for 70 years. Thanks to the door my dear friend and brother, Radhanath had opened for me, by chance.

Later, we met in Delhi and continued our long association; Sadhana and kids also came close to Radhanath and his wife. For Sujata and Seema he was their *Tauji* (uncle – father's older brother) and she *Tai Ji* (aunty – *Tauji*'s wife), a very loving and caring lady.

Radhanath was with the government of India and I was working for *Hindustan.*]

The Chanakyapuri houses had generally two floors, each allotted to different people. We had the lower floor with a front and back yard – with fruit trees and attached garage, extremely low rent (subsidized) with repairs, and free periodic whitewash by the government. The people on the upper floor had the terrace with the same facilities, but no front or back yard.

In addition, occupants of both the floors, each, had a servant quarter – a small one room and kitchen area attached with our houses. The servant quarters were given to the domestic help of our choice.

This spacious accommodation in Chanakyapuri was our home for nine years, 1974-83, till we moved to Indore.

It was about half a mile from the Prime Minister's house. The nearest was the Embassy of Kuwait; Ambassador Issa al-Issa became a good friend, also came to our home for lunch. He was a kind, generous and astute diplomat. Once I remarked about the enormous oil-wealth of Kuwait and his reply was disarming. He said: "Take away all our oil, give us all your greenery."

What a nice compliment and appreciation for India!

The Bhatnagar home had frequent parties and felicitations. Our nearest neighbors, except one journalist, were all senior government officials and diplomats. American, Russian, Chinese, Australian, German embassies had large compounds with offices and some residences of ambassadors. Sadhana and I had been to almost all for parties, receptions, lunch-dinners around Chanakyapuri and other areas where more diplomats and their embassies – late comers – were housed.

I remember when the American embassy building was being built and when it opened – I was a witness and also an admirer of the unique architecture combining aspects (and resemblance) of Mughal structure Itmat-ud-daula (Agra) with modernity. It was designed by the eminent American architect, Edward Stone, who was praised by the world-famous designer and architect, Frank Lloyd Wright himself. Wright's idea was to construct by keeping a combination of Harmony and Humanity.

The American embassy building is exactly that.

Wright also had a beautiful description for the building. He had said that it's "Taj Maria," for the wife of Edward Stone. Yes, it reminds one of Taj architecture, especially of Itmad-ud-Daula, the monument to Shah Jahan's grandfather (Nur Jahan's father), who also happened to be grandfather of Shah Jahan's wife Mumtaz Mahal. [Mughal emperor Shah Jahan got Taj Mahal built for his beloved wife who died after she gave birth to their 14th child.]

So much for the old history – the inspiration for the new.

Coming back to the new building with a history. The corner stone was laid by Earl Warren, Chief Justice of the US Supreme Court, in 1956. The memorable opening ceremony, in 1959, was attended by India's Prime Minister Jawaharlal Nehru.

I was privileged to be present on both the occasions for reporting duty and witnessed a group of laborers presenting an impromptu dance followed by a group of college students performing the vigorous *Bhangra* with the beat of the traditional Punjabi *dhol* (drum.)

Mrs. Bunker also joined in the dance. Caroline (Carol) Bunker was Ambassador to Nepal and was the wife of Ambassador Ellsworth Bunker.

It was fun to watch two American Ambassadors merrily joining the dance group and having a fun-time.

The reasons I mention the long history of the building are two-fold: One, I knew Sardar Mohan Singh, the Indian builder, for this 'joint project' – as described by Ambassador Bunker at the opening – and visited him often at work. Mohan Singh, an unassuming, simple but talented businessman, the owner of Oriental Building and Furnishing Company, Connaught Circus, New Delhi, brought his innovative ideas and expertise to the grand project. He surprised, and also impressed, the American building team.

[Sardar Mohan Singh was also the first distributor/dealer of the newly-introduced Coca Cola. We were always welcomed at his office, and especially made it a point to stop during the scorching heat of Delhi in Summer when coke became scarce in the market. Mohan Singh would immediately order his assistant: *Saheb ke liye paani lao* (bring water – meaning Coke – for Sir).

With the introduction of Coca Cola, started a revolution in newspaper advertising.

For the first time prominent newspapers came out with the most eye-catching full-page ads that sparked everyone's interest. They ran for four days and naturally left a lasting impression. After so many decades, I still remember it vividly. It looked something mysterious.

First day: The caricature of a boy with only the cap of the bottle on his head and just two words in big, huge letters – Hello Folks!

Second day: The same picture with just one word – Thirsty?

Third day: The same picture with just one word - Tomorrow!

Fourth day and the message was clear and the mystery solved: Drink ice-cold Coca Cola *(with the word Coke on the boy's cap.)*

The ads created a big impact and there was no turning back. Ice-cold bottles of Coke became an overnight sensation. It was the first time an ice-cold drink (without extra ice in the glass) was offered. The Coca Cola Company and its dealers had hit a jackpot. The dealers were given big ice-boxes to keep the bottles chilled.

Later, Mohan Singh also headed the New Delhi Municipal Committee, the administrative body for the entire *New Delhi* area and contributed quite a lot to its smooth and effective functioning.]

The other reason for my memories of these buildings is that Sadhana and I visited them many times for meetings and parties. Richard Nixon also held a press conference there which I attended, and met the dignitary. He was Vice President then, later became the President of the United States and brought about the long running – yet unproductive and debilitating - war in Vietnam, in 1975.

[It was a pity he had to give up because of relentless campaign against him in the 'Watergate Scandal,' that was taken to amazing heights of a national disaster worth impeaching the sitting President.

This is American political life and partisan politics at its worst!]

We also visited the beautiful residence of the US Ambassador, next to the Chancery building, named Roosevelt House in honor of the former long-term president.

So much for the 'American Taj.'

Across two streets nearby, is the home of Dr. Karan Singh, the Maharaja of Jammu & Kashmir state and for many years, Cabinet Minister in the Government. Sadhana and I were often invited by Dr. Singh and his lovely wife, Maharani Yasho Rajya Laxmi Devi. Sadhana also attended an impromptu Yoga session where the Maharani, in an instant, squatted on the floor to demonstrate her skills at Yogic exercises.

At the residence of the Australian Ambassador Bruce Grant and his wife, Joan, Sadhana and I played indoor golf, in their rooms with them and some other Australian diplomats.

It was great fun.

In 1974, I was one of the first Indian journalists to visit Australia as a government guest for about 25 days. I went coast to coast – from Perth to

Brisbane, and in-between. It was a most memorable, and informal visit-though I did attend a session of Parliament when Prime Minister Whitlam was speaking and answering questions.

The new Parliament building was yet to be constructed.

I was also in Melbourne after a hectic day of meeting people, including a sister of my Australian diplomat friend, Tonia Shand, toured a zoo, saw a thrilling Kung-fu movie and so on.

One day, after my day-long program, when I came back to Hotel Victoria, and wanted to sleep, I felt miserable. There was nothing that I ate, nothing very strenuous I did, or nothing horrible I saw, but I felt unwell. I don't know what it was but I experienced some kind of a sinking feeling, and breathing difficulty.

I did not want to call the Hotel reception, or the Australian rep that was with me most of the time. I did not want to phone Sadhana and add to her worries.

But I felt something was definitely wrong with me, without any reason. I silently recited some Vedic *mantras,* repeated them and felt some temporary relief.

However, all was not over, and some discomfort persisted.

The reason might be that I was *really* missing Sadhana. I had never felt that kind of discomfort, ever, on any of my visits away, far away, from home, even when I was on the extended four-month plus visit to America and around the world.

[For obvious reasons, what I chose not to mention in my book *Australiana, A Visit to Remember* is *what else I did* to face the situation: I called out Sadhana – also by her several other names like Ashi, Rani etc. For a couple minutes I kept on calling her, quite loudly. It took me a few minutes before I felt some more relief. In another five minutes I was feeling normal. Ved (Sadhana's given name at birth) and Vedic *mantras* did the miracle.

I thanked God and my Ashi with my whole heart. They were my saviors, and she has been my strength all the time.

On my return Sadhana asked me if everything went well – health wise and otherwise.

I told her everything was fine, and it was a very enjoyable visit, except that one day when I felt really miserable.

Before I could tell her anything more, she asked me: Was it *that* day and about *that* time?

I was stunned! How could she *know* what was happening to me on that particular time and day? It clearly was yet another solid proof that Sadhana and I were joined by some unexplained spiritual bond that enabled her to feel my pain even if I was thousands of miles away.]

My Australian visit gave me an opportunity to see the Banana Country – in the East – where a sizable Punjabi (Indian) community lived. The place has an aboriginal name, Woolgoolga. It had two Gurdwaras. I stayed with the head priest of the original Gurdwara, G.S. Atwal. His wife still called India, *Sada Mulk* (our country). Their children, son Rajinder and daughter Randhir Kaur, spoke perfect 'Australian English,' with the peculiar pronunciation.

They were absolutely at ease.

Leaving that small area of Australia as the last part of my trip, I had a unique experience while flying back to the capital, Canberra. I was taken to the small Coff's Harbour airport by Rajinder. (Both the father-and son had earlier welcomed me at the same airport and had brought me to their home, insisting that I stay with them and not at any hotel-motel.)

We reached the airport a little early and saw the doors/gates closed. I was surprised, but we waited.

A few minutes later, the door was opened from inside by a uniformed man who took my bag (as my host bid me farewell) and checked my ticket etc. He loaded my bag onto the small aircraft – I was the only passenger to board from that place, at that time – and asked me to take any seat in, probably, the 20-seater plane. Then he seated himself in the pilot's 'cabin' and flew the plane. It was interesting to see the man playing multiple roles – the doorman, counter-clerk, loader, air crew – and also the pilot. This could only happen in Australia.

[Back in India at one of the meetings we had with the Chairman of Indian Airlines, the former Air Force Chief of Staff, Air Chief Marshal PC Lal, and while talking about cutting costs I mentioned this airlines and the way the staff handled multiple roles. ACM Lal replied: "Can you imagine our pilots doing those A to Z jobs all by themselves even on smaller aircraft flights?"

I knew he was absolutely right.

[In Indian offices, generally, there are peons who take your files and other papers from one desk to the other, one room to the other. I don't know if things have somewhat changed in the preceding decades.]

About four years later, I was able to bring out a book on my visit – *Australiana, A Visit to Remember.* It was indeed a visit with many memories. The then Australian Prime Minister Malcolm Frazer was visiting New Delhi, in 1978, and I was reporting a part of his visit. I took the opportunity to present a copy to him.

PM Frazer happily obliged by signing the book.

My foreign visits that started in Ramesh Nagar, continued while in Rajori Garden, did not stop in Chanakyapuri. My work was progressing nicely. My frequent radio and TV programs and Sadhana's regular radio talks and discussions, and writing articles for magazines, continued.

She would also write poems whenever she got time, or made time.

Meanwhile, I wrote a running commentary when Northern Railway started a Ring Rail all around 22 miles of Delhi area, parallel to Ring Road, in 1975. Earlier it used to be only for goods, later upgraded and used as a commuter train (now extended to the entire National Capital Region touching Haryana and Uttar Pradesh.)

I was first taken around on the train to see and decide.

Later, I finalized the commentary incorporating various stops/places. It was recorded and used to be played as the train chucked along the 'Ring,' describing some important places and their history. It was interesting, I was happy with it and so were the Railway authorities.

The commentary continued for quite some time but (I don't know when) it was discontinued as the circular ring railway itself failed to replace or supplement the existing transport system. I understand it's now being re-discovered, re-constructed and expanded.

Life was going on smoothly and I was working more actively. With a talented wife and two lovely daughters there were no complaints. The girls were doing fine in their school, Holy Child Auxilium School, in R.K. Puram, not far from our home.

There are two instances of what Sujata and Seema were up to.

Sujata loved snakes. There was a snake-charmer who would visit our colony nearly every week. These people, these groups, live everywhere in the country; catching, keeping and showing off snakes was their ancestral business. They go around the community showing their snakes and getting money from people; some give milk for the snakes, especially on a festival – *Nag Panchami* – that traditionally falls during the rainy season, July-August.

The festival of snakes is observed by Hindus of India, Nepal and many other places all over the world.

Sujata would anxiously wait for the snake-charmer who, playing on his *Been* (snake-charmer's special flute), would herald his arrival from a distance. We would make Sujata concentrate in her studies – if she was with her books. However, when the snake-charmer would come right in the lane behind our backyard and stand there playing his flute, we would relent and Sujata would play with the snakes for a while. We will always give some money to him.

I, and sometimes Sadhana too, would drop the girls and pick them up every day. One day Sujata had her board exam at some other center and as we reached there to pick her up we saw what can be described as a scene from a mini-circus.

There was a group of students and the familiar snake-charmer with his big bag of snakes that usually hung from his shoulder. The bag was down and many snakes were peeping out of it, but kept under strict surveillance.

We saw Sujata with a fair-size python around her neck – she had finished the exam early and was waiting for us.

We both were a little annoyed, but also amused.

Ah, the uncommon act of a python around the neck and our girl playing with the soft skin of the big snake!

The snake-charmers make sure to remove all poisonous glands before presenting their acts. They are experts themselves. It's their profession for generations. Our *family snake-charmer* was lamenting the fact that his children were not interested in the ancestral profession.

Thanks Sujata for familiarizing us more with snakes!

Sujata did not end here. In her school, she took part in dramas and often had the lead role. One historical play, organized by the Hindi teacher, Mrs. Beena Mathur, was *Deepdaan*, a story of Panna *Dhai,* the 16th century nurse-maid for prince Udai Singh of Chittaur (Mewar state) who sacrificed her own son to protect the prince and managed to let him escape. Sujata played the emotional and impressive role of Panna *Dhai* and displayed her excellent talent. Seema performed a beautiful dance carrying earthen lamps along with a group of others.

While Sujata played her role like a pro and spoke her lines effectively, Seema could act out every other character's part and render their dialogs with confidence. [There were many occasions when the girls performed parts of the play in front of family and friends with Sujata playing only Panna's part and Seema everyone else's.]

Sadhana and I were in the packed hall to see the program.

The climax of *Deepdaan* was absolutely touching as Sujata had gone deeper into the great role and completely identified herself with the character. Panna got the inkling that the rival, killer-prince, was on his way to finish the young prince - the legitimate heir to the throne. She quickly smuggled the boy out with her trusted associate.

As the killer came with a drawn sword and demanded to know where the prince was, Panna *Dhai* pointed to the bed where she had put her own son. Next moment as the killer did his job and left the room, a heartbroken Panna collapsed.

Sujata enacted the touching scene with deep emotions and as she fell on the floor, we, and the entire audience, gave her a standing ovation.

It was well-deserved!

[It's worth mentioning here that years later, Mrs. Mathur, in another school in Shimla (Himachal Pradesh state) organized and directed the same play,*Deepdaan,* with the lead role of Panna *Dhai* played by a young girl named, Preity Zinta, years later, one of the prominent stars of many hit Bollywood films.

Who would have thought that one day Deepdaan's heroine with cute dimples on her cheeks would become the heartthrob of millions with her memorable roles in *Kal Ho Na Ho, Mission Kashmir, Veer-Zaara, Dil Chahta Hai* and several other Bollywood movies.]

Apart from drama, Sujata also loved to write, and one of her poems, *It's a Handicapped World* was published in Children's World magazine that was widely appreciated. The magazine had multiple language editions.

Seema continued to surprise us with some very interesting things.

One day, after Sujata had passed her exam in flying colors, Seema opened a page of the telephone directory. Those days with no cell phones (mobiles, as they are termed in India) and phone directories were a big source of information with names, numbers and addresses also.

She put her finger on one name – Mohan Lal – and dialed the number.

A man answered. The conversation, in Hindi, followed (fair translation):

Hello.

Can I speak to Mohan Lal *Ji*?

This is Mohan Lal. Who is this?

I am Seema. My sister Sujata passed her 10th class exam with very good marks.

That's very good, I am happy. Congratulations.

Thank you, Sir.

Seema was indeed happy for her big sister. And her happiness continued.

A couple years later when Sujata passed her 12th class examination Seema was happy and could not contain her joy…again.

The phone directory was again handy and, God knows how, her finger fell on the same Mohan Lal, and dialed the same number. (I am sure there were several Mohan Lals listed on the same page of the directory.)

They talked:

Hello.

Can I speak to Mohan Lal *Ji*?

Yes, this is Mohan Lal.

Sir, I am Seema. You remember I called you two years back. Now my sister, Sujata, has passed her 12th class with very good marks.

Yes, yes, I remember. My congratulations! I am happy for her.

Thank you Sir.

We were amused, and also pleasantly surprised, that Seema got the same man again on the same number and talked about the same subject.

What a beautiful co-incidence!

I wish Mohan Lal was still on Seema's radar (or today's Facebook or Instagram type social media) and Seema could continue to keep him informed of all that's happening in our lives.

Thank you Seema for sharing good news with Mohan Lal!

And thanks a lot Mohan Lal *Ji* for responding, remembering Seema and sharing our joy. Where are you now?

Back to the national scene.

There was unrest – demonstrations and protests also – as things in the country were not going smoothly. As I wrote earlier, life doesn't remain constant, it brings changes, some in the family and some in the community, country.

In 1975 the country saw an unprecedented situation with Prime Minister Indira Gandhi suspending the Constitution and declaring Emergency, on June 25. She had lost an election appeal and the Allahabad High Court had declared her election null and void. She retaliated declaring that an unprecedented situation has arisen and she fears "internal disturbance." Emergency rule was proclaimed sanctioned by a pliant president, Fakhruddin Ali Ahmad.

Prominent opposition leaders and thousands of others were arrested and press censorship was imposed. This was unheard of in a country like India, the largest democracy in the world.

Our own magazine, TRAVIANA, had to be closed - a victim of Emergency when restrictions were placed even on a non-political publication. I was asked to submit all the material, every month, for pre-censorship by government officials at the Press Information Bureau.

I clarified to the Censor officers that TRAVIANA was totally non-political but the reply was 'illuminating.'

What if you criticize the government's policy on tourism, aviation and hospitality?

I preferred to close down the magazine than follow the Censor's guidelines and submit everything before finalizing.

It was suffocating. All news was pre-censored by government's press officers and strict restrictions were enforced on meetings, demonstrations or things like that. It was dictatorship of the Prime Minister, her younger son, Sanjay Gandhi and their chosen few. Guidelines were given and some kind of self-censorship was enforced. There were frequent meetings with big bosses of the publishing world where strict directions were given, and repeated. Our Big Boss, KK Birla, was toeing Indira-Sanjay line without any kind of murmur.

[Only Ramnath Goenka of the *Indian Express* courageously defied. First day after Emergency was proclaimed, *Indian Express* editorial space was left blank, and that continued. Goenka and his newspapers challenged Indira Gandhi and her son, Sanjay, at every step. Harassment was heaped on Goenka and was multiplied with stopping of all Government ads, stopping import permits and quotas for legitimate needs for printing, manufactured charges were filed on flimsy grounds but Goenka did not surrender, did not blink, and continued to defy. He went 'eye-to-eye' with the government.]

All kinds of acts took place under Emergency powers and administration was carried on with a heavy hand. Human rights were taken away and even the judiciary was put under Indira Gandhi's newly appointed Chief Justice, AN Ray who had superseded his seniors, a little before she declared Emergency.

However, resistance simmered beneath the superficial peace, order and discipline touted by the government and its henchmen. It was said that during the Emergency trains all over the country ran on-time, crime was negligible, and everything ran smoothly. Members of Parliament, theoretically, were free to speak their mind *on the floor of the House* but the press was not free to report all that was said.

Autocratic rules encouraged forced sterilization and other drastic measures.

Outwardly it seemed things were in order and there was hardly any dissent visible or heard. Beneath the surface discontent was simmering and opposition was restive. Jaya Prakash Narayan (JP), Morarji Desai, Atal Bihari Vajpayee, Lal Krishna Advani and other leaders of opposition were the leading lights of resistance to India Gandhi. There were demonstrations and opposition rallies in several states of India despite Emergency powers exercised by the authorities.

The government was keeping a watchful eye on dissenting or suspected dissenters among the press also and it was rumored that it had prepared a list of newsmen to be arrested in future. Though we were not allowed to write anything critical of the government, dissent was passed on and shared by word of mouth.

A senior official hinted to me that I might be next. It was a little scary as Sadhana and I were opposed to Emergency right from the beginning and used to talk about it frequently, but discreetly. But the major disturbing fact was that my father was staying with us since a few months and I was worried about him, in case I was detained. So, I sent him back to Bombay to rejoin my younger brother, Virendra Bhatnagar and his family with whom he was living for years, anyway.

I used to be a frequent radio and TV personality with talks, commentaries and interviews but Emergency saw me out; I was kind of, black-listed. No radio/TV talks, discussions or interviews. That continued for about two years, practically the entire duration of Emergency.

I did not feel too bad. That is life and that was all politics that I had maintained was always of a temporary nature. Even a formidable leader like Indira Gandhi could be defeated in elections and at the courts. I held on to my views, soundly supported by my wife, unperturbed by results.

Finally, with adverse reaction, internationally, and simmering unrest, internally – that took the shape of a storm – things started changing. With agitation in Gujarat and Bihar among some other Northern and Central states leading the way, Prime Minister Indira Gandhi relented. She was forced to opt for general elections for Parliament (Lok Sabha – 542 seats), in 1977. She must have thought that her Emergency rule had 'chastened' the people and they would vote her again.

She was sadly and gravely mistaken and had to bite the dust, along with her 'heir apparent' Sanjay Gandhi in the elections that followed.

Janata Party, the hastily formed opposition alliance, swept to power with 345 seats in the elections held March 13-19 and vote-counting on March 20. There were major defections in the Congress Party with senior Minister Jagjivan Ram, HN Bahuguna, and Indira Gandhi's close associate Nandini Satpathy, joining the opposition and allying with Janata Party.

Though Jagjivan Ram had formed a separate party called Congress for Democracy, he was part of Janata Party, inspired and motivated by the redoubtable leader Jaya Prakash Narayan and the senior-most former Congressman, Acharya JB Kripalani. All the leaders extensively toured the country appealing to the people to vote out India Gandhi and defeat her party.

Janata Party had come together with merging Bharatiya Lok Dal (BLD), Congress O (Organization – Morarji Desai), Congress for Democracy, Bharatiya Janasangh, and the Socialist Party (George Fernandes) and so on. Even the Marxist Communists decided not to split the opposition votes, and went against Indira Gandhi.

Janata Party candidates fought the election on the BLD ticket as required by the Election Commission, as Janata Party was not yet a recognized and registered, political party. It had fought no elections before. But that was okay as intelligent voters knew what to do.

I kept myself extra busy with meeting these opposition leaders, interviewing them and frequently succeeding in squeezing all those reports in my paper, *Hindustan,* that was still supporting Indira Gandhi.

She had relaxed Emergency a little to allow electioneering all over India.

But things went downhill for Indira Gandhi and her Congress Party. Except for the four South Indian states, Tamil Nadu, Karnataka, Andhra Pradesh and Kerala among the major states, the Janata Party bagged most seats all over Northern India.

On the day of counting, March 20, the whole day, I was at the office or at the Press center and returned home around 5 in the morning when most of the votes had been counted and Congress had suffered an unprecedented defeat. As I expected, Sadhana was up the whole night following the news on TV.

She opened the door for me, smiling; we got into a tight hug, and Sadhana exclaimed: *Desh bach gaya* (the country is saved.)

She had been totally with me on the issue and along with early teenagers, Sujata and Seema we had attended quite a few meetings addressed by Janata Party leaders. Indira Gandhi also had many meetings during the election campaign but there was a clear distinction, as described by Atal Bihari Vajpayee:

"Indira Gandhi and Congress meetings have crowds, we have the audience."

Indeed big crowds for Indira's meetings were arranged by providing buses to bring villagers and given free lunch-boxes. In the photos one could see indifferent, disorderly and uninterested people – many making their way out before Indira finished speaking. In contrast, Janata Party meetings were orderly, people paid attention to the speakers and applauded with perfect understanding.

They were, indeed, audiences. And that paid off for the Janata Party.

As I had surveyed the election scene during the campaign, and written very guardedly, because the restrictions were not *totally* removed (and also because our organization was supporting Indira Gandhi and Congress) it was becoming clear which way the wind was blowing. In one of our meetings, Kuwaiti Ambassador Issa al-Issa asked me directly about my assessment. I had no hesitation in saying that "don't be surprised if Indira Gandhi herself loses her seat."

[Ambassador Issa was Dean of the Diplomatic Corps - the senior most. He was in India for 19 years, a record.]

He was surprised but trusted my reading and analyses and assessment. Later, after the results were out we met again and he complimented me on my assessment. For journalists who mingle with people and talk to a wide cross-section, the signs were clear that an upset was on the cards. Nobody could have predicted accurately but chances were assessed as *very slim* for the Congress and *very bright* for Janata.

I was happy to see Sadhana – and the girls, 14 and 13 – on the same page as I. We all went to Mahatma Gandhi's *Samadhi* (memorial) at Rajghat when all the duly-elected Janata Party members and leaders took the oath to *"remain united always."*

[Of course it turned out just the opposite, and was appropriately described as, "No solemn pledge has ever been broken so speedily and brazenly as this was." That was so sad.]

But on that day, March 24, 1977 at Rajghat, the scenes were jubilant and euphoric and full of faith and hopes for the future.

We were a part of that important historic gathering of enthusiastic people and their supporters who brought a revolution in post-independent India. Congress Party that ruled continuously for 37 years, was dislodged and humiliated and a non-Congress government was sworn-in for the very first time.

I was again on the radio-TV circuit and with added vigor as Prime Minister Morarji Desai, Foreign Minister Vajpayee and others came for interviews by panels of senior journalists, including me. We had access to Ministers and one time just after Morarji Desai was chosen Prime Minister, a couple of journalists – me included – were inside the bedroom of Morarji *Bhai* and asking questions.

It was left to his son, Kanti *Bhai*, to remind us that his father goes to bed rather early and indicating the time for interviews was over.

[This was a far cry from the days of Indira Gandhi and Emergency that the Press got so close to the elected representatives of the people that had toppled the Dictator.]

During the Emergency it had become nearly impossible to meet with Ministers of Indira Gandhi for news and answers to our questions as they themselves were, mostly, tight-lipped and scared about talking to the press and divulging something they should not. As a matter of fact, many of them also did not know a thing – the administration was run by a coterie of close confidantes of the 'Higher Ups' who were close to Indira Gandhi, more particularly to Sanjay Gandhi.

Janata Party's emergence changed the entire scenario. The Prime Minister had the Ministers work and handle their portfolios and deal with the situation themselves. There was democracy, instead of autocracy. There were regular briefings by Ministers, and after every Cabinet

241

meeting a Minister would brief reporters. The Cabinet Ministers were accessible, friendly and ready to listen, get ideas and act.

Of course there was this hastily formed coalition that became Janata Party but there were over ambitious people like Chaudhary Charan Singh of Bharatiya Lok Dal (BLD), and Jagjivan Ram, who left the Congress Party and set up his Congress For Democracy (CFD), who also wanted to be Prime Minister. JP stepped in and discussed with all the elected Members of the coalition (that had become Janata Party) and according to the consensus, declared Morarji Desai to be the leader of the party, and the Prime Minister.

[Yet another instance of Morarji Desai's quick wit was enough to silence all those who thought he was a stern, without any wit or humor, hardened politician and nothing more.

This was Morarji's first press conference immediately after he took the Oath of Office as the Prime Minister (Janata Party government) in 1977. The *Vigyan Bhavan* hall was packed to capacity and journalists were eager to ask questions.

JK Jain, reporter-turned editor of his own paper was a supporter of Indira Gandhi quite a few years back but reportedly tried to join the Janata Party without success. Consequently, he had gone back to Indira's camp with a vengeance. He asked a controversial – and some thought unwarranted – question about urine therapy that Morarji had advocated.

JK asked Mr. Desai: Should a person suffering from sexually transmitted disease (STD) also drink his urine? The attempt was clearly to embarrass Morarji before the crowded press conference, attended by senior Indian and foreign journalists. Many journalists present did not like the question but Morarji said he would give an answer.

Replied Moraji *Bhai*: "For personal problems you can see me after the press conference."

There was a loud laughter. JK must have felt embarrassed as Morarji's wit effectively silenced him.]

Both Charan Singh and Jagjivan Ram were appeased by elevating both as Deputy Prime Ministers. [That satisfied them, but only temporarily.]

Janata Party had seen this divisive trend right from the beginning and it started growing as time passed. The leaders pulled in different directions and some weird decisions were taken like arresting Indira Gandhi without adequate preparation and preparing a solidly convincing charge sheet. The consequence was that a Magistrate released her the next day and Indira emerged as "the helpless, poor woman, victim of a political witch-hunt by Janata Party."

The in-fighting and ideological differences persisted.

The setting up of a high level commission of inquiry into the excesses committed during Emergency and those responsible for the violation of the Constitution, such as Indira Gandhi, was a welcome development. The government appointed the Commission with Justice JC Shah, the former Chief Justice of India's Supreme Court, as Chairman. Justice Shah wanted to complete the finding/proceedings as soon as possible.

However, the Congress put many legal hurdles to prolong the Commission's work, did not cooperate in a legitimate inquiry into the blatant subversion of India's Constitution and total violation of civil rights. On the contrary, it managed to paint itself and its leaders as victims of political harassment and to an extent succeeded in unashamedly fooling the common people.

[The Shah Commission had two prominent persons attached to it – PR Rajgopal as Secretary and the top lawyer, PN Lekhi to assist the Commission. Sadhana and I attended hearings at the Commission daily – I was reporting for my newspaper as well as doing evening commentary on the TV. Sadhana wrote independently and also composed a satirical poem that she recited before Justice Shah and other top people of the Commission.]

Indira Gandhi had one of the top attorneys, Frank Anthony, as her lead counsel. (He was also a nominated Anglo-Indian Member of Parliament.) Lekhi was more than a match for him. They would often clash on facts, politics and peoples' reaction.

On one occasion when Anthony was saying something about the nation and public service – referring to Indira Gandhi's contribution – Lekhi could not contain himself.

He hit Anthony hard by reminding him of his past with the remark: "I was a freedom fighter put in Lahore Central Jail and you were then singing God Save The King."

The audience roared with laughter as Anthony kept silent.

Meanwhile I had been getting wider recognition and honors. The United Nations office in New Delhi offered me a fellowship for about a week to attend and report a UN Conference in Mexico City. The UN rep, Mr. Suszkiewicz, knew me and my wife very well and, probably, he felt I was the only journalist fit for the job at that juncture. A fine man, with wide knowledge of Indian affairs, he had been to our home and had also enjoyed our hospitality.

I attended, and covered the UN Conference for *Hindustan*. It was an experience to see how the UN staff worked to make an international conference worthwhile and meaningful. A plethora of speeches, their simultaneous translation and print-outs in no time and several other demands on the UN staff were mind-boggling. The big number of foreign delegates and their requirements, the host country's ability to handle big responsibility is always tested and challenged. Mexico did an excellent job and all that made a lasting impression on me.

India had been hosting international conferences quite often and very efficiently. I covered many but a UN conference of this size was a first.

[It so happened that the Mexican ambassador to India, Antonio Jose Lara Villarreal was also a good friend of ours and also had been to our home to enjoy Sadhana's tasty food. He was also interested in Hinduism.

Once he asked me if he could also wear the sacred thread (*Janeu* or *yagyopaveet*) and I said, why not? The three strings are a symbol of recognition and respect for three outstanding persons in our lives – our world. They are: your parents who gave you birth, your teachers who gave you knowledge, and the ancient sages (the researchers) who gave you wisdom. This has nothing to do with Hinduism, anyone can wear it. It's a part of traditional 'Hindu culture' because Hindus started it.

Ambassador Villarreal was impressed.

As he came to know about my UN fellowship in Mexico City, he arranged with his government to extend my stay in Mexico as guest of the government for a week. It was, again, an honor and there was no question of not accepting it.

What I saw there amazed me and confirmed the ancient Indian history and heritage of OUR people traveling to faraway lands and making friends there, marrying and cementing our ties with them. That was done not by military invasion, but through the peaceful and amiable exchange of religious texts and popularizing Hindu religion, customs and culture. I met some senior Ministers and also did quite a bit of sightseeing, including the silver mines area in Taxco, about 106 miles south-west of Mexico City.

There are Sun and Moon temples (Pyramids) in Mexico; there is the Maya culture very similar to India. There are names that have their origin in Sanskrit. Sadhana's supervisor at JC Penney store in Los Angeles had the name Nacho – he said it's actually Nachiketa, a name familiar to serious students of ancient Indian history.]

My trip was extended to Romania and Hungary (then under the Soviet sphere of influence) on my way back to India. These presented a different – though well-organized systems – and I had friends there to make me feel good. Those countries had invited me to visit and some of their diplomats were my friends in India. I also stopped in Sofia (Bulgaria) and three days in Istanbul (Turkey), both on my own.

[My Bulgarian trip on government invitation was cancelled at the last moment for some unexplained reason. Since I had already booked my flight, I did not want to cancel the trip altogether, but I made it only a one-day stopover as now I was paying for it.

The next day I saw the Press Chief in his office. He did apologize for the cancellation and graciously presented me with a set of books and other literature about the country. (Little did he realize that he was adding to my problems.)

At the airport, my baggage was found over the limit and I was asked to pay the extra money. What followed next was my countless trips from one counter to another, weighing the baggage, then changing dollars to local currency, back to the first counter to pay and then told to bring the ticket which had already been taken at the first counter where they had checked me and confirmed my flight. To make the matters worse, they said they did not have my ticket – and it was not with me. No one was prepared to help a bona-fide paying passenger whose flight was already confirmed at the counter.

I felt helpless. For the first time, a hardened journalist and a seasoned traveler – me – was nearly in tears. All this drama took nearly 20 minutes, after which, the man at the first counter brought me the ticket and just said, this had somehow gone to another counter. No apologies.

Back in India, I narrated the whole story to the Press Chief of the Bulgarian embassy. Probably, it was undiplomatic on my part but he offered profound apologies.]

Sadhana was shocked and could not believe that something like this could happen, but we took it in stride.

Sadhana, as usual, cared for the family in my absence and didn't complain. Only the kids, especially Seema, was a little mad and managed to send me a message complaining that I keep on extending my trip and to hurry back home, which I did at the first opportunity.

Meanwhile in India politics and political games shamelessly continued to upset Janata Party, whose many leaders were themselves guilty.

These differences encouraged the Congress and Indira Gandhi – experts in all kinds of tactics and political maneuvering right up to the highest level – the President. They worked and Indira Gandhi returned to power by first helping Charan Singh to break away with Janata Party and become Prime Minister with Congress support and then withdrawing support to him.

President, N. Sanjeeva Reddy, who had been elected President as a Janata Party candidate, sided with Indira Gandhi (who had managed to defeat him as Congress candidate earlier and got VV Giri elected as Independent. He dissolved the Parliament (Lok Sabha) to facilitate new elections without inviting Jagjivan Ram (the leader of the single largest Janata Party) to try and form the government.

The dissolution of Parliament and subsequent elections saw Indira Gandhi return to power, in January 1980. Congress won a big victory and Sanjay Gandhi emerged as a redoubtable strong man of the party. Janata Party literally disintegrated and Indira's second innings began.

And then something tragic happened.

Though she did not resort to Emergency again but the same coterie had re-emerged. Then the unthinkable happened. Indira's 'heir apparent' Sanjay Gandhi died in a plane crash within months of the comeback. It was a big unexpected blow – also personally – to Indira Gandhi (it happened very near our Chanakyapuri home, in a forest area.) It was the result of a reckless man flying the plane without taking the required pre-flight steps such as checking the fuel tank.

It was also said that Sanjay was doing some aerobatics – for which he was not fully trained, and therefore lost control of the plane. It also took the life of another pilot, Capt. Subhash Saxena, whom Sanjay took with him on the flight.

The result was obvious.

In Indira's second innings I was once again black-listed – just after the first TV interview. It was with Balram Jakhar, the newly elected (Congress) Speaker of Lok Sabha (Parliament). The interview was crisp, to the point and showed how it should be conducted – fairly, fearlessly, without shredding the man to pieces but asking pointed questions and giving the other side ample opportunity to answer pertinent questions.

I was very fair but undaunted. I asked crisp questions such as, 'Your party was accused of violating the Constitution and taking away people's rights, now that you have come back, how are you going to justify what Congress and its leaders did during the Emergency?' It was an appropriate question, though not to the liking of hardliners and Congress sycophants who did not want to question the leadership.

But Jakhar welcomed my questions as they gave him ample opportunity to defend his party. Asking goody-goody questions would not have elicited the replies he gave. His answers were equally impressive, of course on party-lines.

But the powers-that-be, were mad at my 'audacity' to ask sharp questions. To my pleasant surprise, Speaker Jakhar was extremely happy with the questions because he felt he got ample opportunity to answer.

Since that day Speaker Jakhar acknowledged me at every place and took me as a friend. Sometimes he would address me as *Bade Bhai* (big brother). He gave his staff blanket order to let me in whenever I wanted to see him.

I never misused this kindness and consideration. Politics remained at its place as usual.

The year and Congress victory saw other developments in my office also with my senior, Chandulal Chandrakar, a Congressman, re-elected to Lok Sabha and subsequently appointed a Minister in Indira Gandhi's Cabinet. He resigned as Editor of *Hindustan* and the post that should have been mine on merit and seniority was given to Binod Kumar Mishra, the junior-most member of the News Bureau whose Chief was none other than me.

I was devastated, and so was Sadhana. She had always shared my hopes, and tears and was consistently a pillar of strength for me. She had ample faith in God and in my ability. She told me not to worry, my rewards will come in due course. And that *Hindustan* was not the end of the world.

She and I also toyed with the idea of me resigning and moving out. I even thought of leaving the country but the idea did not go forward. Something else was waiting for me, somewhere else. My Sadhana's firm faith and confidence in me were prophetic. Something bigger was in our destiny.

What happened with my job was sheer political pressure; a weak Birla would succumb to anything that purported to come from Indira Gandhi or Sanjay Gandhi, may be even from a secretary to Sanjay Gandhi.

The same Birla who had decided in my favor when Chandrakar became Editor and his position as Chief of News Bureau fell vacant. Though I was the senior most, with unmatched record of meritorious contribution to the organization and vast experience, two other claimants were also toying with the idea of superseding me. One thought his supposed political connections will help him; the other was depending on family relationship and caste consideration.

The matter went to Birla who consulted Chandrakar and General Manager Sahi. My record was unquestionably solid and KK Birla had no hesitation in confirming my promotion as Chief of News Bureau.

The same Birla succumbed to political pressure; it was probably, a vastly changed climate and mere mention of Sanjay Gandhi and the Prime Minister's office/house was enough for the big newspaper-owner and one of the top industrialists to meekly surrender and do the unthinkable.

It was clearly a political decision dictated by favoritism that I challenged and wrote a letter to Birla. He replied that the other guy was senior and that I had no case. I was mad and sent a counter to Birla stating that the office records would clearly show who was senior and who had merit and that the decision was politically motivated. I also bluntly wrote that political decisions are temporary in nature and they give heartburn to those who work hard - and selflessly.

I did not get any reply to *that* letter. But an interesting development had taken place, meanwhile.

The top government official (Home Secretary), Sundar Lal Khurana, had taken over as General Manager of the *Hindustan Times* group. He was Home Secretary with the Government of India and therefore Emergency was proclaimed under *his* signature. According to legal protocol and rules Emergency declaration and many other important decisions – after the President's approval – had to be issued under the signature of the Home Secretary.

So, Khurana had become the most important official connected with Emergency.

And therefore, he was summoned by Shah Commission, during Janata Party rule, and questioned extensively about his role in the sordid political and undemocratic action.

I was doing a daily commentary on TV about the proceedings at the Commission.

I did that also when Khurana deposed and was questioned, extensively.

[I had not met him when he was Home Secretary.]

A few days after he took over the post with my newspaper, he called me for a meeting. In my mind, I recalled my TV commentary on his testimony and thought that would be my last day in the office. However, to my pleasant surprise, Khurana was very cordial and even talked positively about the TV report. He said it looked that you were not being dictated by TV bosses (under Janata Rule) and your commentary was actually balanced.

I was definitely relieved. Since then our relations were very cordial.

After my last letter to Big Boss Birla, Khurana called and told me that the Chairman (Birla) was unhappy with my letter. I said I am equally unhappy with his action (of depriving me of my rightful post). Khurana said, after all he is the Big Boss and these things do happen and that I should reconcile.

I told him that I cannot and will not work with *Hindustan* for long. Working under someone who was the junior-most in my Bureau was not acceptable to me. I said if you think I am not worthy of the Editor's post, or have no merit and seniority, you can fire me.

Khurana assured me that he didn't question my merit, he knew my worth and also the record of my seniority. However, he said the matter was decided for *other* reasons. He wanted me to reconcile with the situation and continue.

I was gratified that at least this man had sincerely acknowledged my worth, my capability and my seniority, and that I should not take any hasty decision. I let him know that though I cannot reconcile, *I* will decide the future course of action, in due course.

Meanwhile, I continued my work, as diligently as I had been doing all that for nearly three decades with *Hindustan*. Sadhana and I were still as popular as before. She was doing her job of raising the girls and caring for the family and others. Time permitting, I also joined her for vacations and outings.

Meanwhile I got yet another opportunity to go abroad. This was a trip to Taiwan. The breakaway island was made the capital of the Nationalist Chinese government led by Chiang Kai Sheik when he was ousted by the Communists from the Chinese mainland. He was long gone but his Kuomintang Party still in power, asserted its independence. Taiwan was then growing economically faster than mainland China.

I had a wonderful week's visit and meetings with anti-Communist leaders of the world. I made many friends, one of which was Congressman Solomon and his charming wife, Freda. [Solomon was from New York and I had the opportunity to touch base with him – long distance of course, when we arrived in Los Angeles a few years later. He retired from Congress and took up business, and, as happens all the time with me, I lost touch with him after he left Congress.]

One Summer we planned to visit my cousin, Col. VK Bhatnagar, in Siliguri (East India, part of West Bengal, near Darjeeling.) He was posted at the Remount and Veterinary Corps of the Indian Army, a horse/mule breeding center. A top Vet, an excellent polo player and horseman, cousin Vinod had been insisting that we pay him a visit. We finally found time and planned the visit.

I had been going far and wide on my travels but had not been to the closest neighbor – Bhutan.

And then appeared my yet another diplomat friend, the ambassador of Bhutan. [I had met Bhutan's youthful King Jigme Singye Wangchuk a couple times and interviewed him when he visited New Delhi, which was fairly frequent as India and Bhutan had the closest relations.

The ambassador spoke to me and sent an invitation for Sadhana and I to visit Bhutan as the guest of the King. We would be picked up from New Delhi to Calcutta (now Kolkata) to Bagdogra, on our way to Thimphu, the capital of Bhutan.

I had made long-postponed plans to take my family to visit cousin Vinod in Siliguri and explained that to the ambassador.

He came back to me the very next day, bubbling with joy and with an amended program. We all (girls included) would be King's Guests.

I was not much familiar with the route and the ambassador explained. Instead of Sadhana and I going to Calcutta-Bagdogra-Thimphu, we *all* would be picked up at Siliguri – that happened to be on our route to Bhutan – and dropped back there. So the Bhutanese government did not have to pay all the way to Calcutta-Bagdogra and Siliguri and back to New Delhi for the two of us.

It suited all the parties and the family was happy. That was in 1979.

For the girls it would be their first foreign trip and that too, invited by the King of Bhutan.

We had a wonderful visit to Thimphu, Paro and Punakha monastery, saw the town, the rain-prayer-march (where the King leads the parade across the town praying for the rains). We also saw the King's team vs Indian Army team playing basketball (and the King himself playing).

We also met Indian ambassador JC Hiremath and his sweet family. Ambassador Hiremath was one of the finest diplomats and held top posts in various countries. He gave us useful tips about Bhutan, it's very nice people and India's close relations with that country and about his personal relations with its youthful King. He and his wife were well liked by the King and the people.

The visit was topped by a meeting with the King.

[The hotels in Thimphu and Paro were well-maintained and the staff well-trained by India's leading government-run Ashoka hotel. We were well taken care of at all the places. At Paro we were the only guests at that time and had the best of everything – food, desserts, and hospitality. The girls were ecstatic.

The only time Seema was miserable was the long hilly drive from Siliguri to Thimphu when she got exhausted after throwing up several times. A doctor visited and treated her as soon as we reached Thimphu. She was fine the rest of the time. Barring that, it was fun all the way.]

Our meeting with the King was made memorable – by the King himself.

I had asked for, and was assured of, an exclusive meeting with the King. His Secretary picked me up from the hotel and took me to the modestly furnished office of the King.

The first thing after he greeted me was, "Where's your wife?"

I said I thought the meeting was only with me.

He instructed the Secretary to bring Sadhana quickly.

The guy, a well-stocked man, came panting when Sadhana was about to leave the hotel for her painting/sketching hobby and brought her to the King's office.

The youthful King – he was not yet 30 then – greeted her cordially and informally. He asked her to share the ordinary bench with him – opposite his own just a little fancy chair – and asked me to sit in *his* chair. I hesitated but he insisted that I sit where HE wanted me to. I settled down in the King's chair – in his 'Oval Office.'

We talked about various topics for about 20 minutes and I thought I should not overstay and thanked him, hinting that it's okay to leave. He said no, no, let's continue. We did that for another 15 minutes but he again said he wasn't busy and we could continue. It was more than an hour when finally he let us leave but not before I had asked him the important personal question about his marriage.

I said there are reports that a China-born Bhutani girl was being groomed to be his queen. He smiled mischievously and said, you would be among the first to know when I decide to marry.

[That could not happen as we had moved to the United States. He publicly married in 1988. It was reported that they had married privately in 1979. According to the Bhutanese custom, the King marries multiple sisters. (OUR King married four and now has 10 kids.) The King abdicated in favor of his oldest son in 2006 when he was just 51, and the young man only 26. King Jigme Singye Wangchuk himself was 16 when he became the King after his father's death. This King did many appreciable things and has been credited with many reforms in the Kingdom that his son, King Jigme Khesar Namgyel Wangchuck is continuing and expanding.]

As we prepared to leave Bhutan, the King sent his Secretary with a lot of gifts, including exquisitely beautiful scroll of silk with traditional multi-color paintings, called Tankha. He also sent a heavy black slate-stone idol of one of the Bhutanese gods revered in the nation. There was a silver box embellished with pure gold.

We were overwhelmed with the hospitality and the beautiful gifts, couldn't thank the King and the Ambassador enough.

We returned with sweet memories to cherish.

After our Bhutan visit we were back in Siliguri with my cousin and enjoyed another round of relaxed stay and sightseeing in beautiful Darjeeling and Kalimpong. Did some shopping also. We returned to New Delhi with a stopover in Varanasi (Benaras.) In the famous city of Varanasi I had a good friend and a Member of Parliament, Sudhakar Pande, the president of *Nagari Pracharini Sabha* (organization for the promotion of Hindi), an age-old organization my father was also associated with in his time in the 1920s to 1950s. The *Sabha* published valuable books on the language, literature and culture of India. Pande *Ji* gave me several new books for review and comments.

We visited the famous *Ghats* (river front of Ganga) and the Vishwanath temple. Both the places were poorly maintained and even the holy river Ganga was dirty – with thousands of people and animals bathing there every day. We preferred to cross over to the other side to dip our feet in the somewhat clean waters.

[No government or the municipal authority had attempted to clean Ganga and do something meaningful to clean up the roads and passage to the *Ghats* and temples. Only the new government – and Prime Minister Modi who himself got elected from Varanasi, instead of his old state of Gujarat – has initiated some solid work in this direction. A separate Ministry with a Minister in-charge has been created for this job. It is a huge task as all the filth – private and industrial, all along hundreds of miles – is poured into Ganga indiscriminately. So is the state of river Yamuna.]

One miracle had baffled and pleasantly surprised us after we returned to New Delhi and got our things out of the taxi-cab. With all the bags hurriedly accounted for, some paintings and the slate-stone idol were left just outside on the sidewalk. A 'Paris repeated' but with a difference. When I remembered the other items, they had vanished.

We told all our neighbors and the servants about it and requested them to keep an eye on the neighboring servant quarter residents.

A few days later Rati Ram, our gardener, got the info and we took a policeman to that particular servant's quarter. The young man had removed all the things lying on the sidewalk and was trying to sell them. That's how Rati Ram got the wind and everything was recovered from the man.

[Unfortunately a couple of gifts, including the valuable Tankha, were lost in our frequent moves from one place to another, one country to another and one state to another. One of the movers was especially to be blamed but nothing came out of complaints and their promised search.]

Back in Delhi, life was as usual. Politics was getting dirty and my life with *Hindustan*, somewhat uncomfortable. It was some consolation that I had no contact with the new editor – my former junior-most assistant – for news coverage or writing articles. He did not instruct me, or ever ask me to meet with him (a regular practice between an editor and his staff, especially the senior-most man), but it was fine with me. I continued to do my duty – he his, may be getting instructions from his political benefactors and carrying out their instructions to repay the favors.

Two major events – unconnected to domestic politics or my time at the newspaper – happened between 1979 and 1982: The Soviet invasion of our neighbor Afghanistan and our older daughter Sujata's wedding – both very closely connected and both had a profound impact on our lives and our future.

Actually, the two events changed the entire course of our life and family connections. For one, we got a big, extended family now spread in several countries, speaking several languages but sharing the same love and respect. Many from the same families we knew for at least 30 years were present to bid farewell, and pay their last respects, to Sadhana, in 2016, when she left us.

27

The Afghan War and
Sujata's Wedding

I was opposed to the Soviet invasion of Afghanistan right from day one. That also made some of my leftist friends unhappy as they supported the Soviets (Russians) all out in defending their 'empire.' There was somewhat heated discussion at one of the diplomatic/media meetings but I held on to my views.

Well that was political and professional, I never shirked from discussing. Besides, I had good relations with a number of Communist/Soviet-orbit nations and their embassies in India, and mingled with their diplomats.

On a personal level things had to develop and they did very soon.

Rewind:

In 1940 in Bombay, I got another sister, Bimla. She came to my father to study Hindi. Father had started *Hindi Samiti* organization to promote Hindi language in the predominantly Marathi areas. Father 'adopted' her so she became my sister, a very loving and caring young woman.

On Sports Day in my school, I fell from my bicycle and was badly injured. That did not stop me from competing in many other items though I could not figure out why I was not able to give it my best. I came home very tired and immediately laid down and dozed off. After sometime when I opened my eyes, I was deeply moved to find Bimla *behenji* applying coconut oil on my extensive injuries all over the left side of my body to give it a soothing relief.

All along she continued to be a loving and caring sister to me.

Sometime in 1979 one of my nieces (sister Bimla's daughter, Sarojini) was in a local hospital and came in contact with a lady from Afghanistan who was also there.

They became friends and the lady, Razia Mansoori, told Sarojini the story of her flight from Afghanistan and her stay in New Delhi with three little

255

children. Her husband, an aeronautical engineer, was with Ariana, the Afghan Airlines, and had gone to the United States to purchase a plane and train his men. Meanwhile, the Soviets were all over Afghanistan and Mansoori saw no point in returning and getting into trouble.

His family managed to flee and took refuge in India.

One day Sadhana and I went to see Sarojini and she pleaded with me to do something for this scared Afghan family in distress and uncertain about the future.

We met Razia and her family and saw the place she was staying with her two sons about 15 and 10, and a daughter, about five. They called it a guest house. Somehow we didn't like the place; it didn't give us good vibes at all.

Sadhana and I immediately made a plan.

We were strangers but we were human. I told Razia, "From today you are my sister, Sadhana is your *Bhabhi* (sister-in-law) and we are taking all of you home right now."

Sarojini must have given Razia some background info about us, or she herself must have felt our sincerity. There was no hesitation on her part and we brought our 'new family' home. The room Sujata and Seema shared was given to Razia and her boys, Johnny and Jahed. Sweet little Shahla became our dear roommate and would always sleep in our bed, in between Sadhana and me, happily.

She still fondly remembers all that.

The first day when it happened, Sujata and Seema came home to find someone else occupying their room. They were shocked but came around swiftly and accepted them as members of our family.

[Now Razia-Mansoori family lives just a few miles (about 15 minutes) from where I live with Sujata and Mujtaba. We are five minutes away from granddaughter Tamanna Roashan, her husband Khushal, and my cute little great granddaughter, precious baby Aliya.]

This Mansoori family relation has continued for more than 38 years.

There is a history to our relations, and some background.

Razia came from a well-known Kushkaki family holding high positions in Afghanistan. Her sister Sharifa was married to Mohammed Khalid Roashan who was a Minister in the Afghan government for years. All of them were marked figures after the Soviet invasion and occupation and were planning to leave the country. Some had left, others were trying to.

The situation in Afghanistan had become intolerable for them. Thousands of Afghans left their country in search of safety, security and a new life somewhere else. Many went to Europe, many more arrived in America.

This Afghan family became very close and dear to us all. They stayed with us for a few months till Mansoori arranged for their visa and other formalities to join him in America.

Mujtaba, the youngest of four children of Sharifa and Khalid, was a student of Civil Engineering at Chandigarh (Punjab, India.) I sent him a telegram about his *khala – Maasee* (aunty) staying with us. He started visiting her and other cousins at our home in New Delhi.

As they say, the rest is history.

[Mujtaba and Sujata were married on October 8, 1982, in Los Angeles – the same day Sadhana and I married in 1961. Sadhana, Seema and I lived with our son-in-law and Sujata when we moved to America to usher the new year of 1986.]

After Razia and family, there was a stream of Afghan refugees pouring in to India and most of them stayed in Delhi. Some relatives of Razia were at our home and dozens of them, though living in some other areas of the city, visited us frequently. We were privileged to be, kind of, a reception center and a 'contact point' for Afghan refugees, a majority of them became our life-long friends and/or relatives.

Mujtaba's father Mohammed Khalid Roashan came, his younger brother Dr. Ghulam Rauf Roashan, his lovely wife Maliha jan, with their children Yama, Bahram and Ghazal came and stayed with us.

[We missed meeting Zalmai Roashan, the youngest brother and his charming wife Zarifa who were still in Afghanistan at the time. We made up for that while in America.]

Many young men and women would travel miles from their temporary homes in other parts of Delhi to spend some time with us and enjoy Sadhana's tasty dishes. The ones who ate non-veg dishes for breakfast, lunch and dinner, relished all-vegetarian meals at all times, at our home with us.

Among the others were Razia's two brothers Zamanuddin Kushkaki, his wife Samar, sons – Sami, Farid and Wais, and Amanuddin Kushkaki and his wife Nigar, sons – Amin, Hamed and Elyas.

Mujtaba's older brother Murtaza, his wife Shahla and little Husai also came to Delhi but stayed in Mukherji Nagar, miles away from us, which had virtually become a mini Afghan town. We have fond memories of not only them visiting us and enjoying Sadhana's cooking Indian dishes but we also visited their temporary homes and relished their hospitality. Among them was Mansoori's sister Suraya, husband Latif with their two adorable kids, Yama and Metra, Nigar's sister Laila and her husband Aziz, and her brother Mosa. All of them became very close and part of our extended family.

There was yet another young Afghan, Nazir, also became our relative, who met us a couple times. He did small roles in Bollywood movies. He also met us in Bombay as we were leaving for the United States. Nazir is a cousin of Latif, Suraya's husband.

In addition, there were quite a few young men and women, would-be members of our extended family, who loved to meet with us, spend time with us and enjoy Sadhana's tasty vegetarian meals. They were living quite far from us but would often visit. Once we were out and the house locked, but they came, just sat on the grass in the front yard, even dozed off – with a few resting their heads on the stairs when we, finally, returned. There was, usually, no prior notice.

But that was fine with them, and us, we were a family and didn't bother too much about these formalities.

This young, lively and jolly group consisted of cousins of Mujtaba – Waheeda and Parveen, their brother, Masood, Waheeda's would-be-husband Daud, Maryam, Ibrahim, and others.

We went to Agra with many of them to see the Taj Mahal, where the love story of Mujtaba and Sujata began…

They all are very dear to us and visit us whenever possible, especially at times of grief, to comfort us and share our sorrow, along with many others who we met here in the US and who also are very close to us.

Sincere thanks to all these dear ones to help make this world a better place to live.

It was a sense of satisfaction for us that we were there when someone needed us for a shoulder, an ear, a heart – and a home.

We took that as God's planning and our sacred duty. And we had fun too.

Mansoori, Razia and little Shahla paid us a visit in August 1982. They – and we – made it an occasion to deepen the ties and set the 'young people right.' Mujtaba had already gone to America but he and Sujata were in contact with each other and fervently desired a union. Sujata was in her second year in a prestigious college and was doing very well.

But something else was also going on in her head, I felt, and observed.

With Mansoori family's visit we did a quick engagement and opened the door of close relations with a big family.

Dozens of members of this extended Afghan family and their friends came to know us and most of them had come to our home. The close ones had already reached America and were mostly concentrated in Los Angeles. Nearly 40 of them wanted to be at the wedding. However, that being impractical, we ourselves decided to go to America. In a change of wedding format, we took the bride to the bridegroom's place – a reverse *Baraat*, if you will.

It was a lot more expensive and also emotional for us – Sadhana and I, Sujata and Seema flying to America, staying there, arranging the marriage ceremony in a faraway land without much hope of seeing a married Sujata, very soon and frequently – and also without our own blood-relatives present.

However that was, as they say, destiny and we had accepted it.

Before that, Sadhana and I could never think of ignoring our relatives and friends in India, about the marriage and not making them a part of the ceremony. It seemed rather strange that the groom was some 8000 miles away in Los Angeles and we wanted some kind of a party to announce a life-changing happy event.

We innovated. We arranged a 'pre-marriage reception' – an occasion to bless the bride and give a sendoff to the bridal party for the actual wedding ceremony in America.

Over three hundred relatives, friends and well-wishers came to the reception at the prestigious Constitution Club in New Delhi, that basically caters to members of Parliament. There were a dozen senior Cabinet Ministers, ambassadors, and government officials, relatives, and friends from various walks of life and other well-wishers.

The recent arrival of Col. Usman's big family from Kabul added to the color. They also, like the others, became our close friends. The family was conspicuous by their presence as the only representative of Afghanistan and Mujtaba's extended family, to start this loving inter-national relation.

Among the distinguished Cabinet Ministers at the reception were Pundit Kamlapati Tripathi (who was an eminent editor when I was in junior High School), AP Sharma, Maharaja (Dr.) Karan Singh and his wife, Maharani Yasho Rajya Laxmi Devi, and Prof. Sher Singh and his wife Shobha *Ji*.

All who did not know, were curious to meet the groom – 'elusive' as he had to be because of circumstances – and asked about him. We had to explain. It was a unique event – not much heard of – but Sadhana and I had been unique in many ways, so was our marriage, and so that was fine. The guests enjoyed the food and company. Constitution Club's catering was always excellent.

[It was the same place we had celebrated Sujata's first birthday, some 18 years back. It had become historic in our life.]

A couple days later we were on the way to America, via Hong Kong.

We celebrated Seema's birthday, October 6, in Hong Kong. She did not have a grand celebration on her first birthday – like Sujata. However, the positive side was that she was lucky that at least one birthday was celebrated in a foreign country, on a ferry, surrounded by hundreds of people of various nationalities, on the waves of a mighty ocean.

Not many have been that lucky.

The next three weeks we were out of India in Los Angeles, staying with my new sister, Razia and her family who took very good care of us. We were not the bride's party, but family, distinguished guests and dear brother-*Bhabhi* and niece. The big party night at the Mansoori house included many whom we had met and entertained in our home in New Delhi; they were now comfortably settled in Los Angeles.

There were three rituals: A quick Vedic ceremony with me chanting a few *mantras* and a make shift *Havan* (sacred fire) using a 'purified' Barbeque grill; a quicker *nikah* ceremony performed by, probably, a young Mullah; and the third, the next day or so, in a court where a judge pronounced Mujtaba and Sujata husband and wife in the presence of a dozen or so close relatives.

It was triple fun.

Sujata's marriage, also like ours, was not planned out as a Big Fat Indian Wedding where beautiful rituals continue for a number of days, like *roka* (agreement), *mehndi* (henna), *sangeet* (music), *sagai* (engagement), and then *vivah* (marriage) ceremony followed by tearful and emotional *vidai* (farewell to the bride as she departs for her husband's home.)

The short-cut suited us all. Elaborate ceremonies and prolonged rituals, were not practical then. Sujata and Mujtaba, though, have some regrets that they got married so soon after our arrival and did not get any time to 'date,' go out – only the two of them – and have some youthful fun BEFORE they were hitched.

Too bad folks. We gave you a lifetime to do all that you were made to miss initially, in India! You were in a hurry. Sujata didn't get to complete her studies though she had topped in Political Science in her college, Jesus and Mary.

Several rounds of parties followed where we were felicitated and made new friends, renewed old friendships and strengthened our relations. There were hardly a couple Indians in those groups of friends, but we did not miss any.

Three weeks of love, respect, regard – and hospitality no end, Sadhana, Seema and I returned to Delhi and resumed our life. We were naturally more emotional and sad with our first child so far away, the one who took care of her little sister, Seema, like a mother. Naturally, Seema was feeling lonely. But that's life, and that's what you have to adjust to.

Sujata, though, got what she wanted but was also sad that she would have to live so far away from her parents and only sister. [She would often recall the movie song *kahe ko byahe bides* (why did you send me to marry so far in a foreign land) and even added her own version in a letter to us when we were still in India.

You can't keep your daughters with you all their life or yours.

However, we have been lucky to have lived with, or near, our daughters for better part of our life – longer with Sujata than Seema, but that, again, is life. You don't get everything you ask for, wish for, or even deserve. *Kabhi Kisi Ko Mukammal Jahan Nahi Milta,* as I always recall. This is an immortal song from 1980 movie *Aahista Aahista,* beautifully sung by Bhupinder with melody by Khayyam and lyrics by Nida Fazli.

[This separation of mother-daughter gave birth to a beautiful poem by Sadhana. This is one of the finest poems of Sadhana we have included in the collection, a sample proof copy of which we were able to get and show her on her hospital bed.

There is another poem written just before Sadhana conceived for the first time. She wrote that until she conceived she could not depict the feelings on the face of a mother she was drawing. This is also one of the finest and one of my top favorites, also included in *Samarpan.*]

Sujata's marriage and this major change in our lives coupled with whatever was happening in my office and in the country with Indira Gandhi's second round, did not give me much hope for the future. The fact that she came back to power with a vengeance thwarting the united opposition was not quite encouraging.

[Indira Gandhi seemed to have changed, she was not quite herself, especially with the tragic death of her chosen successor Sanjay Gandhi, a couple years before.

Sanjay was reckless, with not much experience or depth as a politician – just like his nephew, Rahul, Rajiv Gandhi's son, entrusted with many responsibilities hard to face and discharge. While Sanjay was able to help his mother regain power in 1980, Rahul has helped his mother, Sonia, lose her power, clout and even relevance since 2014 when Bharatiya Janata Party under Narendra Modi won an unprecedented majority in Parliament as well as in many other states.

Sonia Gandhi is fast losing her trusted associates – because Rahul has made many of them irrelevant without himself being adequately relevant. Her health is nothing to boast of and a 70 year-old Sonia sometimes gives the impression that she is not herself anymore. Who would not, given the situation she is now facing?

One could also sympathize with her – she lost her mother in-law, Indira, her brother in-law, Sanjay, and her own husband, Rajiv.]

28

The Big Change and Moving Out of Delhi

A few months after Sujata's marriage and our return from America I had a meeting with Ramesh Agrawal, the man who, in a decade, took his newspaper chain *Dainik Bhaskar* to the top of Indian newspaper world. He came to meet with me at our Chanakyapuri home along with Jagannath Shastri, his Delhi correspondent.

Ramesh *Bhaisahab*, as he and all the males in his family and his circle of close friends were, fondly and respectfully, addressed, was a simple man. The fact that he came in an auto-rikshaw, not even a taxi-cab, in rubber slippers, spoke volumes for his simplicity. He could have conveniently got a taxi or a luxury car but no, he did not try to impress me with his wealth and prosperity.

I was impressed by his sincerity and simplicity and passion for his plans.

Ramesh *Ji* had planned to start the Indore edition of the paper. *Bhaskar* had three editions already – Jhansi (the original, started by his father), Gwalior and Bhopal (where he lived with his family.) He wanted a known, professional, editor for the new, Indore edition that could be the leader in his group and take the paper to newer heights of excellence and popularity. He wanted new ideas and new passion and also new methods of working.

He was prepared to go all out to have the right man.

I don't know how he came to know about me. May be my 'popularity' traveled faster than my hopes and aspirations. May be the news of my disappointment at the treatment at *Hindustan* after 30 plus years of dedicated and meritorious service, had reached him and he found it a golden opportunity to approach me.

Whatever it was, Shastri and Ramesh *Bhaisahab's* visit helped to change everything. He was persistent, generous and not in a mood to accept NO for an answer. He answered all my doubts, apprehensions and hesitation

263

and seeing me between two minds offered to take me to Indore to let me see and discuss in detail what he had in his mind.

For me it was a big decision. My life in India's capital city with my standing, connections and professional reputation – with relatives and friends – was all set despite the atmosphere at the office.

But Ramesh *Ji* had another 'trump card.' He said he had a claim over me (he had learnt that I was *born* in Indore) and that he wanted me to return to the city of my birth, and a city where my father was once a prominent editor-publisher-community leader and a literary figure.

I was sold, and went to Indore with him. He finalized the deal as I toured the brand new building in a sprawling compound situated on the important Bombay-Agra Road that was soon to be the hub of elite living and shopping in Indore. This was the Press Enclave with several other publications coming up.

On my return I told Sadhana who was very much a part of our meeting in our home and, as usual, was in full agreement with me on whatever I decide best for myself, for the family and for reclaiming my reputation. What I could not get with *Hindustan*, Ramesh Ji was prepared to give me in Indore – Chief Editor of ALL his *Bhaskar* editions, based in Indore.

The salary/ benefits he offered were also much higher.

He didn't leave me with any excuse. There was no room for saying NO. This was an opportunity willingly and generously offered, not through any manipulation or on 'political considerations' or on any promise of favors to be hoped for.

I felt compensated. I felt rewarded. I thought it was the redemption for me. I considered this a fitting reply to those who had wronged me, superseded me and, humiliated me and ignored my long, dedicated and meritorious service to *Hindustan* and also my standing in the profession.

I had over 36 years' experience working for the daily newspapers and magazines. I had also written a number of books and done thousands of radio and TV programs. I had traveled extensively in India and many foreign countries and earned kudos for my prolific reporting and writings.

What more could one expect from a professional eyed as the top man?

I sent my resignation to the General Manager and asked to be relieved in a week's time.

[By then, Mr. Khurana was gone and another younger man had taken over. He also knew me well.]

My accounts were cleared expeditiously. My name card and familiar TV face helped me to get my full Provident Fund in no time as I sat chatting with the Commissioner of the establishment in his office.

[I had heard that people had to wait for months and 'do all kinds of things' to get their own saved and earned money. But I was lucky, the officer was nice, and I got richer before I left Delhi – my home since 1947, and a couple years before that too.

I did not know for sure about the future I was embarking on but I definitely looked forward to one thing: The challenge; and I was prepared to accept it and defeat it.

There were quite a few papers in Indore and one of the biggest, reputed and professionally produced, older newspapers was *Nai Dunia*, with about 160,000 copies printed daily. We were starting with zero, but Ramesh *Bhaisahab* had faith in me and I had the self-confidence - and a record of hard work and professional merits to push me further, and motivate others.

I did not, initially, realize that there could be 'enemies,' there would be jealousy, saboteurs would be lurking in, and I would have to deal with not-so-competent people also. That's why my work was not easy and straight forward. I had to fight and assert, push myself to achieve what was expected of me, and what I was demanding from others, and determined to achieve.

I did not disappoint anyone – myself, my employers, and my readers.

Sadhana supported my decision wholeheartedly. Seema was now in Air Force school and finishing her 12th grade in a couple months and so they both stayed on in New Delhi. Seema was, somewhat, sad leaving Delhi and her friends, especially since Sujata was also not with us. In the end, she proved to be a trooper.

[Why Seema had to leave Holy Child Auxilium School, run by a Christian Missionary organization, and join the Air Force School - and even there an unlikely thing happened - needs to be mentioned.

After Sujata graduated and Seema started her 11th class, Holy Child decided to discontinue teaching Hindi – the Official, National, language of India. Sadhana and I were deeply disappointed but without making it a big issue, took Seema out of that school and quickly got her admitted to the prestigious Air Force Central School, a co-ed institution run by Indian Air Force, mainly for the military kids, but open to others also.

There the drama continued.

As the session started, Principal Henderson announced that he had discontinued teaching of Hindi as hardly any student enrolled for the subject. He had played a trick giving the students a choice between selecting Hindi or Physical Education. Obviously you have to devote more time and pay more attention to learn a language, its literature and grammar etc. PE was more convenient – and of course, interesting for military-kids. And so Mr. Henderson won.

Seema came home and told Sadhana who was upset. When Sadhana told me about it, I decided to act.

The very next day, I sent a letter to the Chief of Indian Air Force, Air Chief Marshal IH Latif.

The letter worked. The Air Force Education Branch Chief, a senior uniformed Air Force officer, at Vayu Sena Bhavan, New Delhi, called me. I told him the full story; he assured me of quick action. Yeah, within a couple days the School re-started Hindi though only two students remained for the subject by then – Seema and Uma Rege, a very good student and her friend.

Sadhana and I always fought for the causes dear to us.]

So, there I was, leaving Delhi where I spent the better part of my life, nearly 40 years, now leaving it with all its attractions – a career that took me near the top, a reputation of being an active, hardworking and popular pressman, and also having a big, close and extended family in the city.

My older sister Prem had already passed away, but her husband, PRK Bhatnagar, my other sister Dr. Preeti Lata and her husband, Dr. Om Prakash Bhatnagar and their families were there. Another doctor couple also in our family is Pankaj and Rashmi, son and daughter in-law of sister Lata and Om Prakash *jeejaji*. Sadhana's brothers – Dr. Indrajit Kumar and his family and Brij and his family, all were there; so were Bimla *behenji's* family, and we were leaving everybody along with a host of friends and colleagues.

It was kind of a new world I was going to explore and function there, and make new friends. Naturally, a feeling shared by Sadhana and Seema.

But it was a decision that *had* to be taken - and make a brand new beginning, set new goals and hope for new achievements. It was kind of uprooting the old trees and trying to plant new seedlings. It was a new future and we didn't know what it was going to bring for us.

But we did take a plunge. We had the confidence.

[Something about sister Lata who had been my friend, protector and guardian whenever mother was not there, more so after she passed away in 1953 at the young age of 52 years. Lata had been there for me all the time, to care for me. She even gave me a thorough wash and clean-up when I was about 8 years old and fell in a sewage gutter – she was just 2½ years older than me. Actually she was the one who taught me to spell my name in English – could be spelt differently – but the one she taught me has continued.

There was one very interesting episode to show how Lata could indeed claim to be my guardian and defender – a memorable one.

I was in third class in a Delhi school and the teacher was a little easy-going. He would give us a Math sum to do, would check the Monitor's answers and ask him to go around checking other students' answers. The Monitor would always mark my answer as wrong with a big X sign.

On a couple occasions I thought I was wrong but the third time I was hundred percent sure I was correct. I went to the teacher, showed my answer to him and was happy when he said it was correct.

However, I was so upset that I dashed home during the short break (home was not far), and told Lata the story.

She was furious.

Lata took me back to school, picked up my bag, and firmly told the shocked teacher:

My brother will not study in your school.

With my bag in one hand and my hand in the other, Lata took me back home and decided to explore other schools the next day.

Nobody questioned Lata's decision as I had felt wronged and humiliated by the Monitor and Lata was justified in her fight with the teacher and bringing me back.

A few days later, I was admitted to another school.

That was my sister Lata.

After marriage, she completely devoted herself to her husband and her husband's siblings, all seven of them. She took care of all of them, helping in various ways including their marriages and their children's.

When I decided to move to Indore she was okay with it as she had lived in Indore since our childhood, and later also she was in a boarding school in that city till she graduated from the high school. However, when we moved to America and for 12 years did not visit India – and she could not visit us – she was heartbroken. She kind of, resigned to this situation, and told Seema when she visited India, that she might not be able to see her brother again. Lata was gone before I could visit India in 1998.]

March 1, 1983 I took over at Indore, months before the first issue was out. I had to interview and hire the staff, set up the office according to my, and the newspaper's needs, professionally. The composing and printing process had to be tested and finalized. These took some time and I had to work 10-12 hours daily, without any days off. I knew things like that will be there and I was prepared and willing to go along.

It so happened that Sadhana, as usual, was concerned about me, my eating, sleeping and so on, and wanted to check on me and see what was going on (though we did keep in touch via phone.) She came and I picked her up from the airport, brought her straight to the office, introduced her to the staff and got busy in my work.

Several hours passed and I did not bother about my wife. Not that I forgot, but things kept me terribly busy and I thought she would make herself comfortable visiting with colleagues and talking to them. I did not even ask her for anything to eat and things like that. For some time she looked at me patiently – and I thought approvingly – but after some time she seemed to have lost her cool and as our eyes met there was something *unfamiliar*. It was about evening and she probably didn't have even lunch – nor did I. However, that had become my Indore routine since she was not with me.

But with Sadhana visiting me this was unacceptable – my behavior.

I got up quickly, left whatever I was doing and sensing her hidden annoyance, took her to my favorite hotel, and the place I was staying. She gave me a look and I, familiar with her every mood, got it. She was conveying to me that it was not appreciated that she was left alone, and that I was trying to make amends on my behavior. But, after all, she was never the one to make a scene.

I admitted my fault and she smiled. I was relieved. It was not the first time something like that had happened - remember the Journalist Union days? But she always gave me the benefit of the doubt and some room to wiggle out.

This was my wife, patience personified. Forgiving forever.

We had one of the best times together, away from home in Delhi, two of us alone. We had a good dinner and the guy who was entertaining the customers with his singing had some of our favorite numbers like *Hothon se chhoo lo tum, mera geet amar kar do* (touch my song with your lips and make it immortal).

[Jagjit Singh's super hit song is one of our all-time favorites from the movie *Prem Geet* (1981) starring Raj Babbar and Anita Raj (no relation). Jagjit also gave music to this song, co-written by him and Indeevar.]

Sadhana left the next day for Delhi and I immersed myself in work.

A couple months later we finally bid farewell to Delhi where I spent nearly 40 years of my life and 22 years with Sadhana. Seema had finished her high school. I brought Sadhana and Seema to Indore, bag and baggage, as the very generous employer, Ramesh *Bhaisahab* had arranged for a comfortable house just across the office in a good area, paying a hefty amount as rent. Ravi Shankar Shukla Nagar was just across *Dainik Bhaskar* office on the main Bombay-Agra road.

The interesting story of our moving to Indore is also memorable and it resulted in unknown people becoming our family, all three generations. Sadhana's reputation of a loving-caring nature knew no stopping. The admiration and love was mutual, and the bonding became strong. It's nearly 35 years since we met these 'strangers' and have continued our relations, though for various reasons not very frequent.

Both families saw tragedies and trials and both shared cheers and tears, together, as we have often done.

It started with our plans to physically move from Delhi to Indore by hiring a truck and finalizing the logistics, packing and dispatching our luggage to reach a day or so after us. We would drive through the notorious dacoits-infested Chambal ravines of Madhya Pradesh state (about 450 miles – 15+ hours non-stop). Munan's younger son, Ajay insisted on sharing the drive with me. He was an expert and I had no objection. He was, even otherwise, very close to us all.

I randomly contacted a transport company – Delhi Golden – and the conversation was something like this:

I want to hire a truck to transport our luggage to Indore, we are moving.

Indore! Okay, that's fine, we are from Indore. Where in Indore?

Ravi Shankar Shukla Nagar.

What? We live in that colony.

That's wonderful.

What's the address?

E-13, HIG colony.

Oh my God! We live in E-12.

And that was the beginning of our close contact. Everything went off very well. The truckers helped with final packaging of our luggage and drove off assuring the delivery in two days, maximum.

The next day we started, Sadhana, Seema, Ajay and I. It was April and summer was heating up everywhere. We stopped on our way a few times. I gulped two bottles of Thumbs Up, a soft drink, and the other three, one each. We had plenty of eats with us.

Luckily we didn't encounter any Gabbar Singh, or Sambha or Kaliya on our way (not that we were disappointed, rather we were extremely fortunate and happy.)

As we reached Indore, and Ravi Shankar Shukla Nagar and E-13, and were freshening up, a lovely young lady with a tray full of snacks, tea and cold drinks came smiling and gave us a friendly welcome. And what a welcome it was!

She said, we are next door, my name is Narindar, we own the transport company that's bringing your luggage.

What a nice gesture! And that was the beginning of a new relation.

From that memorable welcome we became one family. It was a joint family with Narindar's husband, Surjit and their two sons and a daughter, Surjit's younger brother Manvindar, their father and mother, all living together happily. Later Manvindar married Babli, another charming girl that joined the Sethi family.

We were treated like the daughter, son-in-law and grand-daughter. This relation might be confusing as Seema, only a few years younger than Manvindar addressed him as *bhaiya* (brother) and Babli and Narindar as *Bhabhi*. So be it, the love and closeness transcends the definition of relations, just like in the case of Vinod and Alka.

[Remember, in London also we met a Sethi family and stayed with them for about a week. They were nice and friendly, and caring.)

Looks like, Sethis are nice people. I can vouch for it.

29

Settling in Indore,
Hard Work and Fame

It took me, and the management, a few months to get everything in working order and start printing the paper. First the editorial staff, some I added, one I fired before the paper started. Ramesh *Ji* was a dynamic and progressive person. To him old days with either hand-composing or linotype were obsolete. He introduced computerized photo composing and brand new process of printing. All that was new to me also; there were teething troubles we had to take care of and soon.

I had some good people also like Gokul Sharma, Ashok Kumat, Romesh Joshi, Hiralal Sharma, Shriram Tamrakar and Ramvilas Sharma.

A couple months of preparations and a dummy edition was followed by a grand inauguration function where Madhya Pradesh Chief Minister Arjun Singh came from Bhopal, and the Central (federal) government's Minister for Information and Broadcasting, HKL Bhagat, came from Delhi to grace the occasion. Bhagat was an acquaintance, from my long years in Delhi.

There was a huge gathering of the elite of Indore from various walks of life, government, business and the general public.

One notable was my first Editor, Pundit Karuna Shankar Pandya, of daily *Vishwamitra*, my first newspaper in Bombay in 1947, who had retired and was living in Indore. I felt privileged to meet him after 36 years and paid my respects to him by bowing down and touching his feet – and introducing him to the Ministers.

Very soon, Sadhana and Narindar, along with the landlord-family of our home, living next door, the other side, and yet another family living just across the small street in front, became very close. Seema got admission in the Indore University's Devi Ahilya Snatakottar Mahavidyalaya. Because of the higher secondary system in Delhi, she was enrolled in a higher class. This enabled her to get B.A. (Graduate course) degree in two years, instead of the usual three.

[She graduated from College in 1985 and enrolled in M.A. Class.]

Meanwhile Sadhana was in great demand from various women's organizations, art schools, other social and cultural groups and got busy. So much so that when Indore hosted the much-awaited first professional Basketball match between a visiting American team and the Indian team, Sadhana was the Vice President of the Tournament Committee.

There were some other people who were also like a family with their relations with us dating back to the years before my birth. One was the Sharma family; the senior Sharma – Nathulal Ji – was my father's best friend and associate in various social, cultural and religious activities. For us, children, he was *Tauji* (father's elder brother – Uncle). We children were also close, like brothers and sisters.

When we moved to Indore *Tau Ji* had been gone for years, so was his older son, Dr. Om Prakash. But his younger son, Dr. Prakash Chandra Sharma, his sons, Amar and Anand, and his older sister Leela, husband Mr. Pande and daughter were there. Also in Indore was Indu, the daughter of Om Prakash *bhaiya* (brother), and her husband Jugal and their family. Sister Leela was the principal of a girl's high school.

[*Tauji's* younger daughter Kalawati and her family were in Jaipur; we had met them in Jaipur. All were very loving and caring people.]

There was another member of our extended family, Sarla, whom I made a member of *Dainik Bhaskar* family as librarian. Sister Sarla was a cousin of Leela and Prakash. All these close members of our extended family were Indore-based and we got in touch with them quite soon.

Yet another family was my father's 'adopted' sisters Susheela and Rukmani. Susheela *Ji* and her family were there but her older sister, Rukmani *bua* (aunty), had passed away. However, we met her daughter.

A pleasant surprise awaited me as I took over at *Bhaskar*. One day, soon after I reached Indore and was in my office, appeared Neelu, our neighbor in Ramesh Nagar. He was with the federal government in a sensitive department, posted in Indore. He, his wife Santosh and their son, Sonu, also came closer; they were our family since we lived in Ramesh Nagar, New Delhi.

They were with us through thick and thin, all the way. In Indore with all that fanfare and popularity, reputation and recognition there were days of gloom also. Neelu and his family were there for us, at every step of the way. They still are.

As usual, I immersed myself in work; there was a lot to be done before the start of the paper and a lot after I got going.

Seema was busy in studies and Sadhana, as usual, was there for me, even occasionally writing articles for *Bhaskar*. She would accompany me whenever invited, to various other cities for big functions where I would be either the Chief Guest, or inaugurate or give the key-note speech.

In Indore, in addition to my more than 12-hour (self-imposed) shift, I was invited to events, almost every day. It was very difficult to decline, but sometimes had to.

In the beginning, I would refuse almost all invitations as I did not have enough hours in a day to do my work and also go out for others. Then Ramesh *Ji* told me: *Bhaisahab*, please accept as many as you can, as your presence at their functions means wide publicity to *Bhaskar*.

He was absolutely right. With me going to as many events as I could manage, our paper became popular in social, cultural, professional, religious organizations, government departments and educational institutions also. We generously covered their events and they spread the name and fame of *Bhaskar*. It was a win-win situation for us all. The chief rival's monopoly was broken, we gave more space to more events to garner more support and more readership.

In addition, I took up public causes such as extension of TV to Indore, getting a direct railway line to Indore from Delhi and so on.

Bhaskar's varied fare of news, features, editorials and other articles, and personal appearances made the paper more popular day by day. Very soon, starting with zero circulation, *Bhaskar* was touching greater heights in influence, reputation, popularity, acceptability and number.

Our main rival, *Nai Dunia*, a very good publication, professionally and neatly produced, used to mention on their front page below the masthead, the number of copies printed every day. It had a very good daily circulation of over 160,000 copies. After some time the number started going down and when it reached some 130,000, the paper discontinued printing the figure.

It was understandable.

We were fast making new subscribers and getting some from other papers. On extra-ordinary occasions we would print extra special editions and quickly distribute copies to major centers in the city. *Bhaskar,* despite some problems inherent with an 'outsider' brought to do the job, and local issues, forged ahead rapidly.

I had my connections in Delhi, had a huge treasure of rare photos and a zeal to excel. I did not spare any effort to keep raising the bar and devoting my full energy to set and reach new goals. *Bhaskar* took courageous stand on issues, did not care for 'political correctness' and explored new avenues to expand. We did not tread the beaten path and adopted a new format, new style of writing, extensive reporting and forceful presentation.

Because of my connections in Delhi, whenever VIPs from the national capital came, including Ministers, big business people or diplomats, I and *Bhaskar* were there to meet with, report and get ample rewards in popularity, circulation and business.

Chandrashekhar, the leading politician, who later became Prime Minister of India and whom I knew from Delhi, was leading a month's-long march on foot (*Padyatra*) across India. He also passed through Indore. *Bhaskar* office was right there on the same route to welcome Chandrashekhar and his party.

There were senior diplomats and other celebrities visiting Indore, and *Bhaskar* was always there to meet, interview and extend its reach with new and exclusive stories.

In addition, there were members of our extended family and others from Delhi and Bombay also. Among them, we were lucky to meet Sujata's mother in-law, Sharifa *jan*, whom we had not seen earlier. She had managed to leave Kabul, Afghanistan, along with her grandson, Fawad and was in Delhi for some time. We got the information and we invited her to visit us in Indore. Her nephew, Burhanuddin Kushkaki also accompanied them to Indore. As usual, Sadhana was a gracious host offering delicious treats and warm company.

One day Sadhana dressed Sharifa *jan* in one of her sarees, put a *bindi* on her forehead and together they posed for a photograph looking at the wedding picture of Sujata and Mujtaba. They indeed had fun.

During my three-year stay with *Bhaskar* in Indore, though I was supposed to be the Chief Editor of all the four editions of the paper, I could only visit one or two centers for want of time. I would go to several other cities as chief guest.

One of the highlights was my trip to Germany, at the invitation of the German government. That was big news for the press in Indore and regarded as an honor for *Bhaskar* by Ramesh *Bhaisahab*. This wasn't new for me as I had visited a score of other countries, some as guest of their governments.

It was different at *Bhaskar;* there was a different atmosphere, a different Boss, who took it as an honor for *Bhaskar* whose Editor was invited by a foreign government.

It was a first for them.

There was a big reception in my honor at Bhaskar Bhavan (Building), and yet another gathering of the Indore elite, including a few top officials and the Mayor Srivallabh Sharma. Over a hundred other well-wishers, including the Mayor, came to the airport for a rousing send-off to me – the Chief Editor of *Bhaskar.*

Such was the reputation and popularity of the paper we all worked hard to earn. It was also the result of free hand given by Ramesh *Ji* to me to write whatever I deem fit and to lead the staff as I like. I never liked a 'politically correct' policy, as I mentioned earlier. We wrote without fear or favor. That policy paid well for *Bhaskar*. We became pioneers for community welfare and for social, cultural and political causes.

Of course, as I had mentioned earlier, there were hurdles, there were critics, and there were problems created by saboteurs and other sulking elements in and out of the office.

One glaring instance - probably unprecedented - was witnessed at Indore airport itself when I was being given a fond and enthusiastic send off for my German trip. The Mayor and all those hundred plus people gathered to see me off with their good wishes, were waiting, and waiting, and waiting till the plane from Delhi to Bombay overflew Indore without landing – dropping or picking up passengers.

It was quite a few minutes after my flight missed Indore that the airport staff – only on persistent inquiries – told me that the plane didn't land because of the landing gear problem. It could only land once and the authorities decided to land only at Bombay.

That was something rare, and it had to happen *that* day when I was leaving and many of the important people, including the Mayor, were at the airport to see me off! It seemed very strange, quite unbelievable.

However, there was hardly time to argue over the matter, lodge a complaint, give vent to our collective feelings and expect a remedy. That was distant. For me, something had to be done and done quickly. I had to reach Bombay and catch the evening flight of Lufthansa, the German airlines, for Frankfurt.

I thanked the Mayor profusely and requested him to leave and attend to his duties while we work on the problem. He wished me luck and left. We asked many others to do the same. Among the big group was Manmohan Agrawal, the Resident Director of *Bhaskar* and a cousin of Ramesh *Bhaisahab*. There was also a good friend of *Bhaskar*, a senior government functionary with a red beacon on his car.

[Mayor Sharma, sadly, passed away Oct. 2017. He was a stalwart in his Party, BJP. Also held office as State Legislator, Madhya Pradesh.]

The duo quickly decided to drive me to Bombay – a distance of some 330 miles in about 8½ hours, but looked like it was doable with the red beacon flashing.

We three got into the car, the driver was ready and off we started for Bombay racing to catch the flight.

It was not to be.

The driver was not expecting to drive those many miles and therefore had not bothered to fill the gas tank. After about an hour we ran out of fuel in the middle of nowhere. It was early afternoon and no gas station, or even small habitation, was visible as far as our eyes could see. The driver got some good tongue-lashing but that didn't serve any purpose.

There was not even much traffic on the road but, finally, after sometime they hailed a passing truck and decided that I should wait in the car and that the two will find a gas station and take a lift and come back.

They were gone for more than a couple hours. It was scary also as I had my bag with me, and I was alone in the car, at some unknown place with no phone facility (there were no cell phones then.) After what seemed ages they returned with enough gas to take the car to the nearest gas station some 45 minutes away.

By the time we reached Bombay airport the flight was gone for more than two hours. However, Lufthansa staff happened to be very understanding and helpful and I was booked on the next available flight the next day, a full 24 hours late.

There was nothing we could do. All three went to the hotel provided by the airlines and spent the night there. Early morning the two dear friends were persuaded to go back to Indore as my flight was to take off after several hours. They wished me good luck and reluctantly left. I felt bad for them but there was no other option.

I had plenty of time to spend. I did some little shopping I had missed in Indore and went to see my little brother Virendra and his family some 8 miles away in Mahim.

However, destiny had not stopped playing games with me. My brother's home was locked; his wife, Rashmi, was also working and their son, Prafulla must have been in school.

I returned to the airport and waited for the flight. There were no more games and I got the flight and flew to Frankfurt covering the distance in about 9 hours. Luckily the airlines had informed the authorities in Frankfurt about the missed flight and the arrival time of the next. There was a government representative at the airport who welcomed me and took me to the hotel.

There were two other senior journalists – both Editors – one from Bombay and the other from Nagpur city, both in Maharashtra, on this trip as government guests.

The week-long visit was full of meetings and sightseeing and visiting a few other cities, including the capital, Bonn. It was March, still quite cold but there was warmth in our welcome and treatment.

On our return journey we three were on the same flight but for me another game had begun. Since my original flight was canceled, my return flight was also canceled. Nobody in the host government's relevant department thought about it and as I reached the airport, accompanied by the official rep, there was no reserved seat for me on that particular flight.

It took him quite some time to sort things out and there was ample time for it. He finally got me a seat to Bombay on the same flight but not near my friends.

Yet another game was my destiny. Since my original seat was lost I could only be accommodated in the smoking section (in those days smoking was allowed in a separate section.) To test my patience further, and to punish me for some known-unknown reason, the hefty guy seated next to me happened to be a chain smoker – either by habit or nervousness.

I was miserable for the full duration of the flight. There was no other seat available and I did not create a scene. May be if I had done that probably they would have upgraded me, but I did not complain and seek a solution. I thought he would certainly stop after a couple cigarettes but he kept disappointing and surprising me with his addiction.

I don't know if I developed some health problems because of the non-stop second-hand smoke inhalation for 8 hours. If so, I don't feel any. God is kind to me.

On my return I wrote, and *Bhaskar* printed, a series of articles on my German visit – unlike what happened at *Hindustan* when I was on a visit to America in 1965 and had asked the Editor about writing and he had said, no need, just have fun.

It's never *all* fun when a *real* journalist is traveling – even on a *real* vacation. He remains an active journalist. It's just like a soldier or a policeman – never *really* on a holiday, always on duty. And that's how I look at these professions.

An Editor's visit to another country and his experience and observation, account of his meetings with the leaders and common people, and visits to popular places make good story. Any newspaper would be happy to print it. *Bhaskar* did, and naturally the paper's popularity and readership increased. Readers were interested in knowing what I did, whom I met, what did I see. I did not disappoint them – or my Boss who wanted me to accept the invitation, go and, more important, *write* about the visit.

I did what was, and should be, expected. I wanted the full story of what happened before, and after my German visit to come out in book form but could not do that for various reasons; also because of my plans to leave Indore shortly thereafter.

30

More Challenges, More Praise

I like challenges. I always have. But I like to fight them and constantly try to overcome them. You may not be successful all the time but my take on this is, at least try. I have been doing that and if I think I have all the facts, I don't hesitate and plunge head-on in the 'battle.'

Bhaskar gave me more challenges, more opportunities, and I took more of them and displayed a more fearless stand.

There have been several in my three-year stay with *Bhaskar*. I told my reporters and others not to be intimidated, give me the facts, only the facts, and leave the rest to me. I will face the consequences and if we are right, we will prevail.

Once it so happened that my reporter sent me the news that a few students of the local Medical College misbehaved with a group of girls at a popular picnic spot. There was some serious situation and though it did not reach a crisis point it was enough to scare the girls and showed the irresponsible behavior of students of a reputed institution.

Bhaskar printed that news in the morning edition.

A couple hours later an angry group of students armed with hockey sticks descended on *Bhaskar* office and looked for the Editor. I faced them calmly but firmly and they started aggressively arguing with me. They even threatened me with violence and I challenged them with my firm commitment to truth and said the news item grew from your behavior. If someone can claim to be your spokesman and give a rebuttal, with facts and evidence, I would print that.

That argument, obviously, did not find favor with the group and a couple of them became more agitated.

Meanwhile Ajit Jogi, the efficient Collector, appeared on the scene with a handful of policemen. There was nothing more required to be done and the students dispersed without creating trouble.

A couple weeks later, the same Medical College organized their grand Annual function, a gala affair with top class music and dance etc.

Who was the Chief Guest?

Bhaskar Editor Yatindra Bhatnagar – me. Honored and felicitated by the Principal and student leaders. They had become my, our, admirers.

I did not get any further reports of their misbehavior till I was in Indore.

After Indira Gandhi government took strong action to flush out armed militants from the Golden Temple, Amritsar, the holiest Sikh Gurdwara, we covered the news factually. I have always maintained that places of worship cannot be made into an armed fortress – or even a bunker - to fight the lawful authority, the government. In this case, the holiest Gurdwara was made into a war zone with machine guns and other modern weapons stacked and used against the Police and troops of the Indian Army.

It was made into a regular military action. The militants were armed with all kinds of modern assault weapons and took up vantage points to inflict huge losses on the police and soldiers. The government then took more drastic steps and completely cleared the Temple, losing several hundred of their men in the process. The militant leaders, Jarnail Singh Bhindrawale and his chief military lieutenant, Maj-Gen. Shabeg Singh, formerly of the Indian Army, and many of the other armed followers were eliminated.

The situation was so serious that the Army had to be called with tanks. The troops made a successful assault and cleared the Gurdwara. It was a massive, well-thought out attempt when all other efforts had failed. Of course, hardline Sikhs were unhappy, angry and hurt as their holiest Temple was 'desecrated' and almost destroyed. They did not condemn the rebels, rather labelled them as martyrs.

Bhaskar covered the big story faithfully and judiciously and was one of the first to print special editions to keep readers informed about the latest, breaking news.

The hardline Sikhs in Indore were unhappy with *Bhaskar*. They became more agitated and mad when we printed another exclusive report of girls and women being recovered by the Police and Army after the Temple was cleared of militants. These women were forcibly kept inside, some were worshippers who were unlawfully and forcefully detained inside by the militants for 'other' purposes.

Our reporters verified the news from the authorities and waited for my signal. Based on the twice verified report we went ahead and printed that damning story about those militants who supposedly were fighting for Khalistan but behaving like murderers, molesters and terrorists, displaying no religious signs. It was very disturbing and brought a bad name to *their kind* of Sikhism. Secondly, I maintained that these people themselves desecrated the holy place with their own impure conduct.

That was a big story and we reported it accurately, factually and, of course, with the firm stand that the militants were armed terrorists and had to be flushed out. Despite all that we *did not* make that 'bad conduct' report extra sensational. We also did not give it big space, nor a prominent place in our newspaper.

However, a group of enraged, hardline Sikhs came in a fighting mood. As usual, almost all were armed with *kirpans* (small dagger, one of the five essentials for a Sikh) and confronted me. I explained the background, our double verification and our restraint in not playing up the news to make it sensational.

As usual, I stood calm, but firm, and following my habit and policy, gave them the opportunity to refute the news *if they had facts to the contrary* and I would print their statement. That created some kind of split among the group, but most were still agitated and accused me of defaming their faith and maligning the devotees – who were clearly armed militants out to fight, molest and kill.

Again, the same thing happened. Before the situation could go out of control, there was Collector Ajit Jogi with some policemen; his mere presence – coupled with my firm but tactful proposal – made the group retreat quietly.

I heaved a sigh of relief as sometimes mindless agitators would do crazy things. I once again thanked Collector Jogi who was always on top of things; nothing happened in the city that escaped his attention.

A few months after Operation Blue Star (storming of the Golden Temple) Indira Gandhi was assassinated by her Sikh body guards. This was a signal for supporters of Mrs. Gandhi, agitated Congressmen and other anti-social elements to target Sikhs in Indore, in Delhi and dozens of other cities. In Delhi some 3000 Sikhs were brutally murdered. Estimates of those killed vary from 5000 to 10,000. It was widely suspected that several Congress leaders and activists were behind these organized anti-Sikh killing and destruction of their property.

Bhaskar was in the forefront in blasting the revenge-killing of innocent Sikhs and severely criticized the leadership that incited the riots. We took a bold stand and condemned the looters who were bent on killing and destroying. [There was widespread looting of Sikh properties everywhere and the looters did not spare even our Sikh neighbors – Narindar's family and their home, next door to us.]

Realizing *Bhaskar's* courageous and correct stand in support of Sikhs and the paper's severe condemnation of anti-Sikh riots and those rabble-rouser Congressmen that were behind all that mayhem, a bigger group of Sikhs visited *Bhaskar's* office and had no hesitation in praising the Editor and the paper profusely.

I only expressed my firm views of siding with truth and supporting the cause of the innocents and blasting the wrong-doers.

On this occasion we didn't need Ajit Jogi. He must have been busy elsewhere doing his duty.

However, he was very much there when during the anti-Sikh riots some Sikh-owned and run shops, right along the walls of the historic 18th century palace of the Holkar Maharajas, were torched. It resulted in a big portion of the palace itself being burnt and destroyed.

Rewind a little bit:

As I was born in Indore and was proud of my connections with the city, the palace and its grandeur, I was sad to see the palace lacking proper care and maintenance. It was largely occupied by a few government departments. The maintenance was so bad and irresponsible that beautiful murals on the walls were painted over and hidden. Overall it was a disappointing site and the palace no longer had its grandeur when I took my post with *Bhaskar.*

Soon many activists – me included – raised their voice for taking back the Palace (Rajwada) and restoring its grandeur and making it again the pride of the city. A high-power committee was formed with several former Maharajas and prominent community activists, senior government officials and prominent business persons for the purpose.

I was unanimously selected as Convener of the restoration committee. Former Maharaja Madhavrao Scindia (Sindhia) of Gwalior, whom I knew well, was among the prominent members of the Committee. It also included the former Maharaja of Dewas and some others.

We had our meetings in the beautiful glass hall, with glass walls all around; everything made from material imported from Belgium. It was like a gorgeous movie set for an enchanting performance.

The 1984 riots saw the glass hall and all the area surrounding it destroyed in the unfortunate fire.

I rushed to the spot and found Jogi himself handling a big hose and spraying water to put out the fire but, alas, the flames had engulfed the beautiful glass-hall and a large portion of the palace.

[I have a photo of the beautiful glass hall and our meeting somewhere in my unopened boxes of books and important photos and files.]

A little bit about an alleged curse. There was rivalry/enmity between Gwalior and Holkar Maharajas and a 'curse' was widely talked about that if the Gwalior Maharaja ever came to the Holkar Palace it would be destroyed. At our meeting at the Palace, in the glass hall of the same Palace, Maharaja Madhavrao Scindia was present. He also went around with me to see the parts that badly needed renovation and systematic restoration.

When the fire broke out and could not be quickly and fully controlled, all the rooms and corridors that Maharaja Scindia visited had been destroyed by fire. Some maintained that the curse had come true. In any case, the Palace was in ruins, badly burnt.

As long as I was in Indore with *Dainik Bhaskar* I continued my efforts to somehow rebuild and restore Rajwada but it was too much. Maharani Usha Devi, the daughter of the last Maharaja, Yeshwantrao Holkar (who merged his state in 1948, like hundreds of other princely states, with newly independent India), was living in Bombay, married to a businessman. The merger also ended their formal titles. The 'successors' nominally kept their titles of Maharajas, Rajas, Nawabs and so on. Maharani Usha Devi, occasionally visited Indore and kept the movement to restore Rajwada alive. She was there a few days after the big fire had destroyed it.

[I saw a report that the damaged palace was rebuilt and renovated in 2007 by the Maharani bringing back its grandeur and stately architecture and making it again the pride of Indore and the best tourist attraction.]

Back to Indira Gandhi's assassination, on October 31, 1984.

Journalists are always after *news*, the more tragic, the better opportunity to display and comment, to follow and keep reporting, keep the momentum, and fully exploit the situation. It's not callousness, it's the challenge and rising to the occasion for presenting the news quickly, completely, extensively, to excel and attract more readers and beat the competition.

Bhaskar beat all other newspapers in reporting the event and brought out a special supplement, late afternoon, as soon as her death was *officially* announced. Our reporter, Jagannath Shastri and the agencies had already conveyed the information that Indira Gandhi was shot multiple times from close range and there was absolutely no possibility of her surviving.

In the light of the confirmed news of body-guard Satwant Singh emptying his machine gun on Indira's body, I made a calculated decision to get the edition ready. With selected photos and with formatting the pages quickly in a couple hours, we were ready. As soon as the official announcement of death was made in New Delhi, *Bhaskar* press started rolling and in minutes, the Extra Special was out in the market.

It took the city by storm.

It had never seen such a quick response to an absolutely stunning news.

The next day the major streets of Indore witnessed *Bhaskar's* front page hoisted over with strings looking down on people excited, in mourning, angry, or sympathetic – but all praising the coverage we gave to the important story.

That day *Bhaskar* press just kept on printing extra copies almost the whole day to quickly reach the entire city and beyond.

I had a host of photos of Indira Gandhi that, probably, none else had. On subsequent days we kept the editions distributed everywhere in larger numbers than ever before and printed touching editorials, well-informed articles and commentaries. Later, we brought out an extra, magazine-size collection of photos – mostly exclusive – that was distributed along with the copies of *Dainik Bhaskar,* the ever growing newspaper that was creating history in Journalism.

It's said that bigger the event, more horrible the happening, newspapers' job is to report and feature it extensively and 'cash the event.' We did it, and we did it in a manner that was not sensational and insensitive, but sobering and touching, not melodramatic but soothing, and of course quite impressive.

As anticipated our circulation crossed a hundred thousand copies – a record performance in a little over one and a half years.

Indore had given me, Sadhana and Seema new opportunities to function and flourish. Initially, both the women were not happy being in a smaller city with no close friends and relatives but, quickly got accustomed to things and became experts in adapting to the situation.

Neelu and family would persuade us to go on picnics and movies. I would join whenever possible. Sadhana and Narindar would go shopping; Seema had her own circle of friends to hang out with. They both played badminton in the adjoining open space along with neighbors, our landlord's son Suresh, his sisters and others.

I was constantly invited to lay the foundation stone of buildings and other places, preside over the opening of bank branch, be the chief guest of big social and educational functions and so on.

Indore University planned to start a post-graduate degree course in Journalism and the Vice Chancellor (President) of the University invited me and another senior journalist, Jawaharlal Rathore to prepare the syllabus for teaching. After weeks of discussions we finalized the syllabus and the University started enrolling students. [The same I did for Delhi University.]

We not only were the 'fathers' of the Journalism course but also were persuaded to join the Faculty and teach for at least the first year.

It was an honor to do that. I took one class of reporting technique and shared my experience with the students. *Bhaskar* hired a couple of students from the first batch of graduates. It was a first for Indore University and I was proud to be one of the pioneers of this project.

As stated earlier, during the unprecedented and dastardly, politically-motivated attacks on Sikhs in many parts of India, and also Indore, as an aftermath of Prime Minister Indira Gandhi's assassination, our dear neighbors also suffered. Their home was looted, and totally destroyed by the ruffians who were raising slogans in praise of Indira Gandhi. Sadhana had asked them (at that time only Surjit, Narindar and their little son, 'Kaju' were home) to come and 'hide' in our home. They were with us for days till I asked the Commissioner who arranged a police transport and got them escorted to a temporary, well-protected Camp for Sikh families in danger.

That was one of the most disturbing, depressing and unforgettable events for Sadhana and me.

How can people get so much worked up and be so cruel to other innocent people in their own community?

How can a political party and its leaders be so callous just to promote their party's interest in the next election? Of course that worked.

[Indira's body was put for 'viewing' for three days by her son, Rajiv Gandhi, and the tremendous sympathy wave got the Congress Party an unprecedented majority in the parliamentary elections held just after seven weeks of her death. The Congress bagged more than 404 seats out of 533; it was 50 more than the last election.]

After the ordeal was over, Surjit and his family showed remarkable spirit and rebuilt their home and their transport business that was affected severely. With faith in God and in their own hard work they overcame catastrophic situation and again came on top.

Surjit was full of sincere praise and admiration for Sadhana during this calamity. One day he reminded Sadhana: our tradition is that the brother always protects his sisters, but here a sister has protected her brother and his family.

What a touching sentiment!

Sadhana said, I did what every sister, brother or neighbor should have done. I am proud of my brother and his family - my extended family.

Narindar always addressed Sadhana as *Didi* (big sister). Surjit's mother (Beeji) was like our mother and loved us dearly. Sadhana was the special one for her and Papaji (father).

They all couldn't be anything else.

I was with Sadhana all the way despite danger for us also because we shielded and hid our Sikh neighbors in our home. Sadhana was determined to protect them, come what may. I was in the office when she asked this dear family to come and stay with us, with 'Kaju' asked not to make noise to attract outside attention and invite trouble.

The poor boy kept mum.

At least twice the enraged mob had confronted Sadhana and me saying that they knew the Sikh family lived next door and we said, no. Two days later someone who had worked for them betrayed and confirmed that the E-12 belonged to the Sikhs. It was then the mob broke open the locks and looted everything. What they could not carry, they destroyed. They carried their fridge dragging it on the road raising slogans like "Indira *Maiyya ki jai* (hail mother Indira) etc.

This was an ugly spectacle. It was brutal. It was unprecedented and inexcusable in a civilized democratic country.

Later the looters re-visited our home and demanded we hand the Sikh family hiding with us over to the mob. We said they don't stay with us. Somehow the rowdy bunch went back but when it looked imminent that they might, out of frustration – and also suspicion – attack our home, I arranged for the family safe passage to the Camp. It took several days to control the situation – of course full normalcy took several weeks. However, hundreds had been killed, and homes destroyed and severely wounded the conscience of an otherwise peaceful nation.

[The wounds are still there but hardworking Sikhs have worked their way back to build their lives and continue to serve their country, India. Few left for other countries and continue the movement for a separate homeland for Sikhs – Khalistan – the root of the armed struggle that resulted in storming of the Golden Temple in the first place.

By and large, that movement is no longer significant in India. Punjab state, where a vast majority of hard-working Sikhs live, is peaceful, prosperous and patriotic.]

The Sethi family always treated Sadhana as their daughter. (Their father and mother, fortunately, were away when these ugly events took place.) They were always very loving and caring and so were the two brothers and their wives. The children were respectful and after their older son, Bablu, married, his charming and intelligent wife, Rani, followed the family tradition.

[Sadhana and I visited India, and Indore, in 2007 and stayed with them as family. The ladies would go shopping and engage in other activities continuing the same love and consideration as before. Rani was there for us everywhere with the car. Narindar, as usual, was the perfect picture of the best host, and a loving sister.

The whole family has remained wonderful.

This was typical of Sadhana and it also goes to the credit of the Sethis who continue to be special for us. When we were leaving Indore the patriarch (Papa *Ji*) said to me: leave my daughter here for the impending marriage of her *Veer* (brother – Manvindar.) We will send her after all the ceremonies are over.

Our relations with the Sethi family are this close.

Neelu and his family had moved to Delhi and we were treated there also with the same love and hospitality. Sonu was pre-teen in Indore and I had taken him to watch the first India-West Indies One Day international cricket match in the city. When I introduced him as *my* grandson his eyes glowed. He was the one who got my cowboy boots and cowboy hat the Texans had given me in 1965-66 when I was in the US. None else would have been the right kid to get them. We were told that he went to bed with the shoes and the hat on.

I love you Sonu for that too.]

Something about some of my colleagues in *Hindustan*, some senior to me: There was Sita Charan Dixit, always encouraging me to write something special. (His son, JN Dixit became a senior officer with the External Affairs Ministry, ambassador and the Spokesman for the government. We attended his wedding; he and his wife also came to our place to taste Sadhana's cooking.)

Apart from Chandrakar, there were some others such as Banke Bihari Bhatnagar (no relation), Shiv Kumar Vidyalankar, Krishna Chandra Mehta, Vidyasagar Vasishth, Kshiteesh Kumar, Yashpal Gupta, Satish (Dattattreya Tiwari), Som Dutt Shukla and others who were quite close to me. I wasn't married then but they all treated me as a member of their family. It continued after Sadhana came into my life. She was respectful to my senior colleagues and treated those younger like Anand Sharma and Anand Dikshit as her *Devars* (husband's younger brothers) or like her own little brothers.

A few of them – especially their wives (my *bhabhis*) - were keen to get me hitched to some nice girl in their circle or among their relatives. One senior colleague had two or three daughters and one day, without any initiative from me, said: you know I have three daughters, you can choose anyone.

I was not keen to get married at all and the matter ended there. My friends, kind of, gave up on me about marriage.

A year or two before Ved (Sadhana) came on the scene we had a young girl, Purushottama Kapoor – hired as a reporter. The News Editor, Jagannath Gupta asked me to get her started, take her with me on assignments and make her familiar with certain beats and so on.

That re-kindled my colleagues' interest in my marriage. They thought – some said openly – that it's a matter of time before I (Yatindra) would be hitched. (They obviously thought about Miss Kapoor.)

They were right. I got married within a year or so, but to another young girl, Ved (Sadhana).

[I can't forget an amusing incident involving Miss Kapoor.

She was with me on one of the party-assignments. As we entered, one of my diplomat friends and another senior journalist came rushing and almost together, exclaimed: Oh, oh, this is the first time I am meeting your wife.

I had to clarify that she was *not* my wife. They apologized.

Later I said to Purushottama that I was really sorry and that I had never given them any such impression.

Her answer puzzled me.

She said, I don't mind.

[She was married after a few years to a Canada-based Indian; Sadhana and I attended the ceremony in Delhi. There was a name-change, Miss Kapoor became Anita Singh. Once we touched base after we came to the US but since have lost contact with her.]

BB Bhatnagar had become Editor of the weekly *Saptahik Hindustan* and would always ask me to write for the magazine. I did, and both were happy. Outside writers were paid for their articles etc. but that was fine with me as I was a staffer in the same organization.

Two other eminent writers-poets on our staff were Gopal Prasad Vyas and Ramanand Doshi. Vyas *Ji* was basically a writer-poet specializing in humor. Doshi wrote romantic poetry. Both were very popular in poetic seminars. Both have been my very good senior friends. Sadhana too often met them and enjoyed their poems.

There was an interesting anecdote about Doshi. One day he borrowed some money from me and said that he was meeting someone and would tell me something interesting later.

He returned after more than an hour and told me: a young woman from Jalandhar, Punjab, came just to hear two lines from one of my poems. Of course I recited several and entertained her at our favorite restaurant, Milk Bar (just two minutes from our office.)

Those were very touching lines, and I quote:

> *Jeevan dardeela karne ko pehla pyaar bahut hota hai,*
> *Jeevan bhaar bahut hota hai*

(First love is enough to bring pain to your life, now life is a big burden.)

Doshi was a dear friend and wrote beautiful poetry. He was later editor of our sister publication, *Kadambini*, and made me write often and do book reviews also for his magazine.

During my career I had the privilege to know and meet many more, see their work and often report. I knew and met one prominent scholar Dr. Raghuvira, also a Member of Parliament. He was a top linguist knowing a dozen plus languages, collected rare manuscripts in Sanskrit and was an institution himself. (So is his illustrious son, Dr. Lokesh Chandra. I had the honor of meeting with him also, quite often.)

Once the visiting Mongolian Prime Minister Tsedenbal, was felicitated at his world famous Institute, the International Academy of Indian Culture in New Delhi. Prime Minister Jawaharlal Nehru accompanied him to the function where Dr. Raghuvira welcomed the distinguished visitor in his own language – Mongolian.

There were many more such as 'Mahapundit' Rahul Sankrityayan, the 'father of Travel Literature in Hindi.' An avid traveler, he was also a linguist, expert in ancient Indian history, Buddhism, and India's close connections with Tibet. I read four of his books on travel and discoveries, when I was not yet 11 years-old.

The other luminary was Nirad Chandra Chaudhuri, the eminent Indian writer in English language who later settled in Oxford, England and was honored by the British government with an OBE (Order of British Empire). There is a plaque put by the local Council proclaiming that Nirad Chaudhuri lived there.

We met Nirad *babu* and his wife, a down-to-earth couple, several times while in Ramesh Nagar; they would attend parties organized by OP Bhagat, our dear neighbor and colleague, and we would have lively discussion with him. He died in Oxford, UK, just three months short of his 102nd birthday, in 1999.

Reading one of his books and the minute details and description of roads and landmarks of places in England, the British envoy had asked Nirad Chaudhuri, how many years he had spent in England. His answer stunned the ambassador: I have never been to England.

Yes, till then, not a single day he spent in England, but his knowledge and grasp were phenomenal. He was an admirer of England.

Yet another distinguished person I met, interacted with and was privileged to get an autographed copy of his autobiography *(Life and Myself)*, was Harindranath Chattopadhyay – a great writer, lyricist, freedom fighter and also a film personality. He had acted in several movies such as *Ashirwad, Bawarchi, Tere Mere Sapne* etc. One of his famous songs is *Railgadi*, picturized on the old-time great Ashok Kumar. The other is *Surya Ast Ho Gaya.*

Harin *Babu* was the younger brother of Sarojini Naidu, the first woman President of Congress, India's age-old political party. She was also a Minister in Indian cabinet and I had the honor to meet with and report her meetings and briefings.

Mr. Chattopadhyay's wife, Kamaladevi, was another eminent leader, a pioneer for women's movement, and a social reformer of repute.

I will be amiss if I don't mention another unforgettable two hours with the most prominent classical dance-guru of India, Shambhu Maharaj. Former Maharani, Ripjit Kaur (Singh), of one of the states in Punjab, and a great admirer of Shambhu Maharaj, had invited him at her apartment in

New Delhi for an informal meeting-demonstration for her and her small select group.

I happened to be at the right place at the right time. I had varied interests ranging from politics and sports to fine arts and literature and was invited to several events.

Shambhu Maharaj then was in his late fifties.

The 60 minutes or so Shambhu Maharaj devoted to show the intricacies of the classical Kathak dance form left an indelible impression on me. This simple, unassuming Guru, an expert in his art, demonstrated the soft, intricate and varied *mudras* (moves) in a charmingly impressive manner amazed us all. For simple actions, like tying an arm-band, you must be graceful, use the soft touch and use your lips to hold one end in a delicate move to make a difference.

He would address the gracious hostess: Rani, *iski nazakat dekho* (see the delicate touch.)

It was a rare privilege to see Shambhu Maharaj (Shambhunath Mishra) in an informal and small gathering and be mesmerized.

Among his several prominent disciples are his illustrious nephew, Birju Maharaj, Damayanti Joshi, Maya Rao and Uma Sharma. Birju Maharaj also choreographed the dance sequences in some of the classic movies like *Devdas*, Umrao Jan and Bajirao Mastani. He is 79.

[Shambhu Maharaj died in 1970 when he was about 60.]

A story about Kapurthala state and its Maharajas – unconnected with Shambhu Maharaj or Rani Ripjit Kaur (Singh) – is worth mentioning.

This happened in 1968 while we were in Ramesh Nagar. I was introduced to the former Diwan (Prime Minister) of Kapurthala and Patiala states, Diwan Jarmani Das. One day he and his wife, Susheela, well-known in social circles, came to our home. Diwan Sahab was trying to publish a book about his years as Diwan in Kapurthala and Punjab state and related stories. He wanted me to go through his manuscript, give suggestions and edit it.

I asked him to meet me in a couple days.

After I finished reading the manuscript I was astonished about what went on in the life of a sovereign Maharaja in pre-independence India's princely state. It's not that all the states and all the Rajas and Maharajas led the same, or similar, lives but this one was amazing.

Diwanji and his wife met us again in my home and I gave my frank opinion: This book is explosive. You have narrated stories of luxurious life, escapades almost every other month to Paris (with you in tow), and having an extremely 'good time' there for decades. This book has events from private lives. I think you better consult an attorney first to make sure no defamation/libel cases are filed after the publication. Once cleared, I would be happy to edit it.

I did not hear from Jarmani Das. A few months later I came across the book titled *Maharaja*, written by the same Diwan Jarmani Das. It contained all that I thought was defamatory, and the publication risky.

Obviously, the author must have been advised to go ahead and get the book published as, probably, nobody in his sane mind would think of a court case and get more extensively exposed in public with more juicy stories from their past.

Jarmani Das not only went ahead with *Maharaja* but also had the sequel, *Maharani,* published shortly thereafter. Both became best sellers, obviously, with juicy stories of a colorful past of some rulers.

That 'encounter' left me in amazement how outrageous things could be published without any risk of court cases.

Among the other political celebrities were Prime Minister Atal Bihari Vajpayee and Deputy Prime Minister Lal Krishna Advani, whom I knew very well from as early as 1952. They were then in their early years in politics, I in journalism.

I had free access to both afterwards.

The interesting thing about Advani *Ji* is that we had a fair resemblance and one could be confused. (Not much now, I think.) That resemblance became well-known and even he realized it. One day Advani *Ji* himself said: When I am required at a meeting and I cannot go, I tell the people to invite you, instead. Well, he did have a good sense of humor.

We both, and Sadhana too, enjoyed his comment and the somewhat rare resemblance.

I had many more interactions with Advani *Ji* as I was regularly reporting the Parliament and he was a Minister and member.

[The last time I met Advani *Ji* was in 2007 when I just showed up at the official residence of the Deputy Prime Minister of India. I was told by the secretary that the DPM was in a meeting with the Army Chief and the Governor of Jammu and Kashmir, and immediately after the meeting, would go to the Parliament. I gave him my business card to show Advani *Ji*. As soon as the meeting ended, I was called in and we spent some time talking. He had not forgotten me from those good old days.]

Sadhana and I were also privileged to have attended some memorable events where outstanding music-maestros performed. Among them were Pundit Omkarnath Thakur, Bhimsen Joshi and MS Subbulakshmi. Their concerts were arranged by JC Mathur, the very popular Director General of All India Radio (AIR), in New Delhi. Mathur himself was a lover of music. Often the big lawns of *Akashvani Bhavan* had coal-laiden heaters to warm the winter evenings for these out-of-this-world concerts.

31

Sujata's Visit, Seema Goes with Her and Then...

By the time Sujata and nine-month-old baby Tamanna visited us in Indore, in September 1985, things had become normal. The Sethis had rebuilt and restored their home and expanded their transport business with added vigor.

I went to Bombay to receive and bring Tamanna and Sujata to Indore.

Sadhana was overjoyed to see her first granddaughter, and first daughter. So was Seema and I. We had seen Sujata after nearly three years – the video of baby Tamanna mailed to us *from America* earlier was *sent back* by Bombay Customs department despite my visiting their office.

Rewind a little:

We got info that a video is waiting for us at Bombay Custom Office – they will not mail it to me in Indore. Wow! Bombay was the Custom clearance hub.

I went to Bombay to collect it.

Then the rigid bureaucracy came into play.

The officers at Bombay Customs wanted me to play the video for them to prove that there was nothing 'objectionable.' I had no gadget to play it (they will not provide one – don't know if they had).

The result: they refused to give it to me and returned it to the sender – Sujata Roashan in America.

It was disgustingly disappointing. A baby's video returned because of some stupid bureaucratic procedure! How rigid and insensitive the government functionaries behaved, despite my telling them it was a baby's video for her grandparents.

Nothing worked. I didn't throw my weight around, and I don't know if that would have worked. I don't even know if somebody needed a bribe – nobody gave me a hint about it – and in any case, I wouldn't have paid a dime for the video howsoever valuable it was for us. But I couldn't do anything at all.

However, now Sujata and Tamanna were with us and we enjoyed their stay. Sadhana got busy taking care of Tamanna – as Sujata does these days with her granddaughter, Aliya, Tamanna's first child. Sadhana took over almost all the duties of a caring, nurturing mother, baby sitter and Nanny, right from her arrival. Tamanna was no longer dependent on Formula; India's natural and nourishing milk suited her, so was regular massage by Sadhana, her dear *Nani* (grandma).

Seema too, took her turn to pamper her first niece whom she adored. [She still does it for the third generation - now that Tamanna has her own very cute baby, Aliya.]

Seema, meanwhile, continued to be a very good student at her college excelling in making charts, and presentations besides contributing to other activities. She, even otherwise, is more involved in expertly making beautiful designs, doing cross-stitch work, making scrap books, collages, photo albums, calendars with very appropriate quotes to add to the beauty. [She made some with Sadhana's paintings and sketches when she was alive, and one after, that family and friends received and enjoyed.]

She took these incredible skills with her to America and also perfected and expanded them. She excels in hosting parties, organizing events and outings. Our family re-union at the world famous Niagara Falls was such an incredibly memorable event beating professional and experienced tour-operators also. She does these things with love and always gives a beautiful personal touch.

Her creativity knows no bounds.

During Sujata and Tamanna's stay with us in Indore, Mahesh Saini, Sadhana's nephew, came and was present when Tamanna had her *Mundan* (first haircut). She quite comfortably sat in the lap of her Mahesh *mama* (uncle). He is with Hindalco Industries in India.

I, meanwhile, continued with my diligent work with *Bhaskar*. In between I took the family to Delhi for a couple days.

Sujata and Tamanna were with us for about two months. We had a great time with them. Nothing could be better. We did not know that dark clouds were hovering around the horizon.

On the 'other side' something was definitely not right and I got an inkling that would ultimately change our lives. We had to change our plans about everything in Indore and India.

Sujata took Seema with her to America in November, 1985. Then we did not know that in a couple months we would also leave India and join them in America and make that country our home for the rest of our lives.

It has been more than 31 years since then.

Something about what seemed to be brewing on 'the other' side:

As I wrote earlier, I was leading *Dainik Bhaskar* the way I thought proper – fearlessly, independently, not blindly supporting the ruling Congress Party, in Madhya Pradesh state (with Chief Minister Arjun Singh) and at the Center, headed by Indira Gandhi who, more or less, was a one-woman-government. Once, a critic summed up the situation succinctly: "In the Central Cabinet there is *only One Male* – Indira Gandhi."

There were many skeletons in her closet but none outside the coterie could, or would, do anything about it. Top investigative journalists were not found easily, those who could dare to publish uncomfortable truth were a rarity.

There were some self-imposed restraints, too.

Ramesh *Ji* had given me a free hand and said if some higher-up political leader complained about it, nine out of 10 times I would not even mention it to you; only once I would tell you – and there the matter would end; nothing further.

That was a clear signal for my complete independence.

[I did not want to go *overboard* with that freedom. I never misused that freedom and power, nor got any *personal* benefit out of it.]

And that was also the reason why the then rulers might be unhappy with me. They needed sycophants, and they would be rewarded. I was not one of them. On major national issues, I was a solid nationalist, a patriot – not a *socialist*. On local issues, I was a community activist working for the common people, not particular special interests and power-hungry opportunistic politicians. I was, therefore, not one to hang around with the 'big ones.'

That also might be annoying for some 'big ones' who thought all journalists – including the Editors – are 'for sale.' The price may vary, here and there.

The ruling party, and its entrenched politicians - and maybe some special interest groups - did not think the way I did, or still do. I presumed, a majority of right-thinking politicians respected my writings and were friendly to me in New Delhi and Indore, even if not totally agreeing with me on issues. That was alright.

I didn't know that some elements were working against me behind the scenes. Those might have included some jealous and disgruntled people, 'vested interests,' and their hangers-on, hand-in-glove with them.

I don't know exactly what happened.

I also don't know the main force behind what all that happened later.

[It did change my life –*our* lives.]

I would just mention one.

The Chief Minister of Madhya Pradesh, Arjun Singh, was the Chief Guest at *Bhaskar's* grand inauguration, in 1983. We printed an exclusive interview with him as the main front-page story.

That was that. Our coverage of local, national and international affairs was factual, unbiased, and always on the side of truth, of course as we saw it and interpreted accordingly.

My editorials, commentaries and analyses were pointed and hard-hitting.

Bhaskar encouraged and welcomed opposite views also with articles and comments. I personally inspired new writers. I respected and gave space to the established and well-known writers but I also had a soft corner for newcomers. On issues like Afghanistan and the Soviet Union's (Russian) invasion, I was vehemently opposed to it. That was also the policy of the United States, so what.

It wasn't that I was blindly supporting America.

But there were people who thought otherwise. 'Socialism' was still in fashion very much.

I was on a visit to Delhi (as I did frequently to touch base with my contacts – and as Ramesh *Ji* also wanted me to do) and was planning to return to Indore in a day. Somehow, I sensed something was not right. I hurried back and probably unintentionally 'escaped' the net the authorities had laid out for me.

Once in Indore, I got a message that the investigative agency of the Government of India wanted me to be in touch with them in connection with some inquiry. I smelled a rat and that confirmed my suspicion.

The first thing I did was to dispatch Sujata-Seema-Tamanna to America. I saw them off at Bombay and returned to Indore. That was Nov. 1985.

A communication was waiting for me to be in New Delhi to assist in investigation of something. I was given all the support by the management to do the needful.

Once in New Delhi and *Bhaskar's* office in Connaught Circus, an officer from the Intelligence agency came and handed me an order from the Lt. Governor of Delhi (the Chief appointed official for the territory) to 'assist' in two-day investigation.

A copy of the order was not given to me and I was taken in an official car, with my carry-on bag, to their offices where I was met with about half a dozen people. They took turns to interrogate me on a wide variety of issues. Their aim seemed to be to pin on me some kind of serious charge, like if I was a foreign agent, indulging in some kind of espionage against the country passing on 'national secrets,' a traitor, or involved in economic offense and getting money from foreign sources.

There was no clear-cut explanation or methods. It was clearly a 'fishing expedition' to find 'something' against me and also against another person who was, I gathered, their 'prime' target.

Instead of two days, I was kept for six days, without a known extension of Lt. Governor's order. I was taken to a few places and kept in a guest house watched by a car-load of plain-clothed policemen at the gate. I was fed alright, but could not communicate with anybody – even my wife Sadhana, or even an attorney if I wanted to. First I thought I was assisting in some kind of investigation but, it quickly dawned on me that *I* was the 'suspect' and they were trying to pin me down and slap some charge, something serious, some scandal on me.

Sadhana, alone in Indore, was in panic. She didn't know anything about my whereabouts, was worried sick as she could not even reach me. She went, as they say, from pillar to post (*Bhaskar* management, some of the VIPs she knew, Neelu Bhagat and so on, but nobody could help – nobody knew except, I think, Neelu, but even he didn't know where exactly, and how long. And since the matter was being handled by Delhi-based intelligence officers, Neelu couldn't do anything, despite the fact that he knew *everything* about me and my work for the last 25 years - since his childhood.

Finally, Sadhana contacted one of my journalist friends in Delhi and they decided to approach the court first thing next morning to move a 'habeas corpus' petition to ask the government to produce me, *immediately.*

That was not needed, as the intelligence officers had extracted some kind of statement from me, something akin to their last point of *justification* for my interrogation – the American connection. Their point was that I was writing articles for which the American embassy was paying me a fee. A similar statement I was asked to give to a magistrate while a policeman was waiting for me outside the court. It was supposed to be *on my free will*. Ha!

[I had Deep Feature service functioning while I was in Delhi for which a regular subscription was paid by the recipients; the remuneration for the articles published in newspapers was paid by the papers. Clips of published articles were also available to the American officials, among others, for additional payment. With me moving to Indore, I discontinued the feature and clipping service.

Deep Features was not even functioning for the last three years when I was summoned, and no payment was received since 1983. Whatever payments were received, they were all legitimate remuneration for published material.]

The interrogators wanted to know how many foreign diplomats I knew and have been meeting. I explained that external affairs was one of my regular beats and I knew, and frequently met scores of them, from various embassies, including Americans, Australians, Chinese, Germans, Koreans, Hungarians, Romanians, Russians and so on. They also specifically asked me about my American and German visits. I told them the invitations were routed through the Government of India, and the Reserve Bank of India (Federal Reserve).

Whatever I wrote was public property, published in my newspapers.

They also tried to book me for possibly leaking defense information. I told them I was accredited to the Defense Ministry also and top military officers regularly briefed me, and few other very senior journalists, but we never printed anything that we were not supposed to print. Moreover, we rarely got any information that was NOT supposed to be printed – some issues were discussed and some things were shared *just as background information.* We, and I, in particular, never ever shared the info with others not entitled to know, much less with foreign countries.

The investigators lacked any evidence to implicate me even on this count.

The interrogators seemed so naïve as to believe that our Generals and other top military officers were stupid enough to share *'really classified'* material with even the senior journalists already cleared by the Ministry of Defense.

They were definitely just fishing.

They then changed their tactics. They pointed out my name printed on an invitation and a pamphlet about a defense-related seminar to be inaugurated by former Prime Minister Morarji Desai. [These types of Think-Tank activities, talks, seminars, discussions etc. are something routine in a democracy. But here, I was the target of investigation and they *had to do something.*]

I told them that I got a letter inviting me to be on the panel and attend the seminar but I had declined because I had no time. (I would have attended if I had time, and even my consent to be on the organization committee was no crime, though that *also* I had declined for lack of time for any meaningful role I could play.)

The seminar was a public event for which several former military officers were also invited to attend or speak. Even holding a seminar such as that *was no crime* – everything was open to the public which has a right to discuss any topic of national or international importance. It did not involve any current military officer and there was no private briefing by them, at all.

So there was nothing to incriminate me but during their relentless interrogation, at least three times they threatened me with, 'we will send you to jail for 14 years' if you don't tell the truth and give facts. I had told them whatever were *the facts*, and the *truth*. Nothing had come out to nail me, and charge me of any 'crime.' They did charge the other guy, organizer of the seminar, activist Rama Swarup.

They took him to the court where *even he was totally acquitted of all the charges* falsely slapped on him.

So much for the 'espionage' or other supposed 'offense!' Clearly it was a case of harassment and attempt to implicate me in *anything* to tarnish my untarnished reputation.

They did succeed in that. The 'case' got publicity and adverse comments followed. Those Intelligence officers had 'justified' their salaries.

[Deep Features, when functioning, did not print anything sent directly by any foreign source. We would go through vast material freely available publicly, choose our topics and write independently. I was subscribing to a number of newspapers, periodicals and reports from a wide variety of sources. I was doing an immense amount of reading and writing. Yes, I was not a Communist, socialist and did not toe the line of the Soviet Union. I was independent. But, as I mentioned earlier, Deep Features had stopped three years back.]

The political climate in India, for years, was pro-Soviet. It was fashionable to admire the Soviet Union and denounce the United States. Pro-Moscow, and a socialist, were the signs of a 'progressive person.' Nobody would raise an eyebrow. However, if you supported America on *any* issue, or spoke against the Soviet invasion of Afghanistan, or 'hard line Soviet hegemony' over East European countries, you would be immediately labeled as CIA (American) agent by the 'fellow travelers,' leftists, socialists and 'progressives.'

I was, therefore, seen through the colored lens by the 'progressives' and the Reds, the Left. I didn't care, though many of the leaders on the 'Left' knew me well and I also knew their opportunistic policies, too well.

[Some so-called pro-Soviet ignoramuses hailing the Russians and their policies didn't even know what the abbreviation, USSR, meant. One of the very vocal 'socialists' in my office, *Hindustan*, who often eyed me as pro-America, showed his utter ignorance when I asked him what USSR stands for.

His answer would make Lenin and Stalin and Khruschev (Khruschov) turn restlessly in their graves. It also exposed his shallow love for the Soviets, and his superficial knowledge about that country. Without hesitating, he proudly and unhesitatingly announced: USSR is United States of Soviet Russia.

The ignorant sycophant didn't know USSR stood for 'Union of Soviet Socialist Republics.']

However, the pro-Soviet and anti-West (or American) climate in New Delhi had persisted.

This disturbing political atmosphere followed me. And my critics had their chance they might have been waiting for a long time.

In addition, the changes in *Hindustan* editorial set-up with somebody way too junior to me, Binod Mishra, appointed as Editor was perhaps part of the same conspiracy.

A little about the man who had taken over. He was from the caste-ridden state of Bihar and himself a Brahmin, proud of his 'high caste.' For me, it didn't matter. I used to give assignments and also pass on certain leads for good news stories to reporters working in my News Bureau. Mishra was the junior-most.

One day DP Yadav, a Minister in the Government of India, told me about a certain new scheme he had finalized and asked me if I could assign a reporter to cover the story for our paper.

I asked Mishra to go and interview Yadav.

The instant reaction of Mishra was shocking, and also disturbing. He blurted out: Should I go to that *Ahir* ? (low caste, milk-seller.)

[Yadav belonged to a backward class that, traditionally, tended to cows and buffaloes and sold milk. (Even Lord Krishna was raised by Yadavs). This Minister was educated, seasoned politician who had won his seat in Parliament and was *not* selling milk. I don't know if he ever handled the milk business.]

I was not amused at the reaction. I was disgusted, and I firmly asked him to get that interview.

He did go but produced an insignificant story written reluctantly.

The people with that kind of mentality are not only extremely narrow-minded but also fond of keeping a grudge.

Something about one of those others whom I suspect of being behind all that happened to me in Indore - Arjun Singh! He may or may not be the culprit, but one of my good friends, JK Jain, a former Member of Parliament, also had his complaint about the then Chief Minister of Madhya Pradesh, in later years, conniving and manipulating things that affected Jain.

There might be others behind this unhappy development, I don't know, but the impact on me, Sadhana, my reputation, and my family was big.

Something damning about Arjun Singh: He was three times Chief Minister of Madhya Pradesh; also Governor of Punjab, a Parliamentarian, and finally, a Central Government Minister. Everywhere scandals followed him. He was alleged to be involved in several scandals of corruption and dereliction of duty, favoring his relatives; even harassing his granddaughter-in-law, Priyanka Singh.

A case under the Anti-Dowry Act was registered against him.

He was the one in the Churhat Lottery scandal involving his relatives in raising money through a lottery and misusing the funds for building his own palace and other activities. He was involved in another corruption in the form of Deemed Universities scandal (gave many institutions 'University status,' 44 of them were later disqualified.)

Yet another, more scandalous, and a cowardly act was also his fate.

Arjun Singh was the CM when the Bhopal Gas Tragedy (a big leak of gas in a plant of pesticides owned by the American company, Union Carbide) took place. It was considered the world's worst industrial disaster affecting more than 500,000 people, with the immediate death of 2259 people and total gas-related deaths of 3787. There were 558,125 injuries.

Other estimates say that 8000 people died within two weeks and another similar number died from gas-related diseases, following months and years after the gas-leak.

The tragedy happened on December 2-3, 1984, in Bhopal. As soon as it happened and gas started leaking, Chief Minister Arjun Singh was reported to have fled to his palace away from Bhopal. His government failed to act quickly, did not handle the situation properly, did not evacuate people speedily and had no clue as to what all was needed to be done, immediately. What could the rest do when the Big Boss himself was reported to have fled the scene?

The government could not cope with the tragedy, thanks to the leadership of the Chief who was absent.

On top of that, Arjun Singh even helped the Union Carbide Chief, Warren Anderson, to flee Bhopal, and India. The Pilot who flew Anderson, testified in court later that the order to whisk Anderson away came from the CM's office. Incidentally, it's also a significant fact that Union Carbide had donated Rs.150,000 to the 'social' organization floated by Arjun Singh and his relatives that also raised funds through Churhat Lottery.

So much for the man who later was elevated as a Central Government Minister and joined many others who were also similarly known for personal and political corruption in a corrupt government set-up the like of which was seldom seen before in India.

Back to my situation: The week-long ordeal left me disillusioned, distressed and disappointed. I was put in a situation where there seemed to be no remedy, no appeal, no complaint. Though Ramesh *Ji* was totally convinced of my innocence and was fully sympathetic, and understanding, my professional image and personal integrity had taken a severe, undeserved beating.

I told Ramesh *Bhaisahab* that, even unintentionally, I have damaged you, and *Bhaskar*. (I was firm that I would not put him and the paper in any embarrassing situation, anymore.) He reluctantly agreed to relieve me; in any case my three-year contract was also ending in a few weeks.

Ramesh *Ji* was generous with his words and his check book and arranged a grand farewell party for me in the office and I said good bye to *Bhaskar* and to Indore.

However, that's life, and ups and downs - for whatever reason - are a part of our destiny.

Sadhana always stood by me. She faced the situation calmly when she did not hear from me for six days – though extremely worried – and this finale also could not make her question me or blame destiny.

She was with me every step of the way, and together we took the major decision of our life -- to leave India and join Sujata's family in America.

Sadhana has been with me through every phase of my life, every moment of ecstasy and agony. I can't imagine anyone could find, or get, such a wife. I was able to face the situation, the heart-break and an uncertain future just because Sadhana was by my side. Her ever present total love and absolute faith gave me fresh courage and hope. These qualities are something to be immensely proud of. I couldn't have expected any better.

Not many deserve and get a wife like her.

I gave her several pet names – beside Ashi – like Rani, Paru, even Raja and told her that she was my 'charger;' every now and then I have to come and kiss you and re-charge myself.

[My love and admiration for Sadhana remind me of a song much later heard in America, that I would, without hesitation, proclaim:

Jag ghoomeya thaare jaisa na koi

(I have traveled the world but there's none like you).

These touching lines of the song by Irshad Kamil from the movie *Sultan* and sung by the top singer Rahat Fateh Ali Khan, Salman himself and Neha Bhasin, show the depth of my love for my Sadhana.

In America when we celebrated our 50th wedding anniversary and Sadhana's 60th and 75th birthdays, I wrote poems about her. She had written some outstanding poems, some about me, the kids and other topics, all compiled in *Samarpan*. A final edition of the book with all the poems and their English translation is due for publication.]

In the next few days we disposed of whatever we could. I gave away my large treasure trove of books, some rare and collectibles, some on various national and international topics, quite a few reference books and others. Sadhana got rid of her large collection of dresses, household things, beddings, furniture and crockery. She also gifted some of her larger paintings to the studio of the eminent artist, Bendre.

As I prepared to leave Indore everything from my birth, visits and stay in Indore and the happy-unhappy developments, and sweet-sour memories involving my family came to my mind.

A little over four years after my birth we lived in Indore. Then about four more years in Mussoorie-Dehradun. About a year in Delhi and about a couple years with mother and two younger siblings – a sister and a brother – in Indore and a few months in Mhow, a military town near Indore. Later I moved with father to Bombay while others were with mother in Agra and elsewhere.

When I was in Indore for the second time, around 1937-38, I was a student of Islamia school, a junior school with 5th as the highest class. I was the only Hindu out of 500 plus Muslim boys and enrolled in 5th, We got along well, though I was more fond of playing than studying, and some of the teachers more fond of punishing than teaching and paying more attention to boys like me.

I was good at English, and even without studying, got the highest marks – 62 out of 100 in the class examination. Also I had a good singing voice and was one of the two who would sing the school prayer song daily. It ran something like this:

Aie do jahaan ke aali, ai gulshanon ke maali,
tere he faiz se hai, sarsabz daali daali

(O Lord of both the worlds, O gardener of all the orchards, it's because of your glory that every branch of the tree is green.)

A great *universal* truth!

[Because of a confusion, I took Islamic History in Junior College but that gave me a chance to study Islam and Prophet Muhammad.]

My other older sister, Lata, was in a boarding school in the city – the school I attended when 4 and had become fond of my first teacher, Chhoti Bai. I didn't know her real name but remember she used to take me to her room to wash my hands (after a busy time at play) and face and apply some powder. Chhoti Bai was a friend of my mother and so our family was close to her.

Lata, a few years later, graduated from the same high school, also run by the United Church of Canada Mission that ran the same hospital where many of us, siblings, were born, and where the only *Nani* I ever knew, was the Chief.

When I was in Indore in 1983-85, Lata paid us a visit – she had become a medical doctor and was in Delhi working for the Government medical service. Her husband Om Prakash, was also a medical doctor. She was happy to visit her old school – though with no familiar faces left.

She and Om Prakash *jeejaji* (brother in-law) were married in Bombay at the same place where father and I lived since 1940 and where he and my two younger siblings were still living. The marriage of Lata was a grand affair graced by, among others, the 'Grandfather of Hindi movie industry' – Prithvi Raj Kapoor, an old and dear friend of my father.

Prithvi Raj Kapoor (we all addressed him as Papaji) acted in some great movies like *Sikandar* and *Mughal-e-Azam*. His sons (Raj, Shammi, and Shashi), grandsons Randhir, Rishi and Rajiv, great grand children (Karisma, Kareena and Ranbir) have been, and are, some of the top movie stars of Indian film industry with many memorable performances.

One can say that the Kapoor family has ruled the Hindi movie industry for four generations. Even Prithvi Raj Kapoor's father (we all called him Bade Papa Ji) was featured in one of the Kapoor films. So this makes five generations! Right!

Another top movie star of his time, Jeetendra (Ravi) was our next-door neighbor in the same building, in Bombay. He was just about two months-old when his mother brought him from Punjab –traditionally daughters give birth at their parents' home, not in-laws'). His mother, Krishna, was like my older sister and loved and cared for me. Jeetendra played in my lap, and later when I left Bombay in 1947 he and my younger brother Virendra became pals, being almost the same age. By the way, Jeetendra is his filmy name, his real name is Ravi and he is also a Kapoor – no relation to Papaji.

Indore had seen ups and downs for me and also my father. He was on top in publishing-writing- literary world, social and community activities, and was well respected. However, he had to face a shocking situation centered on the marriage of my other older sister, Prem Lata, and was dragged to the court. That event shattered him and made him, and me, uncomfortable in our relations with people very close to us, and who had been with our family through thick and thin.

But, again, that's life and life's phases of sunshine and darkness, for us.

[However, my father was very kind and magnanimous – he forgave Prem and my mother for that shocking development. I probably, wouldn't be that generous. Perhaps Sadhana understood father completely and when he stayed with her, and Sujata-Seema while I was in the US, they had detailed review of the events. Father had great love and respect for Sadhana, as a person, as a daughter-in-law and as the mainstay of our little family.

Father was a cleanliness freak, extremely particular about a clean home environment, and personal hygiene – going to the extreme. It was heard around him that even after a glass of water he has to rinse his mouth.

I have inherited *some* of this habit.

Father and mother had spent a big part of their lives separately – partly because of weather, jobs and probably also some differing views, and their priorities. I could over-simplify this divergence: father was more pro-community, and mother was pro-family. For father community included families while for mother families made a community. There was not much basic difference between the two views but the emphasis and priorities created a gap.

My mother died very young, in 1953, when just 52 year-old.]

Sister Prem's marriage controversy brought father and me to Bombay in 1940-41.

Following that unpleasant event father also had another devastating experience, professionally.

A successful businessman of Bombay, Sitaram Poddar, had invited father to start a Hindi newspaper as Editor. They finalized the plans and father was asked to wind up his Delhi-Indore affairs and move to Bombay.

In a couple weeks father did the same and arrived in Bombay only to find that the world had changed. He went to meet with Poddar and got a shock – Sitaram Poddar was no more. He had passed away just a day before.

His son knew about the whole plan to bring out the newspaper with *my* father as Editor, and that *his* father was financing the publication, totally. In any case, he was not at all keen to honor his father's pledge, and the newspaper plan died.

With that an uncertain future emerged.

However, my father, Dwarka Prasad Sewak (he never wrote Bhatnagar), decided to stay on in Bombay and continue what he was best at – writing, publishing, spreading Hindi language, and actively participating in religious, social and community activities. He worked with Nalanda Publications, bringing out a few books. He then was the Editor for a magazine *Maheshwari* and gave it his best.

As I wrote earlier, father would always take me to demonstrations, political meetings, and other events to listen to leaders – social, political, religious, literary and so on.

He also took me to a Yoga Guru to learn physical fitness, do Yogic exercises and conduct myself with strict discipline, mainly during the summer vacation in school.

This was 1942 and a couple months later the big "Quit India" resolution was passed at the Congress session in Bombay. Mahatma Gandhi had given the call "do or Die" and my father, some of his close associates, like Guru *Ji* (Dhyandhar Gupta) and Kundan Lal *Ji* (not yet married) were also involved in this freedom struggle.

Guru *Ji's* gym (Hind Yogashram) was locked down by the authorities and he went underground traveling and working with other freedom fighters.

But before that he had taught me quite a lot. A quick learner (when I wanted to) I became an expert in several kinds of exercises, Yogic *asans* (postures) and stick-play besides doing incredible number of push-ups and sit-ups.

Guru *Ji* was also an excellent archer. I would have graduated to this form in addition to astonishing yogic exercises I had already learnt.

As I mentioned earlier, I was also a tiny party in the freedom movement. I was in school and only 13 when 'Quit India' movement started. We formed a 'revolutionary' group named Azad Party (Party of the Free) and organized. We would oppose monthly tests, sing nationalistic songs instead of the usual school prayer, would boycott regular studies, and go out trying to close other schools. We would hold meetings and make speeches. This was our way of defiance, fighting the British government.

I was the youngest of the core group. We all pledged our allegiance to each other and to the goal of freedom. Our dedication and passionate adherence to our goals were tested with a burning candle and by putting our arm/wrist on the flame. I was the youngest at 13 years and my record was less than 15 seconds, but it was applauded.

The oldest member had the incredible tolerance for about 35 seconds. Another, about 3 years older than me, did about 25 seconds, the second highest. Both had big blisters that took months to heal and left big scars. I also had a small ugly blister I hid from father and later wore full-sleeve shirt to hide it.

All over 5 seconds tolerance were admitted.

I was voted as 'treasurer' – collector and custodian of weapons (we had access to only knives) we never used. They were only to boost our own morale and give us confidence and psychological sense of bravery.

The news of Azad Party activities reached the Principal and the Managing Committee of the school summoned three of us, the leaders, for a 'meeting.' We were questioned for a long time, charged with gross indiscipline and threatened with expulsion. We pleaded 'not guilty' and stated our burning desire to be a part of – and contribute just a little – to the freedom movement. We refuted the allegation of destruction of public or private property.

Letters were then handed over to us for our fathers about the allegations, inquiry and possible punishment. We did not know the exact contents, we were asked to give the letters to our fathers/guardians.

I did not ask the others about the letters. I had dutifully given the letter to my father.

Next day the Principal asked me about the reply. I said you did not ask me to bring a reply; I have given your letter to my father. He asked me to bring the reply next day.

Reaching home I asked my father about the letter and his reply. He looked at me straight and said in a firm voice: Tell your principal that *mera baap bhi yehi karta hai (*my father does the same thing.)

My joy knew no bounds. I knew something similar would come from father and I felt proud of him.

Next day I saw the Principal. He asked me about the reply. I said my father told me to tell you: *mera baap bhi yehi karta hai.*

The Principal was furious and asked me to leave at once. I left feeling a sense of victory and did not think of any consequences.

Luckily, there were no consequences other than a stern warning to keep away from violence and destruction of property (we never indulged in that conduct, anyway). For me there was another 'punishment.' The Principal, otherwise an excellent teacher who taught English and Sanskrit in the final class (High School) and would involve students in his class to perfectly learn what he taught, never once looked at me directly and never asked me a single question the whole year he taught us.

It must be said to the credit of Principal Mr. AV Jakhie, that he did not bar my participation in the school's sports teams (cricket, table tennis, volleyball and kabaddi) where I was among the best, and Captain of the last two.

My defiance and love of freedom persisted though India did not gain freedom while I was in high school.

My sticking to principles, and standing firm for legitimate causes, has trickled down from our parents, especially my father, to my children, Sujata and Seema.

I am proud of both the girls.

[It was more than 10 years later that I met Guru *Ji* in New Delhi when he came to my office with Kundan Lal *Ji*, Bimla *behenji's* husband and my brother-in-law.

In the intervening years, this family had grown and in addition to Sarojini, there were four other dear nephews and nieces – Jatinder, Virender, Rajinder and Suman. Sarojini is no more and her other brothers are well settled with their families in Delhi. Sujata and I met Jatinder (who was named after me – a little variation of spelling) with wife Krishna at Virender and Kusum's home/office in November, 2016, while in India for *Asthi Visarjan* (immersion of Sadhana's ashes.)

Virender aka VK Arya is the CEO of AVK Global Trainers, his own very successful company and works from his impressive home office. He took us upstairs and insisted that I sit in his chair and offer my blessings.

Virender retired from BSNL as a Senior General Manager.

All these children and their wives were loving and respectful. Sujata recalled the days we spent while growing up in New Delhi, especially when Sarojini was getting married and Jatinder was in charge of the arrangements. At her special request, he made sure that her favorite dish with huge Paneers (Indian cheese chunks) was prepared and served.

Jatinder is also a member of my Two Daughters' Club with one daughter –Ankita, a successful RJ (radio jockey) working with Radio Zindagi in Northern California. The other, Akansha is in India.]

Back to my story.

My father also worked for Prithvi Raj Kapoor's Prithvi Theatres as advisor on languages and helped the actors with correct pronunciation of Hindi and Urdu. He was well-versed in both the languages – and had also studied Farsi in his earlier years as that was the language of the Mughal *darbar* (Court – Kingdom). Almost all educated Kayasthas (our sub-caste) learnt Urdu-Farsi as a big number of them were associated with government under the then rulers, for generations.

Sewak *Ji*, as he was popularly known for his decades-long role as a social-servant (activist, worker), remained in Bombay. For about seven years I was with him and later he lived with my younger siblings, sister Priyalata (Chhutta) and brother Virendra (Rana). After Priyalata got married and left to live with her husband, Radhakrishna Prabhu, father continued to live with Virendra, his wife Rashmi and son Prafulla.

Chhutta and Virendra, both excellent singers, often performed at their college functions and also on other occasions on public stage.

Chhutta is also an accomplished Indian classical dance performer – Kathak, Bharatanatyam and Manipuri, now 'retired,' though her sense of humor has not.

Interestingly, when just a six-year old, she acted in a Sanskrit drama on the life of Kalidas, (or Kalidasa), the renowned Classical Sanskrit writer, widely regarded as the greatest poet and dramatist of his time, some 1600 years back.

'Kalidas' was staged at the famous Opera House theatre in Bombay. The actors' team from Varanasi included some distinguished academics and writers. Prithviraj Kapoor, a lover of theatre and himself an actor, was also associated with the team and helped stage the play. It was widely appreciated.

Beautifully dressed as a princess in the drama, Priyalata had a short dialogue and was very excited about it. Some 75 years later, she still remembers the line – me too:

'Asti kashchit vagvisheshah?'

(Is there something special you want to say?)

Whenever Sujata-Seema, Sadhana and I visited Bombay or met my brother, Rana on his visit to Delhi, which was rare, there was a special song we always begged him to sing. It became his 'signature song' as a matter of fact, and he sang it with great depth and emotion – two distinguishing traits of Talat Mahmood, the original singer who is loved and admired by so many even today. This beautiful composition was written by Majrooh Sultanpuri, music by SD Burman, filmed on the brilliant actors – Nutan and Sunil Dutt – in the award-winning director Bimal Roy's 1959 film – *Sujata.*

> *Jalte hain jiske liye, teri aankhon ke diye*
> *Dhoond laaya hoon vahi, geet mai tere liye*

(For the one that shines the light of your eyes, I have managed to find that very song for you.)

Sadhana often told Sujata-Seema and teasingly reminded me that it was due to my love and admiration for the beautiful Nutan and the outstanding roles she played especially in these films, that I chose to name our daughters – Sujata and Seema. Incidentally, I saw almost all the Nutan films with Sadhana and she seemed to echo my sentiments.

It so happened that on our way to Karna Lake, a major tourist attraction in the neighboring state of Haryana, about 80 miles from our home in Delhi, we were racing with a car (Munan's son, Ajay on the wheel) and playing games like overtaking it and slowing down sometimes for fun. We did not know the passengers in the other car.

As we stopped at the lake, the other car also arrived and lo and behold, who steps out?

Nutan along with Suresh Oberoi, another popular actor.

They looked tired but graciously gave autographs. I did not let go of the opportunity to introduce my daughters and remind her of the titles of her movies – Sujata and Seema. All the while Sadhana kept smiling and later found another chance to tease me.

It's worth mentioning here that the legendary character in *Mahabharat* – Karna, is believed to have bathed in this lake and this is where he gave away his protective armor to Indra, The Godfather of Arjun, though that resulted in his defeat.

[I do have many regrets in life. I feel those who proclaim with a straight face they don't have any are either the top saints or not telling the whole truth. There are places you wanted to revisit but couldn't, chances you missed, acts you did or didn't do, wanted to call/or write to someone but didn't, promises you made – to yourselves or others – but could not keep, things you wanted to give to someone but didn't or couldn't etc. Big or small doesn't matter.

I have many in my life. One is I didn't do anything for my younger siblings – Chhutta and Rana – when I could. Even for my father. Not that they wanted any, or needed, but that's beside the point.

But what can you do *now?* Just add on to your list of regrets.

The moral of the story: Do it now so that you might not regret later of not doing something at the right time, right place for the right person.]

I had visited Indore, and Ujjain also couple times before (years before joining *Bhaskar),* to report on election campaigns for various parties.

By the end of 1985 all that remained were the latest events that had left us shattered and ready to sever ties with the city and the country.

Only two families – Neelu and his wife Santosh, and my staffer Sudha Salunke and her husband – were present at the railway station when we left Indore for Bombay.

A far cry from the days when hundreds were present when I took over and *Bhaskar* was inaugurated, and when I left for Germany. It happens when some adverse and unsubstantiated reports are published widely.

One of the reports published in the widely circulated magazine, Blitz, of Bombay said: "The American Embassy quickly issued green cards to Bhatnagar and his young wife and whisked them off to America." This report was from one of my good friends in Delhi, A. Raghavan, who knew me well. The truth was that we traveled to America by spending

316

our own money and we received the green cards years later when our daughter Sujata sponsored us.

We left for Bombay to spend a couple days with Priyalata and Virendra and their families and then to leave the country that we have loved, and will always love.

The first day of 1986 saw us at New York JFK airport from where I called Sujata-Mujtaba and told them where we were and that we will take the next flight for Los Angeles. They had just some inkling about our leaving India but were not aware of the fast moving events and our departure from India for an uncertain future abroad.

However, they were ecstatic and so were many members of their extended family who met us in India, and some who had only heard about us.

A warm welcome awaited us as Sadhana and I, two weary, disenchanted and somewhat confused people, but still very much in love and determined to explore new grounds and face new challenges, arrived around midnight at Los Angeles airport. Some two dozen relatives and well-wishers with their cars and some with their families, gave us a reception and hope one could die for.

A new phase of our existence was starting. A new chapter of our life was being written. New challenges were anticipated but also new successes were being planned by a superior power.

One does have apprehensions, fears and uncertainties looking into the future. I have tried to live up to what I read in my junior high school.

A renowned Hindi poet, Pundit Ayodhya Singh Upadhyaya 'Hariaudh,' (1865-1947) in one of his poems wrote:

> *Jyon nikal kar badalon ki god se,*
> *thee abhi ik boond jo aage badhi'*

(A drop of rain-water left the lap of the clouds and proceeded.)

And the drop was thinking what's going to happen to me? I might fall in a heap of dust and be lost forever.

People often think about the uncertain future when they are forced to leave their homes but .....

Ek sundar seep ka tha munh khula,
Voh usi mein ja padi moti bani

(It fell in the mouth of a beautiful open oyster and became a pearl.)

[It was an honor to recite my short poem of tribute at a largely attended memorial service for this great poet recalling his contribution to literature. I was barely 17 then.]

Something similar was also on our minds when we left India.

We had taken this first step in our 25 year's life together. With Sadhana as my inspiration, my love, my pillar of strength, companion, my partner and everything, I wasn't worried about anything. And then our little immediate family – Sujata-Seema-Tamanna-Mujtaba – was with us, backed up by a long list of well-wishers in the extended family.

Sadhana and I both felt assured and extremely at ease with that welcome, but there was something more to come. That, probably, none would have heard from their sons-in-law. But Mujtaba was different.

As soon as we got our bags and all 'hellos' and 'welcome to America' were said and hugs done, Mujtaba said in a loving, caring, determined and sincere tone:

"Papa-Mumma, from today you are my responsibility."

It was not easy to hold back our tears.

[Mujtaba has faithfully kept his promise ever since that memorable night. He has been with us, for us, in Los Angeles, in San Francisco Bay Area, visiting us in Houston, back again in California. We have been living with Mujtaba and Sujata. He has been a son, a dear son, to us, and so has been Sujata – a daughter but very much taking care as a son would, and should, do.

Seema, though, had to live far away after her marriage, has not missed any opportunity to be with us, spend time with us, and arrange re-unions. She and her family would visit for a get-together two or three times a year – and singly in-between. So does her husband, Dr. Randeep Suneja, whenever he gets time. They have done a lot for us (bought a house for us in Houston, Texas, where we lived for five years) and took care of us. Both are very dear to us and so are the kids, Arjun, Nisha and Shivani.

We never thought that we would find ourselves surrounded by loving and caring people even out of India – Sujata's in-laws who are spread over a vast area but would be there for you whenever you needed them.

So would be Seema's in-laws. Her mother-in-law, Usha *Ji*, Randeep's older brother Pradeep and his wife Amita (both top doctors) and their children are very close to us and are our family.)

Among my American friends I can happily count Dr. Scott and Pamela Abramson and Bob-Lisa Cohen. Scott has been with me for years as a caring and loving friend and a doctor. In San Leandro, Northern California, he often came to check on us, Mujtaba-Sujata and me, made it a point to see Sadhana and share our views on world affairs.

God has been kind to us, notwithstanding my complaints.

Any one asking Seema for her real wish will always get the same determined answer: to live with my parents and Mujtaba *Jeeju* (brother in-law) and Sujata *Didi* (sister).

Her answer remains the same even if her mother is no more with us. She looks to me and Mujtaba-Sujata as her *maika* (parent's home.) And she adores her niece, Tamanna and her daughter, Aliya.

Who could have asked for more?]

Years back, I had given a small book by Louis Weber, of Publications International (Illinois) to Sadhana on one of her birthdays.

The first page said:

The day you became my wife, my world became blessed.

I also said, and meant every word of it, and I read this to Sadhana, and she read it back to me. It added:

I am infinitely blessed that in a world full of different people,
        You have chosen to give your heart to me.
I am forever grateful that in a world full of different paths,
        You have chosen to walk beside me.
I am eternally joyful that in a world full of different opportunities,
        You have chosen to create a life with me.

She echoed every word for me.

That was my wife, my Sadhana, my love.

That's all my dear children, my dear friends.

That's OUR Fairytale Love Story.

I can only add:

> *Teri meri, meri teri prem kahani hai lumbi,*
> *kuchh pannon mein ye simat na paye.*

(Our love story is very long; it cannot be squeezed in a few pages.)

Books by Yatindra Bhatnagar

Bangladesh, Birth of a Nation
Mujib, the Architect of Bangladesh
Australiana, A Visit to Remember
Korean Experience
Autumn Leaves (a collection of own poems)
Yugpurush Tito (Hindi)
Vikas ki Yatra (Hindi)
Romania, Desh Nivasi aur Yaadein (Hindi)
Kranti ke Swar (collection of poems in Hindi, with Sadhana Bhatnagar)

Translations from English to Hindi

Sudoor Porva (History of the Far East by Prof Paul Clyde)
Syngman Rhee (a biography)

Editor/Co-Editor/Contributing Editor/Advisor

Dr. Zakir Hussain (Former President of India)
Middle East Business
Where to Stay (in Middle East)
Samarpan (a collection of Sadhana Bhatnagar's poems)
Global Intelligence

Contributions

Discovery in Europe
Into the Sun
Great American Poetry Anthology
The Golden Treasury of Great Poems

Publications

TRAVIANA (Travel, Aviation and Adventure magazine)